TRANSIT COOPERATIVE RESEARCH PROGRAM

TCRP REPORT 111

Elements Needed to Create High Ridership Transit Systems

TranSystems
Medford, MA

WITH

Planners Collaborative, Inc.
Boston, MA

Tom Crikelair Associates
Bar Harbor, ME

Subject Areas
Public Transit

Research sponsored by the Federal Transit Administration in cooperation with the Transit Development Corporation

TRANSPORTATION RESEARCH BOARD

WASHINGTON, D.C.
2007
www.TRB.org

TRANSIT COOPERATIVE RESEARCH PROGRAM

The nation's growth and the need to meet mobility, environmental, and energy objectives place demands on public transit systems. Current systems, some of which are old and in need of upgrading, must expand service area, increase service frequency, and improve efficiency to serve these demands. Research is necessary to solve operating problems, to adapt appropriate new technologies from other industries, and to introduce innovations into the transit industry. The Transit Cooperative Research Program (TCRP) serves as one of the principal means by which the transit industry can develop innovative near-term solutions to meet demands placed on it.

The need for TCRP was originally identified in *TRB Special Report 213—Research for Public Transit: New Directions,* published in 1987 and based on a study sponsored by the Urban Mass Transportation Administration—now the Federal Transit Administration (FTA). A report by the American Public Transportation Association (APTA), Transportation 2000, also recognized the need for local, problem-solving research. TCRP, modeled after the longstanding and successful National Cooperative Highway Research Program, undertakes research and other technical activities in response to the needs of transit service providers. The scope of TCRP includes a variety of transit research fields including planning, service configuration, equipment, facilities, operations, human resources, maintenance, policy, and administrative practices.

TCRP was established under FTA sponsorship in July 1992. Proposed by the U.S. Department of Transportation, TCRP was authorized as part of the Intermodal Surface Transportation Efficiency Act of 1991 (ISTEA). On May 13, 1992, a memorandum agreement outlining TCRP operating procedures was executed by the three cooperating organizations: FTA, the National Academies, acting through the Transportation Research Board (TRB); and the Transit Development Corporation, Inc. (TDC), a nonprofit educational and research organization established by APTA. TDC is responsible for forming the independent governing board, designated as the TCRP Oversight and Project Selection (TOPS) Committee.

Research problem statements for TCRP are solicited periodically but may be submitted to TRB by anyone at any time. It is the responsibility of the TOPS Committee to formulate the research program by identifying the highest priority projects. As part of the evaluation, the TOPS Committee defines funding levels and expected products.

Once selected, each project is assigned to an expert panel, appointed by the Transportation Research Board. The panels prepare project statements (requests for proposals), select contractors, and provide technical guidance and counsel throughout the life of the project. The process for developing research problem statements and selecting research agencies has been used by TRB in managing cooperative research programs since 1962. As in other TRB activities, TCRP project panels serve voluntarily without compensation.

Because research cannot have the desired impact if products fail to reach the intended audience, special emphasis is placed on disseminating TCRP results to the intended end users of the research: transit agencies, service providers, and suppliers. TRB provides a series of research reports, syntheses of transit practice, and other supporting material developed by TCRP research. APTA will arrange for workshops, training aids, field visits, and other activities to ensure that results are implemented by urban and rural transit industry practitioners.

The TCRP provides a forum where transit agencies can cooperatively address common operational problems. The TCRP results support and complement other ongoing transit research and training programs.

TCRP REPORT 111

Project H-32
ISSN 1073-4872
ISBN: 978-0-309-09885-4
Library of Congress Control Number 2007927801

© 2007 Transportation Research Board

COPYRIGHT PERMISSION

Authors herein are responsible for the authenticity of their materials and for obtaining written permissions from publishers or persons who own the copyright to any previously published or copyrighted material used herein.

Cooperative Research Programs (CRP) grants permission to reproduce material in this publication for classroom and not-for-profit purposes. Permission is given with the understanding that none of the material will be used to imply TRB, AASHTO, FAA, FHWA, FMCSA, FTA, or Transit Development Corporation endorsement of a particular product, method, or practice. It is expected that those reproducing the material in this document for educational and not-for-profit uses will give appropriate acknowledgment of the source of any reprinted or reproduced material. For other uses of the material, request permission from CRP.

NOTICE

The project that is the subject of this report was a part of the Transit Cooperative Research Program conducted by the Transportation Research Board with the approval of the Governing Board of the National Research Council. Such approval reflects the Governing Board's judgment that the project concerned is appropriate with respect to both the purposes and resources of the National Research Council.

The members of the technical advisory panel selected to monitor this project and to review this report were chosen for recognized scholarly competence and with due consideration for the balance of disciplines appropriate to the project. The opinions and conclusions expressed or implied are those of the research agency that performed the research, and while they have been accepted as appropriate by the technical panel, they are not necessarily those of the Transportation Research Board, the National Research Council, the Transit Development Corporation, or the Federal Transit Administration of the U.S. Department of Transportation.

Each report is reviewed and accepted for publication by the technical panel according to procedures established and monitored by the Transportation Research Board Executive Committee and the Governing Board of the National Research Council.

The Transportation Research Board of the National Academies, the National Research Council, the Transit Development Corporation, and the Federal Transit Administration (sponsor of the Transit Cooperative Research Program) do not endorse products or manufacturers. Trade or manufacturers' names appear herein solely because they are considered essential to the clarity and completeness of the project reporting.

Published reports of the

TRANSIT COOPERATIVE RESEARCH PROGRAM

are available from:

Transportation Research Board
Business Office
500 Fifth Street, NW
Washington, DC 20001

and can be ordered through the Internet at
http://www.national-academies.org/trb/bookstore

Printed in the United States of America

THE NATIONAL ACADEMIES
Advisers to the Nation on Science, Engineering, and Medicine

The **National Academy of Sciences** is a private, nonprofit, self-perpetuating society of distinguished scholars engaged in scientific and engineering research, dedicated to the furtherance of science and technology and to their use for the general welfare. On the authority of the charter granted to it by the Congress in 1863, the Academy has a mandate that requires it to advise the federal government on scientific and technical matters. Dr. Ralph J. Cicerone is president of the National Academy of Sciences.

The **National Academy of Engineering** was established in 1964, under the charter of the National Academy of Sciences, as a parallel organization of outstanding engineers. It is autonomous in its administration and in the selection of its members, sharing with the National Academy of Sciences the responsibility for advising the federal government. The National Academy of Engineering also sponsors engineering programs aimed at meeting national needs, encourages education and research, and recognizes the superior achievements of engineers. Dr. William A. Wulf is president of the National Academy of Engineering.

The **Institute of Medicine** was established in 1970 by the National Academy of Sciences to secure the services of eminent members of appropriate professions in the examination of policy matters pertaining to the health of the public. The Institute acts under the responsibility given to the National Academy of Sciences by its congressional charter to be an adviser to the federal government and, on its own initiative, to identify issues of medical care, research, and education. Dr. Harvey V. Fineberg is president of the Institute of Medicine.

The **National Research Council** was organized by the National Academy of Sciences in 1916 to associate the broad community of science and technology with the Academy's purposes of furthering knowledge and advising the federal government. Functioning in accordance with general policies determined by the Academy, the Council has become the principal operating agency of both the National Academy of Sciences and the National Academy of Engineering in providing services to the government, the public, and the scientific and engineering communities. The Council is administered jointly by both the Academies and the Institute of Medicine. Dr. Ralph J. Cicerone and Dr. William A. Wulf are chair and vice chair, respectively, of the National Research Council.

The **Transportation Research Board** is a division of the National Research Council, which serves the National Academy of Sciences and the National Academy of Engineering. The Board's mission is to promote innovation and progress in transportation through research. In an objective and interdisciplinary setting, the Board facilitates the sharing of information on transportation practice and policy by researchers and practitioners; stimulates research and offers research management services that promote technical excellence; provides expert advice on transportation policy and programs; and disseminates research results broadly and encourages their implementation. The Board's varied activities annually engage more than 5,000 engineers, scientists, and other transportation researchers and practitioners from the public and private sectors and academia, all of whom contribute their expertise in the public interest. The program is supported by state transportation departments, federal agencies including the component administrations of the U.S. Department of Transportation, and other organizations and individuals interested in the development of transportation. **www.TRB.org**

www.national-academies.org

COOPERATIVE RESEARCH PROGRAMS

CRP STAFF FOR TCRP REPORT 111

Christopher W. Jenks, *Director, Cooperative Research Programs*
Crawford F. Jencks, *Deputy Director, Cooperative Research Programs*
Gwen Chisholm Smith, *Senior Program Officer*
Eileen P. Delaney, *Director of Publications*
Hillary Freer, *Senior Editor*

TCRP PROJECT H-32 PANEL
Field of Policy and Planning

David A. Lee, *Connecticut Transit, Hartford, CT* (Chair)
Alan Castaline, *Massachusetts Bay Transportation Authority, Boston, MA*
Richard L. Dreyer, *Tindale-Oliver & Associates, Inc., Tampa, FL*
Eric T. Hill, *Metro Plan Orlando, Orlando, FL*
Douglas Holcomb, *Greater Bridgeport Transit Authority, Bridgeport, CT*
Ronald Kilcoyne, *Greater Bridgeport Transit Authority, Bridgeport, CT*
David M. Luskin, *University of Texas - Austin, Austin, TX*
Jan Maynard, *Utah Transit Authority, Salt Lake City, UT*
John F. McGee, Jr., *Southeastern Pennsylvania Transportation Authority, Philadelphia, PA*
Rosie Sanford, *Loxley, AL*
Richard F. Stevens, *Fairfax County (VA) DOT, Fairfax, VA*
Elizabeth Day, *FTA Liaison*
William B. Menczer, *FTA Liaison*
Richard Weaver, *APTA Liaison*
Karen Wolf-Branigin, *Other Liaison*
Peter Shaw, *TRB Liaison*

AUTHOR ACKNOWLEDGMENTS

The research described in this report was performed under TCRP Project H-32 by TranSystems Corp., with assistance from Planners Collaborative, Inc., and Tom Crikelair Associates.

Daniel Fleishman of TranSystems was the Principal Investigator for the project and the primary author of this Guidebook. Also contributing to the research and preparation of the Guidebook were James Wensley, Rick Halvorsen, Larry Englisher, Stephen Falbel, Carol Schweiger, Bruce Kaplan and Kathleen Fay of TranSystems; Scott Hamwey, Dan Rabinowitz, Nicole Buxton and Don Kidston of Planners Collaborative; and Tom Crikelair.

The guidance of Gwen Chisholm Smith, the TCRP Program Officer for the project, and the Project Panel is also acknowledged.

FOREWORD

By Gwen Chisholm Smith
Staff Officer
Transportation Research Board

TCRP Report 111: Elements Needed to Create High Ridership Transit Systems describes the strategies used by transit agencies to create high ridership and includes case studies of successful examples of increased or high ridership. The case studies focus on the internal and external elements that contributed to successful ridership increases and describe how the transit agencies influenced or overcame internal and external challenges to increase ridership.

This report includes a companion interactive CD-ROM that contains a database of individual transit agency ridership strategies linked to the strategies and examples presented in the report. The CD-ROM also contains a brochure that outlines the key elements identified in this report for increasing and sustaining ridership. These materials have been designed to assist transit managers and staff, as well as policymakers and other regional stakeholders, by identifying strategies that can be used to increase ridership.

Increasing ridership is a national goal of the Federal Transit Administration and a high priority for all transit systems. Increasing ridership is important to sustain public investment in transit, particularly in a resource-constrained environment. Ridership is generally used by public authorities as the basis for measuring the effectiveness of public transportation investments. In addition, strong transit ridership supports a wide variety of public policy goals, including energy conservation; air-quality improvement; congestion relief; mobility for transportation-disadvantaged groups; and promotion of livable communities, economic development, and sustained growth initiatives. Increasing transit ridership also improves the efficiency of the overall transportation system by using available capacity. Transit agencies throughout the United States and abroad have had success at generating higher-than-usual rates of ridership growth, through innovative use of service improvements, marketing techniques, fare policy and technology initiatives, and partnerships with other entities. This report identifies transit ridership "success" stories that can be emulated and describes the types of actions that can be taken to sustain or increase transit ridership.

Daniel Fleishman of TranSystems was the principal author of this report. Also contributing to the research and preparation of the reporrreport and CD-ROM were James Wensley, Rick Halvorsen, Larry Englisher, Stephen Falbel, Carol Schweiger, Bruce Kaplan, and Kathleen Fay of TranSystems; Scott Hamwey, Dan Rabinowitz, Nicole Buxton, and Don Kidston of Planners Collaborative; and Tom Crikelair of Tom Crikelair Associates. Under TCRP Project H-32, "Determining the Elements Needed to Create High Ridership Transit Systems," the research team conducted a comprehensive review of literature, practice, and findings related to producing and sustaining high transit ridership. Based on the information gathered, this report provides information on the effective use and effects of a broad range of strategies on ridership and provides guidance on selecting appropriate strategies to sustain or increase ridership.

CONTENTS

Chapter 1 Introduction and Overview — 1
- Introduction — 1
- Industry Research/Dissemination Efforts — 2
  - Industry Research — 2
  - Information Dissemination Efforts — 3
- Case Studies — 4
- The Guidebook — 4

Chapter 2 Factors Affecting Ridership — 6
- Introduction — 6
- Factors Affecting Ridership — 6
  - Previous TCRP Studies — 7
  - Mineta Institute Study — 11
  - Other Studies — 13
  - Findings from the Case Studies — 14
  - Categorization of Factors Affecting Ridership — 17

Chapter 3 Identification of Service Needs and Opportunities — 22
- Introduction — 22
- Evaluation of Existing Services — 22
  - Service Evaluation — 22
  - Needs Assessment of Marketing/Information and Fare Systems — 27
- Identification of Needs & Potential Markets — 28
  - Conducting Demographic and Travel Pattern Analysis — 28
  - Conducting Market Research — 29
  - Identifying Market Segments — 32

Chapter 4 Selection of Strategies — 37
- Introduction — 37
- Service Environments and Strategies — 37
  - Identifying Types of Service Environments — 37
  - Identifying Strategies for Different Service Environments — 39
  - Identifying Relative Cost-Effectiveness of Potential Strategies — 41
  - Evaluating Ridership Impacts — 41
- Elements of Successful Strategies — 43
  - Characteristics of Successful U.S. Examples — 43
  - Successful Examples from Abroad — 50
- Conclusions — 51

Chapter 5 Operating/Service Adjustments — 52
- Introduction — 52
- Design/Implementation Guidelines — 52
  - Applicable Settings — 52
  - Planning/Research Activities — 52

53	Design and Performance Measures
56	Cost Estimation Considerations
57	Expected Ridership Response
58	Routing/Coverage Adjustments
58	Increased Route Coverage
61	Route Restructuring
62	Improved Schedule/Route Coordination
65	Scheduling/Frequency Adjustments
66	Increased Service Frequency and Increased Span of Service
67	Improved Reliability/On-time Performance
68	New Types of Service
68	Improved Travel Speed
70	Targeted Services
72	Improved Amenities
73	Passenger Facility Improvements
75	New/Improved Vehicles
76	Increased Security and Safety
78	**Chapter 6** Partnerships/Coordination Initiatives
78	Introduction
78	Guidelines and Examples
78	Partnerships
79	University/School Pass Programs
81	Travel Demand Management Strategies
84	Subsidized Activity Center Service
85	Coordination Initiatives
86	Consistent Regional Operating Policies
87	Coordination with Social Services Agencies
88	Coordination with Other Transportation Agencies
90	Promotion of Transit-Supportive Design and TOD
92	**Chapter 7** Marketing & Information Initiatives
92	Introduction
92	Design/Implementation Guidelines
92	Applicable Settings
94	Planning Activities
94	Expected Ridership Response
95	Marketing/Promotional Initiatives
95	Targeted Marketing/Promotions
97	General Marketing/Promotions
101	Information Improvements
101	Improved Printed Informational Materials
103	Improved Customer Information and Assistance
103	Automated Transit Traveler Information
109	**Chapter 8** Fare Collection/Structure Initiatives
109	Introduction
109	Design/Implementation Guidelines
109	Applicable Settings
110	Planning Activities
110	Fare Collection System Design Process
112	Fare Structure Development Process

113	Cost/Revenue Considerations
114	Expected Ridership Response
114	Fare Collection Improvements
114	Improved Payment Convenience
120	Regional Payment Integration
121	Fare Structure Changes
121	Fare Structure Simplification
123	Fare Reduction

CHAPTER 1

Introduction and Overview

Introduction

Increasingly, public transit ridership supports a broad range of public policy goals, including air quality improvement, energy conservation, congestion reduction, provision of mobility to the transportation-disadvantaged, access to jobs, and promotion of economic development and sustained growth initiatives. As transit is often undervalued by policymakers as an important component of the local transportation system, attracting and sustaining high demand therefore represents transit's best weapon in the fight for scarce public funding. However, evaluating the direct impact on most of those goals is difficult at best. Instead, measures related to usage (e.g., systemwide ridership levels or ridership per capita) or productivity (e.g., riders per revenue vehicle hour) represent the best indicators of transit "success" and are typically considered the primary measures of the effectiveness of a transit investment.

For this reason, it is important that transit operators—as well as funding partners—are aware of the various types of strategies that have been effectively used by their peer agencies to increase ridership on their systems. Transit agencies all around the country have had success at generating relatively high per capita ridership rates and at promoting higher-than-usual rates of growth, through service improvements, innovative marketing techniques, and policy changes. A number of agencies have also developed partnerships with other entities (e.g., universities, developers, tourist attractions, and employers) to expand usage, and many agencies have developed arrangements to provide service to special events.

If every agency were able to generate a ridership level approaching that of the best-performing systems (operating in similar environments), overall transit usage in the United States would see a dramatic increase. The purpose of Transit Cooperative Research Program (TCRP) Project H-32 (Determining the Elements Needed to Create High Ridership Transit Systems) was thus to develop guidance materials that effectively (1) identify the full range of types of actions, initiatives or special projects that offer the potential to create high ridership and (2) provide examples of their effective usage and impacts. The research sought to address the following key questions, among others:

- What are the major factors, both within and outside transit agencies' control, that influence transit demand?
- What types of strategies—and combinations of strategies—have proven successful in different types of operating environments (e.g., rural areas, suburban towns, large cities, and college towns)?
- What are the types of tradeoffs an agency may have to make in pursuing high ridership versus promoting other goals (e.g., cost control, increased revenue, and improved equity considerations)?

This Guidebook and the accompanying interactive CD have been designed to facilitate an understanding of the full range of actions and initiatives available, and provide guidance on selecting appropriate strategies. The remainder of this chapter (1) identifies key transit industry research and information dissemination efforts, (2) summarizes the case studies conducted as part of the project, and (3) presents the outline of the remainder of the Guidebook.

Industry Research/Dissemination Efforts

Industry Research

There has been considerable research over the years on the various types of strategies that have been used to spur ridership growth. For instance, a number of TCRP projects have focused on such topics as ridership-building initiatives in general, marketing and market segmentation strategies, fare policy/technology developments, traveler information technologies, and transit amenities. These and other studies have reported on many transit agencies' success at producing significant ridership increases, while also exploring the influence of various internal and external factors on ridership.

The research team has conducted a comprehensive review of relevant literature, practice and research findings related to producing—and sustaining—high transit ridership. Key categories of reference materials and other sources of information are identified below; specific reference documents are listed in the appendices, with key sources included in the Annotated Bibliography (Appendix B) and other sources presented in Appendix C. The findings from these materials are discussed in Chapter 2.

TCRP Studies

A number of TCRP studies closely related to this topic have been undertaken; the most directly related studies are as follows (these documents are summarized in Appendix B, Annotated Bibliography):

- *TCRP Research Results Digest 4: Transit Ridership Initiative* (1995) identifies key factors and initiatives that led to ridership increases at 27 transit agencies between 1991 and 1993.
- *TCRP Research Results Digest 29: Continuing Examination of Successful Transit Ridership Initiatives* (1998) follows up on the above study and identifies key factors and initiatives that led to ridership increases at 42 transit agencies between 1994 and 1996.
- *TCRP Research Results Digest 69: Evaluation of Recent Ridership Increases* (2005) follows up on the above study and identifies key factors and initiatives that led to ridership increases at 28 transit agencies between 2000 and 2002.
- *TCRP Report 27: Building Transit Ridership: An Exploration of Transit's Market Share and the Public Policies that Influence It* (1997) explores a variety of public policies and transit management actions that can potentially influence transit ridership.
- *TCRP Report 28: Transit Markets of the Future: the Challenge of Change* (1998) identifies potential effects of anticipated demographic, geographic, economic, technological, and societal trends on transit ridership and services; the report also identifies future transit markets resulting from those trends and the most appropriate types of services to address these markets.
- *TCRP Report 36: A Handbook: Using Market Segmentation to Increase Transit Ridership* (1998) presents an overview of market segmentation for transit professionals, including a discussion of the different types of data used for defining market segments.
- *TCRP Report 46: The Role of Transit Amenities and Vehicle Characteristics in Building Transit Ridership* (1999) identifies and describes how passenger amenities and vehicle characteristics attract transit ridership.

- *TCRP Report 55: Guidelines for Enhancing Suburban Mobility Using Public Transportation* (1999) identifies, assesses, and documents current practices used by transit agencies to better serve suburban travel needs; the report also categorizes the different types of suburban environments and discusses the application of types of service to each.
- *TCRP Report 70: Guidebook for Change and Innovation at Rural and Small Urban Transit Systems* (2001) focuses specifically on rural and small urban systems and (1) identifies elements that can produce a "culture of innovation" in this type of environment and (2) describes examples of initiatives and innovation at small transit agencies.
- *TCRP Report 95: Traveler Response to Transportation System Changes* (2004) represents a compilation and discussion of previous analyses of the impacts of various types of transportation system actions on demand. Individual chapters of the overall study have been published as stand-alone reports. Four of these reports (*Chapter 9—Transit Scheduling and Frequency, Chapter 10—Bus Routing and Coverage, Chapter 11—Transit Information and Promotion,* and *Chapter 12—Transit Pricing and Fares*) are particularly relevant to this study. Each of these chapters presents and discusses the results of analyses and agency experience regarding the nature of traveler response to a particular type of strategy.

Because of the range of factors affecting ridership and types of actions that can be pursued, a number of other TCRP reports also provide information that is applicable to this research; these are listed in Appendix B.

Other Research Efforts and Sources of Information

The research team has also reviewed related research efforts undertaken by other entities, including individual transit agencies. Several key reports are summarized in Appendix B.

The research team has also compiled information on national ridership trends, as well as recent and current initiatives implemented (and planned) by individual transit agencies and localities. Key sources of this information include the following:

- Federal Transit Administration *Innovative Practices for Increased Ridership* database/website—FTA has developed this interactive website/database that highlights examples from around the country; FTA has solicited input from local agencies, through its regional offices, in an effort to document success stories from various sizes and types of transit services. The projects reported on in the database represent a key source of examples discussed in Chapter 4 and Appendix A of this Guidebook. (link: http://ftawebprod.fta.dot.gov/bpir/).
- APTA Transit Ridership Reports—quarterly ridership figures for U.S. transit agencies (link: http://apta.com/research/stats/ridership/).
- FTA's National Transit Database Reports—annual demographic and service operations and usage data profiles of individual transit agencies, as well as national-level summary data (link: http://www.ntdprogram.com/NTD/ntdhome.nsf/Docs/NTDData?OpenDocument).
- Presentations at (and proceedings from) conferences (e.g., the APTA Bus/Paratransit, Rail and Fare Collection Workshops; the TRB Annual Meeting; the Canadian Urban Transport Association Conference; and state transportation conferences).
- Articles in transit-related journals (e.g., *Passenger Transport, Metro,* and *Mass Transit*).
- Individual agency websites and discussions with various transit agency, MPO, municipality, and state transportation department staff and officials.

Information Dissemination Efforts

Recognizing that achieving and maintaining high ridership should be a national goal and a high priority for all transit systems, the FTA and APTA have introduced several other initiatives intended to disseminate information about effective ridership strategies. These initiatives represent another source of information for this study. These efforts include

- Regional workshops—FTA has sponsored regional workshops presenting examples of various types of ridership initiatives.
- Transit Ridership Best Practices Webinar—FTA and APTA held a "webinar" on this topic, featuring presentations on several key projects.
- Individualized Marketing Demonstrations—FTA selected four agencies (WTA in Bellingham, WA; GCRTA in Cleveland; Sacramento RTD; and TTA in Research Triangle Park, NC) to demonstrate the promotion of transit usage through targeted marketing methods.
- BRT Research Project—FTA has conducted research to determine which features are most cost-effective in increasing ridership.
- "United We Ride" Initiative—FTA developed this five-part initiative to assist communities and states in the establishment of coordinated human services transportation services.

Chapter 2 discusses the key findings of the industry review.

Case Studies

The research team conducted case studies of a dozen U.S. transit agencies that have deployed various strategies to promote ridership growth; the case study agencies were as follows:

- Advance Transit (Wilder, VT);
- BAT Community Connector (Bangor, ME);
- Baldwin Rural Area Transportation System (Robertsdale, AL);
- Capital Area Transportation Authority (Lansing, MI);
- Greater Cleveland Regional Transit Authority (Cleveland, OH);
- Orange County Transportation Authority (Orange, CA);
- Ride On (Montgomery Co., MD);
- Transfort (Fort Collins, CO);
- Tri-County Metropolitan Transportation District (Portland, OR);
- Utah Transit Authority (Salt Lake City, UT);
- Ventura Intercity Service Transit Authority (Ventura, CA); and
- Whatcom Transportation Authority (Bellingham, WA).

The goal in selecting case study sites was to choose agencies that represent (1) a range of system sizes (i.e., covering each of the major operating environment categories), (2) different modal combinations (i.e., bus only as well as multi-modal), and (3) a range of types of strategies. The case studies also reflect a variety of specific market orientations (e.g., college towns and suburban areas). The individual case study reports are presented in Appendix D. The overall findings are discussed in Chapter 2.

The Guidebook

The contents of the Guidebook are as follows:

- Chapter 2, Factors Affecting Ridership, synthesizes the key findings of ongoing and previous research and information dissemination efforts—as well as the findings of the case studies conducted for this study—and includes (1) a review of industry-wide ridership trends; (2) a discussion of the internal and external factors/elements affecting ridership; and (3) a categorization of the different types of strategies, actions, and initiatives that have been effectively utilized by transit agencies.

- Chapter 3, Identification of Service Needs and Opportunities, provides guidance related to evaluating existing service needs and identifying market opportunities. This includes identifying gaps/deficiencies in existing services, as well as understanding the characteristics and service needs of different market segments.
- Chapter 4, Selection of Strategies, addresses the process of identifying appropriate strategies/actions/initiatives to attract and/or retain riders. The chapter includes a discussion of successful agency examples, by service environment size (i.e., large city, medium city, and small town/rural area) and category (i.e., metropolitan, suburban, downtown/CBD, or regional).
- Chapter 5, Operating/Service Adjustments, describes the strategies that fall under this category.
- Chapter 6, Partnerships/Coordination Initiatives, describes the strategies that fall under this category.
- Chapter 7, Marketing & Information Initiatives, describes the strategies that fall under this category.
- Chapter 8, Fare Collection/Structure Initiatives, describes the strategies that fall under this category.

The following appendixes are included on the CD-ROM that accompanies this report:

- Appendix A, Successful Examples—This appendix identifies and describes examples of transit agency strategies, actions and initiatives that have proven successful at generating high ridership levels and/or significant ridership increases.
- Appendix B, Annotated Bibliography—This appendix identifies and summarizes the most relevant research reports related to the production and retention of high transit ridership.
- Appendix C, Other References—This appendix identifies additional sources not included in Appendix B.
- Appendix D, Case Studies—The individual case study reports are presented here.
- Appendix E, Using the Interactive CD—Accompanying this report is an interactive CD that contains a database of individual transit agency ridership strategies linked to the strategies and examples presented in the written report. The CD's contents and usage instructions are described here.

CHAPTER 2

Factors Affecting Ridership

Introduction

As indicated in Table 2-1, ridership on all U.S. transit systems has risen substantially over the past decade. Based on APTA's ridership reports, total national ridership increased by over 22% between 1996 and 2005. As shown, ridership peaked in 2001, dropping somewhat over the next 2 years and then rising again in 2004 and reaching the high point for the decade in 2005. The growth during the late 1990s generally coincided with the economic boom during that period—and the subsequent ridership decline in the next 2 years similarly paralleled the economic downturn beginning that year.

While most agencies experienced at least modest ridership growth during the late 1990s, many agencies were able to sustain demand even between 2001 and 2003. As is discussed below, factors associated with the economy are certainly among the many influences on transit usage; one specific factor contributing to the resurgence of demand in 2004—continuing in 2005—was the sharp rise in gasoline prices. However, the research conducted in this study and elsewhere has shown that transit agency strategies have also played major roles in increasing ridership. This chapter reviews the external factors that affect ridership and the types of internal strategies agencies can use to build and retain ridership.

Factors Affecting Ridership

The research in this area has considered both internal and external factors that have contributed to demand for transit services. Agencies have utilized a broad range of internal strategies (i.e., actions planned and implemented by the agencies) related to service design, marketing, pricing and other types of efforts to help spur ridership growth. However, external factors outside of the agencies' direct control (e.g., local economic conditions, cost/availability of alternative transportation modes, and land use/development patterns and policies) have also exerted a strong influence, both positive and negative, on demand levels. The relationship between external factors and ridership can be quite straightforward; for instance, population and employment growth in a region can raise transit demand simply by expanding the potential ridership base. Alternatively, certain factors (e.g., fuel prices, parking availability and prices, and regional development patterns) affect transit ridership by influencing the relative attractiveness of transit versus automobile use. While an agency may not be able to explicitly control these external factors, it can monitor them, anticipate their potential impact on transit demand, and take actions to mitigate—or take advantage of—them.

Given the importance of these different types of factors, it is useful to understand the nature of the relative impacts of internal versus external factors. As transit demand is influenced by a combination of factors, it is a challenge to isolate the impact of any particular action or factor.

Table 2-1. Annual US transit ridership totals, 1996–2005.

	1996	1997	1998	1999	2000	2001	2002	2003	2004	2005
Ridership (000s)	7948	8374	8750	9168	9363	9653	9623	9427	9586	9708
Change from previous year	—	5.4%	4.5%	4.8%	2.1%	3.1%	-0.3%	-2.0%	1.7%	1.3%
Cumulative change (from '96)	—	5.4%	11.0%	15.4%	17.8%	21.5%	21.1%	18.6%	20.6%	22.1%

SOURCE: *APTA Transit Ridership Reports*, 1997 - 2005

However, a number of the studies identified in Chapter 1, as well as the case studies conducted for this project, have examined the relative influences of external and internal factors on transit usage. The key findings from these studies are reviewed below.

Previous TCRP Studies

As indicated in Chapter 1, a number of previous TCRP studies have investigated the factors affecting transit ridership growth. Several of these have considered in particular the relative impact on demand of internal versus external factors—as well as the impact of individual types of agency initiatives. *TCRP Research Results Digest 4: Transit Ridership Initiative*, for example, reports that, based on interviews with senior staff at 27 transit agencies, "forces traditionally outside the control of transit planners, managers and even policy makers may have greater impacts on ridership than any combination of traditional fare, marketing, service design, or operational initiatives" (p. 5). On the other hand, the study also notes that "the introduction of nontraditional services and planning initiatives in many areas seems to suggest, however, that progress can be made in terms of both absolute ridership and market share, even in the short term. This is particularly true in communities that are pursuing strategies that better match an increasing variety of services with diverse markets" (p. 5).

A follow-up study, described in *TCRP Research Results Digest 29: Continuing Examination of Successful Transit Ridership Initiatives*, considered the ridership trends over the next few years (1994–1996) of 22 of the agencies examined in the above study—along with trends at 20 additional agencies. Based on interviews with officials at these 42 agencies, the report notes that "external forces continue to have a potentially greater effect on ridership than system and service design initiatives" (p. 1). This report further suggests that the most important external factors (at least for the period covered by the study, 1994 through 1996) were

- "The resurgence of local and regional economies, which has spurred ridership growth;
- Reductions in federal transit operating assistance, which have suppressed ridership growth; and
- Integration of public transportation with other public policy initiatives and program areas (e.g., welfare-to-work, education, and social service delivery), which has spurred ridership and eased some funding constraints." (p. 1)

However, this study also found that various types of agency actions and initiatives "have played a significant role in recent ridership success stories" (p. 1). The categories of agency actions/initiatives identified were as follows:

- **Service adjustments.** Types of service adjustments most frequently mentioned in the survey were
  - Reallocation of service to the most productive routes
  - Increased frequency of service

- Enhanced passenger amenities
- Introduction of transit center-based route structures
- **Fare and pricing adaptations.** Frequently mentioned actions included
  - The introduction or expansion of deep discount passes
  - The expansion of outlet sales
  - Cooperative programs with businesses or other organizations or institutions
- **Planning orientation.** Frequently mentioned examples included
  - Community-based planning activities
  - Strategic plans
  - Comprehensive operational analyses
- **Marketing and informational initiatives.** These initiatives included "approaches ranging from broad public information campaigns to programs tailored to specific markets or specific services" (p. 12).
- **Service coordination, consolidation and market segmentation.** These initiatives "are intended to highlight instances in which integration is occurring across a broad spectrum of transportation service providers and others, or where the needs of specific submarkets or user groups are being targeted." (p. 13).

While the report observes that "most systems experiencing major ridership increases attribute the increases to various combinations of strategies" (p. 1), it also notes that "route and service restructuring" was a prominent factor contributing to ridership increases during the study period (1994–96) and that "many of the systems experiencing significant ridership increases between 1994 and 1996 instituted or expanded deep discount fare policies along with efforts to make passes more widely available throughout their communities" (p. 2).[1]

A second follow-up study, described in *TCRP Research Results Digest 69: Evaluation of Recent Ridership Increases*, reviewed the 31 U.S. transit agencies experiencing the greatest ridership increases between 2000 and 2002. This included 15 of the 42 agencies examined in the previous study. Based on interviews with senior managers at 28 of these agencies, the study authors found that many of the factors observed in the previous study continued to play key roles in influencing ridership. As was found in the earlier studies, service adjustments represented the type of initiatives most widely cited as having influenced ridership, with service expansion mentioned by three-quarters of the agencies; more than half of the agencies reported service coordination and partnering (especially with universities), and half cited fare and pricing adaptations (including introduction of new fare media and technologies). Nearly half of the agencies suggested that shifts in planning orientation (including strategic planning and customer-oriented planning) were key factors. The one area that was not seen as important in increasing ridership by at least half of the agencies was marketing and information initiatives: one-sixth of the agencies "indicated that stand-alone marketing campaigns or initiatives were significant factors in ridership increases."[2]

TCRP Report 27: Building Transit Ridership: An Exploration of Transit's Market Share and the Public Policies That Influence It, reported on interviews with managers at 50 transit agencies—and subsequent case studies of 8 selected agencies. Like *TCRP Research Results Digest 29*, this study identified a range of specific internal transit strategies with the "potential for increasing transit ridership or market share" (p. 7). These strategies are shown in Table 2-2.

---

[1] The ridership changes over the past several years for the examples reviewed in *TCRP Research Results Digest 29* are considered in Appendix A provided on the accompanying CD-ROM.
[2] *TCRP Research Results Digest 69*, p. 2.

Table 2-2. List of potential transit strategies for building ridership (from *TCRP Report 27*).

Category	Type	Strategies
Service improvements	General	Increased route structure Increased frequency Service cutbacks Dynamic scheduling Increased speed Improved security Improved comfort Increased capacity
	Suburb to suburb	High-occupancy vehicle lanes/facilities Transportation demand management programs Suburban activity centers
	Suburb to central city	Feeder services Fare integration Service coordination (timed transfers) Unitickets Station parking provisions
	Within central city	Core services
Information to customers	Real-time information services	Location Schedules
	Low technology	Tailored schedules Bus stop information
	Medium technology	Computerized information systems Kiosks
Marketing and promotion		Fare incentives Education New resident promotion Image advertising Cooperative promotions
Public policy changes		User-side subsidies Parking pricing/regulation Income taxes Fuel/carbon taxes Dedicated operating support Land use policy Local area bus services
Road pricing		Various

SOURCE: *TCRP Report 27: Building Transit Ridership: An Exploration of Transit's Market Share and the Public Policies That Influence It* (1997), p. 8

In analyzing basic mode choice decisions, *TCRP Report 27* concluded that "transit ridership, in particular, has been found to vary with five general types of factors:

- **The levels of travel-inducing activities.** Since travel is predominantly a derived demand, as the levels of those activities that require passenger transportation change, so can the demand for transit service be expected to change.
- **The price and other characteristics of the service.** The price and various aspects of the level of service provided by the transit system have been shown by substantial previous research to affect the level of ridership.
- **Other transportation options.** The price and service characteristics of substitute and complementary modes of travel may also be expected to influence transit passenger volumes.
- **The characteristics of the population served.** The market for transit services comprises individuals with heterogeneous tastes, and the level of demand can be expected to vary between different demographic and socioeconomic subgroups of the population.
- **Other factors.** Other determinants of transit patronage levels that are not easily classified into the above four categories include, for example, the weather and changes in public tastes over time." (p. 25)

However, in considering these mode choice factors, the authors conclude that "transit-side strategies alone are insufficient to achieve a large modal shift" (p. 11). This is attributed primarily to observations that:

- "The private vehicle's quality of service is valued very highly.
- The range of transit service improvements is quite limited.
- The automobile ownership decision dominates the mode choice hierarchy." (p. 11)

TCRP Report 27 also explains that "land use and related factors are very important" (p. 11). Three factors in particular are suggested as "affecting the interrelationship between land use and transit ridership: urban expressway capacity, urban core density, and downtown parking availability" (p. 11). Moreover, "ridership levels and market shares are very strongly associated with development densities, and are, therefore, highest in the core areas of the nation's most densely developed cities" (p. 22). Finally, this report considers how various types of public policies (enacted at the federal, state and local levels) affect mode choice—and thus influence transit demand. Table 2-3 summarizes the mode choice impacts of the different types of public policy initiatives.

TCRP Report 95: Traveler Response to Transportation System Changes represents a compilation and discussion of previous analyses of the nature of the impacts of various types of transportation system actions on demand; the study does not specifically address external factors. Individual chapters of the overall study have been published as stand-alone reports. Four of these reports (*Chapter 9—Transit Scheduling and Frequency, Chapter 10—Bus Routing and Coverage, Chapter 11—Transit Information and Promotion,* and *Chapter 12—Transit Pricing and Fares*) are particularly relevant to our study. Each of these chapters presents and discusses the results of analyses and agency experience regarding the nature of traveler response to a particular type of strategy. (The key findings from these chapters are discussed in Chapters 5 through 8.)

Table 2-3. Summary of mode choice impacts of public policies.

Transportation Investment Policy
• Infrastructure spending directly affects the relative attractiveness of each mode
• Transit operating assistance can help maintain, improve or expand services
• Research and development funding provides innovations in the provision of transportation services
Transportation Pricing Policy
• Taxes and tolls make automobile use more expensive
• Local policies dictate taxi fares, and indirectly, service levels
• Local parking pricing and availability are very important components of the cost of driving
Environmental Policy
• Federal/state emissions standards increase new car prices
• Local air quality mandates require programs to reduce single-occupant vehicle use
• Local policies influence development patterns and transportation pricing
Energy Policy
• Minimum average fuel economy standards increase new car prices and decrease operating costs
• Alternative fuel vehicle and research and development provisions of Energy Policy Act are unlikely to affect choices made by consumers/households
Tax Policy
• Income taxes affect economic activity and disposable income, thereby influencing the affordability of various travel choices
• Preferential parking cost deductions promote automobile commuting over transit
• Sales taxes affect automobile costs and may support public transit
• Mortgage interest deductions influence housing location choice
• Property taxes may support local roadway infrastructure
Land Use Policy
• Provisions of zoning laws (lot size, use) affect the viability of public transit
• Design reviews and other restrictions can require definitive plans for addressing transportation issues in new developments

SOURCE: *TCRP Report 27: Building Transit Ridership: An Exploration of Transit's Market Share and the Public Policies That Influence It* (1997), p. 33

Mineta Institute Study

The Mineta Transportation Institute study cited earlier (*Increasing Transit Ridership: Lessons from the Most Successful Transit Systems in the 1990's*) provides the most comprehensive review of the relative impacts of external and internal factors on transit ridership. Utilizing a range of methodological approaches (a literature review, an analysis of nationwide transit data/trends, and a survey of transit agency officials and in-depth case studies), the researchers consistently found that "the most significant factors influencing transit use are external to transit systems" (p. 105). Through an analysis of the National Transit Database (NTD) data for all U.S. transit agencies, the researchers found, in particular, "extraordinarily strong correlations between ridership and three external factors related to economic activity: unemployment rate, real hourly wage and real GDP" (p. 105). These correlations are summarized in Table 2-4. However, the researchers also found "a relatively high degree of correlation between transit ridership and the internal factors tested" (p. 105). The internal factors tested were related to average fare and service provided (revenue-vehicle miles and revenue-vehicle miles per person); these correlations are also shown in Table 2-4. The authors note, though, that the correlations to the amount of service "do not necessarily imply causality." They point out that "increased service should increase ridership, but increased demand should also motivate transit managers to increase service" (p. 34).

The Mineta Institute researchers conducted a survey of the 227 U.S. systems that gained ridership between 1995 and 1999; 103 usable responses were obtained. Consistent with the findings from the other methodologies, the survey responses indicated that ridership increases could be attributed to a combination of internal and external factors. The following basic categories of external factors were identified through this survey (p. 57):

- **Population growth.** Specific factors include increased immigration and rising transit dependency (due to aging populations, for instance).
- **Strong economy and employment growth.** Specific factors include increased tourism and greater demand for travel in general.
- **Changing metropolitan form.** Specific factors include increased suburbanization and residential/employment relocation.
- **Changes to transportation system.** Specific factors include increased congestion, reduced parking availability and increased costs, increased gas prices, and construction projects and time delays.

The internal factor categories identified were as follows (p. 57):

- **Fare changes and innovations.** Specific factors include fare decrease or freeze, universal fare coverage programs, and introduction of new payment options.

Table 2-4. Correlation coefficients of internal and external factors and transit ridership: 1995–1999.

	Unlinked Trips	Unlinked Trips/Person
Internal Factors		
Real average fare (2001$)	-0.61	-0.81
Revenue vehicle miles	0.81	n/a
Revenue vehicle miles per person	n/a	0.37
External Factors		
Unemployment rate	-0.70	-0.16
Real hourly wage (2001$)	0.96	0.70
Real GDP (2001$)	0.79	0.24
Real GDP per person (2001$)	0.82	0.29

SOURCE: Mineta Transportation Institute, *Increasing Transit Ridership: Lessons from the Most Successful Transit Systems in the 1990's* (2002), p. 4 (source of data in table: calculation using National Transit Database data)

- **Marketing and information programs.** This category includes advertising, niche marketing/market segmentation, survey research and customer satisfaction feedback mechanisms.
- **Service improvements.** This category includes expansion of routes (geographical/temporal), introduction of new/specialized service, and route restructuring.
- **Amenities/service quality.** This category includes development of transit centers, development of park-and-ride facilities, increasing frequency/reliability of service, cleanliness of service, new vehicles, and bus stop improvements (e.g., signage, shelters, and benches).
- **Partnerships.** This category includes community outreach/education, planning and strategies, and intra-agency cooperation.

The results of the survey, in terms of frequency with which each of the internal factors was cited, are shown in Table 2-5. As indicated, the internal factors mentioned most often by the survey respondents as contributing to ridership increases were service expansion and route restructuring; these were followed by advertising/information programs. In general, internal factors were mentioned more often than external factors—as could be expected from transit managers. However, external factors were acknowledged as having an impact; the most commonly mentioned external factors were economic/employment growth, population growth and worsening traffic congestion.

The final element of the study was a set of case studies of a dozen of the "most successful" U.S. transit agencies (in terms of ridership growth during the study period). The major factors cited by these agencies as being primarily responsible for their ridership growth are summarized in Table 2-6. As indicated, there was considerable variability in the major causes identified, although "several agencies were forthright in attributing the bulk of their ridership increases to external factors such as rapid population increases and economic growth" (p. 103).

Table 2-5. Frequency of internal programs contributing to ridership growth (from Mineta Institute survey of U.S. transit agencies).

Type of Program	Size of Transit System					Total (n=103)	% of Systems Mentioning Program	Rank
	Very Small (n=29)	Small (n=13)	Medium (n=22)	Large (n=17)	Very Large (n=22)			
Service Improvements								
Service expansion	23	13	17	14	16	83	81%	1
Route restructuring	19	12	11	12	6	62	60%	2
Introduction of new/specialized services	14	10	10	6	11	51	50%	4
Fare Innovations/Changes								
New payment options	7	5	2	8	7	29	28%	6
Universal fare coverage program (UFC)	2	6	6	5	9	28	27%	7
Fare freezes/decreases	12	1	1	2	4	20	19	9
Marketing								
Advertising/information program	20	9	12	7	11	59	57%	3
Market segmentation/niche marketing	2	0	0	6	2	10	10%	10
Partnerships								
Employer-based partnerships (including UFC)	3	7	6	9	8	33	32%	5
University-based partnerships (including UFC)	3	4	7	5	6	25	24%	8
Community outreach/local government	2	0	3	2	0	7	7%	11
Social service collaboration	1	1	0	1	2	5	5%	14
Service Quality and Amenities								
Reliability/shortened headways	1	0	2	3	1	7	7%	11
Park and ride lots	1	2	1	0	2	6	6%	13
Rail development	0	1	0	0	4	5	5%	14
Bus stop improvements	1	0	1	1	0	3	3%	16
Safety, cleanliness	0	0	0	3	0	3	3%	16
New buses	1	0	0	0	1	2	2%	18

Note: Since there are multiple responses per transit system, "% of Systems Mentioning Program" does not sum to 100%

SOURCE: Mineta Transportation Institute, *Increasing Transit Ridership: Lessons from the Most Successful Transit Systems in the 1990's* (2002), p. 58 (source of data in table: survey of 103 transit agencies that reported ridership increases between 1995 and 1999)

Table 2-6. Causes of ridership increases reported by case study agencies (from Mineta Institute case studies of U.S. transit agencies).

Agency (location)	Major population/ employment increases	Major fare structure change	Flash pass system instituted	Coordination with major employers	Extensive public participation	Extensive use of market research	Major capital investment	Land use policies	New fixed rail routes	Major route reconfiguration
ATC (Las Vegas, NV)	++									
AMA (San Juan, PR)										++
Caltrain (SF Bay area)	++			+						++
Gainesville (FL) RTS		+	++		+		+			
Green Bus Line (Brooklyn, NY)		++								
Long Beach (CA) Transit		++					+			
MARTA (Atlanta, GA)	++			+						
Milwaukee Co. (WI) Transit		++	++	++						
MTA-NYCT (NY City)	++	++					+	++		
OMNITRANS (Riverside, CA)							+			
Pace (Chicago, IL)		++		++						
Tri-Met (Portland, OR)							+		++	++
% cited as major factor	33%	42%	17%	17%	0%	0%	8%	8%	8%	17%
% cited as secondary factor	0%	0%	0%	17%	8%	33%	8%	0%	0%	0%
% cited as factor	33%	50%	17%	33%	8%	33%	17%	8%	8%	17%

++ denotes cited as major factor   + denotes cited as secondary factor

SOURCE: Mineta Transportation Institute, *Increasing Transit Ridership: Lessons from the Most Successful Transit Systems in the 1990s* (2002), p. 99 (source of data in table: interviews with managers at case study agencies listed)

Other Studies

A number of other studies have considered the relative impacts of internal and external factors on transit ridership. For example, Gomez-Ibanez ("Big-City Transit Ridership, Deficits and Politics Avoiding Reality in Boston," 1996) analyzed ridership changes at the MBTA (Boston) in the late 20th Century, and found the agency's ridership to be considerably more strongly influenced by downtown employment levels and real per capita income levels than by changes in service levels or fares. He estimated that, for each 1% drop in employment, MBTA ridership would be lowered by 1.24 to 1.75%, and that each 1% rise in per capita income would result in a 0.70% drop in ridership. In contrast, Gomez-Ibanez determined that a 1% increase in the amount of service provided would result in a gain of 0.30 to 0.36% in ridership, and a 1% reduction in fares would generate 0.22 to 0.23% in additional ridership.

A study by Kain and Liu (*Secrets of Success: How Houston and San Diego Transit Providers Achieved Large Increases in Transit Ridership*, 1995) analyzed data (for the years 1968–1992), to ascertain why ridership in both cities generally increased during the early 1990s—a time when many transit systems were suffering significant ridership losses. The researchers attribute much of the increases in both cities to a combination of two internal transit factors (average fares and revenue vehicle miles of service) and three external factors (i.e., regional employment levels, fuel prices, and automobile ownership levels). In an earlier study of transit in Portland (OR), Liu (*Determinants of Public Transit Ridership: Analysis of Post World War II Trends and Evaluation of Alternative Networks*, 1993), considering the same types of variables (using data from

1976–1990), found that several external factors (per capita income, automobile ownership, and suburbanization of residences and employment locations) had a greater impact on demand for transit than did internal factors (i.e., annual transit miles and average fares).

Finally, regarding the relative impact of internal strategies, a major regional bus study in the Washington, DC area (TranSystems Corp. et al., *WMATA Regional Bus Study – Final Report*, September 2003) included an analysis of the various types of service improvements and their relative potential contributions to an overall goal of doubling ridership over the next 20 years. The results of this analysis are shown in Table 2-7. As indicated, "expand fixed route coverage" was expected to have the largest relative impact among the service improvements, followed closely by "improve frequency"; note, however, that "normal expected ridership growth" (due to non service-related factors) was expected to have the largest impact.

In considering the factors affecting transit demand and productivity, the WMATA study also concluded that "For bus routes, and indeed for transit in general, perhaps the most important single factor affecting ridership is the *density of development* in the corridor served by the route. Density is so important because a fixed-route service has, by definition, a limited service area. It is limited because people (1) don't like to walk and (2) don't like to transfer." (*WMATA Regional Bus Study – Comprehensive Operational Analysis Summary Report*, February 2001, p. 67)

This study further evaluated the relationship between ridership/productivity on specific routes and several selected land use and demographic factors along these routes. Regression analysis was conducted involving five independent variables (related to residential density, employment density, household vehicle ownership, number of senior residents, and proximity to regional activity centers) and three ridership measures (i.e., ridership, peak productivity, and off-peak productivity). None of the variables alone were found to explain much of the variation in ridership or productivity. However, the analysis confirmed that ridership and productivity tend to be higher in areas that have a greater-than-average percentage of households with no vehicles; it also indicated that ridership tends to be higher for routes that serve regional activity centers. (p. 77)

Findings from the Case Studies

As discussed in Chapter 1, a key element of this project was a series of case studies of U.S. transit agencies that have deployed various strategies to promote ridership growth.[3] Table 2-8 shows the types of ridership strategies deployed by these agencies. As indicated in the table, the case study agencies used various combinations of strategies in their efforts to increase ridership, and most agencies used strategies in all major categories. All twelve agencies deployed partnership/coordination initiatives, eleven used operating/service adjustments,

Table 2-7. Relative contributions of service improvements to doubling of ridership in Washington region (over a 20-year period).

Strategy/Factor	Estimated % Increase
Normal expected ridership growth	36%
Expand fixed-route coverage	23%
Improve frequency	19%
RapidBus, priority and strategic corridors	8%
Enhance image of bus systems	8%
Extend span of service	4%
Introduce flexible-route service	2%
Total	100%

SOURCE: TranSystems Corp., *WMATA Regional Bus Study Final Report* (Sept. 2003), p. 42

---

[3] The case study reports are included in Appendix D which is provided on the accompanying CD-ROM.

Table 2-8. Types of strategies used by case study agencies.

Category/Subcategory/Type of Initiative	AT	BAT	BRATS	CATA	GCRTA	OCTA	Ride On	Transfort	Tri-Met	UTA	VISTA	WTA	No. of Strategies
Operating/Service Adjustments													40
Routing/coverage adjustments													17
Increased route coverage	X	X		X		X						X	5
Route restructuring	X	X		X	X		X	X		X			7
Improved schedule/route coordination	X	X	X					X		X			5
Scheduling/frequency adjustments													12
Increased service frequency	X					X	X		X	X			5
Increased span of service		X				X	X					X	4
Improved reliability/on-time performance	X					X				X			3
New types of service													7
Improved travel speed/reduced stops	X	X							X	X			4
Targeted services	X	X		X									3
Improved amenities													4
Passenger facility improvements						X		X	X				3
New/improved vehicles						X							1
Increased security and safety													0
Partnerships/Coordination													27
Partnerships													18
University/school pass programs	X	X		X	X	X	X	X		X		X	9
Travel demand management strategies	X		X		X	X	X	X	X				7
Privately subsidized activity center service	X			X									2
Coordination													9
Consistent regional (inter-agency) operating policies						X				X			2
Coordination with social service agencies		X						X					2
Coordination with other transportation agencies	X						X	X					3
Promotion of transit-supportive design/TOD	X								X				2
Marketing and Information Initiatives													23
Marketing/promotional initiatives													12
Targeted marketing/promotions				X		X		X	X			X	5
General marketing/promotions		X		X	X	X			X	X	X		7
Information improvements													11
Improved informational materials	X	X		X		X		X					5
Improved customer information/assistance				X		X		X					3
Automated transit traveler information				X				X		X			3
Fare Collection/Structure Initiatives													14
Fare collection improvements													9
Improved payment convenience		X		X	X	X		X		X	X		7
Regional payment integration							X			X			2
Fare structure changes													5
Fare structure simplification		X											1
Fare reduction	X			X		X			X				4

ten marketing/promotional and information initiatives and nine fare collection/structure initiatives. The most common type of strategy was operating/service adjustments (40 separate actions, strategies or initiatives implemented by all of the case study agencies), followed by partnership/coordination initiatives (27), marketing/promotional and information initiatives (23), and fare collection/structure initiatives (14).

The most widely used subcategories were partnerships (18 separate initiatives among all the case study agencies) and routing/coverage adjustments (17). Other commonly used subcategories included scheduling/frequency adjustments (12), marketing/promotional initiatives (12) and information improvements (11). The least used were improved amenities (4) and fare structure changes (5). With regard to specific types of action, the most common was university/school pass (9 separate initiatives), followed by route restructuring (7), travel demand management strategies (7), general marketing/promotions (7), and improved payment convenience (7).

The case studies examined, to the extent possible, the effect of specific strategies on ridership at each agency. In some cases, however, strategies are too recent to allow for any assessment of the ridership impact. In other cases, particularly where agencies have simultaneously implemented several strategies, it was not possible to isolate the impact of individual efforts. At several of the agencies, multiple strategies actually comprised elements of a single comprehensive ridership enhancement program. For example, OCTA's "Putting Customers First" campaign included service adjustments, marketing efforts and fare collection/structure improvements. Similarly, TriMet's "Frequent Service" program included a range of marketing and informational efforts as well as service adjustments.

Based on the cases where sufficiently detailed data were available, it was determined that the most significant direct impacts on ridership have come from different types of operating/service adjustments (particularly increased route coverage, route restructuring, and increased service frequency) and as a result of partnerships with various local entities (particularly universities). Although marketing/promotions and information improvements seldom had a major direct effect on ridership, they invariably represented important complements to the introduction of any service improvements—and were often instrumental in the establishment of key partnerships. For example, establishing and maintaining a positive image of the transit agency in the community was seen by several agencies as a crucial element both in attracting/retaining riders and building key partnerships. Fare collection and fare structure initiatives similarly were not typically seen as having major ridership impacts on their own, but also represented important "pieces of the overall puzzle."[4] (In actuality, the distinction between categories is often blurred; for example, a key result of many partnerships is some type of new fare payment mechanism.)

In addition to reviewing the specific strategies—and ridership trends—at each agency, each of the case studies assessed the effect on ridership of various external factors (e.g., gasoline price trends, regional employment/unemployment levels, and population growth in the service areas). The key findings regarding external factors are as follows:

- Gasoline prices fluctuated somewhat between 1995 and 2004, experiencing a net increase, but averaging a less than 5% increase per year through 2003. Although gas prices were presumably one of many factors affecting people's decision to use transit, there is no clear relationship in any of the case study locations between gas price and transit demand through 2004. However, the precipitous rise in gas prices (53%) between October 2004 and October 2005 has been a more important factor contributing to the ridership growth during that period. The retail price of regular gasoline reached a high average price of over $3 per gallon in September 2005; this represents an increase of over 185% since 1995, and the price has more than doubled just since 2002. Although the price subsequently fell significantly (the average was approximately $2.15, as of December 2005), the earlier sharp rise doubtless led many people who previously might never have considered using transit to reconsider their modal decisions—and to use transit for at least a portion of their trips. Thus, the fuel price increase through much of 2005 was clearly a factor affecting transit ridership.
- In most of the case study regions, the unemployment rate peaked in 2002 or 2003 and has declined somewhat since then. However, in a few places (i.e., Lansing, Cleveland, and Bangor), unemployment has continued to rise over the past couple of years. Ridership has grown in these locations—despite the increase in unemployment—as well as in locations that saw a drop in unemployment. Thus, while unemployment is certainly a factor affecting demand,

---

[4]Although not observed in any of the Case Studies, Chapter 8 points out that fare-related strategies can have significant effects on ridership; in particular, reduction of fare levels (e.g., introduction of free transfers) has in several instances resulted in considerable jumps in demand. For example, the introduction of free bus-rail transfers and a variety of prepaid options in New York City in the late 1990s led to a 15% ridership gain.

there was no discernible direct relationship between the unemployment trend and ridership in any of the case study systems.
- Regarding population changes, the case study areas varied considerably: one area (Cleveland) experienced a small loss (3%) between 2000 and 2004, two others (Bangor and Lansing) stayed roughly even, and the others all saw significant growth (from 3% in Advance Transit's area to Ventura County's 13%). Population growth doubtless contributed to ridership increases in most of these locations, although the percentage ridership growth generally far outstripped the percentage population increase. In comparing the rate of population change to the demand trend, there is no direct relationship between the two factors; for example, the agency that saw the greatest percentage rise in demand (Advance Transit) had one of the lower population increases, and the second largest ridership rise (CATA) occurred in a region that had very little growth during the review period.
- However, population and economic growth associated with particular trip generators did appear to have an effect on ridership in a couple of the case study locations. These included growth/expansion of college campuses and medical centers. For instance, significant expansion of the Dartmouth campus and two medical centers—and the resulting increase in traffic congestion and limited availability of parking—directly contributed to increased transit demand at Advance Transit. Meanwhile, increasing enrollment at University of Maine would seem to be a key factor affecting ridership on one of BAT's key routes.
- Specific events affected demand at two of the case study locations: (1) The presence of the Winter Olympics in 2002 caused an overall increase in economic activity in and around Salt Lake City, and a marketing campaign encouraged local residents to use transit rather than driving. This contributed to an increase in UTA's ridership in 2002 despite the economic recession occurring in 2001–02. (2) A period of particularly heavy rainfall in Ventura County washed out roads for a week in 2004 and made many routes inoperable; while there was still ridership growth in 2004–05, it occurred at a rate somewhat lower than that of the previous years.

Thus, although certain specific developments or events apparently directly affected transit use at several of the case study locations, and broader trends (e.g., related to gasoline prices, employment/unemployment levels, and population changes) certainly contributed to ridership increases at all locations, the overall finding from the case studies is that these external factors had less of an effect than the agencies' own initiatives on ridership growth during the review period.

The next section discusses the categorization of specific internal and external factors affecting transit ridership.

Categorization of Factors Affecting Ridership

Mode Choice Parameters

Thus, as indicated by the above research findings, transit demand results from a combination of a broad range of factors, some within an agency's direct control and others not. In categorizing the specific types of factors/strategies of both types, it is also useful to review the parameters that contribute to mode choice decisions, particularly those that influence the decision to use transit. The basic considerations involved in mode choice decisions are the characteristics of the mode and the characteristics of the individual traveler and can be summarized as follows:

- Price and availability of each mode. This includes factors such as
  - The availability and cost of automobile use (i.e., day-to-day costs such as fuel, parking cost/availability, and tolls, as well as long-term costs such as purchase/lease, maintenance/repairs, insurance, taxes, and registration; also, nature of employer subsidy if any) and

- The availability and cost of transit (i.e., fare, employer or other subsidy, if any, and parking cost, if applicable).
- Quality of service of each mode. This includes factors such as
  - Travel time (i.e., the door-to-door time required to make a trip);
  - Convenience (i.e., the effort needed to access and use the transit service, including the need to transfer and the walking distance to/from a stop/station at both ends of the trip; also, ease of accessing schedule and other types of information, amenities such as bicycle racks, guaranteed-ride-home provision for transit or ridesharing);
  - Comfort (e.g., crowding/amount of space, seating arrangements, privacy, shelter at bus stops, and personal entertainment possibilities);
  - Service reliability (i.e., the predictability of the travel time and schedule from day to day);
  - Perceived personal security/safety; and
  - Perceived overall "image" of each mode (e.g., courtesy/helpfulness of transit personnel, and cleanliness of transit vehicles and stations).
- Trip characteristics for each particular trip. This includes factors such as
  - Trip length and purpose,
  - Number of people to be making the trip, and
  - Whether there are multiple destinations involved.
- Personal (sociodemographic) characteristics of the traveler. This includes factors such as
  - Income;
  - Origin and destination locations; and
  - Status (e.g., employed, student, or retired).

Clearly, the majority of the specific parameters in these categories lie outside of the transit agency's direct control and thus represent external factors. Nevertheless, it is important to realize that the transit agency can control key parameters in the first two categories. In other words, the crux of the challenge in generating high ridership for transit services is to make transit as competitive as possible in the areas of *pricing* and *service quality*—while developing a clear understanding of how best to address the considerations in the latter two categories.

Categorization of External Factors

As indicated above, industry researchers have identified a range of factors outside of transit agencies' direct control that have a strong influence on transit demand. Essentially, these factors can be divided into two general classifications, those that affect demand for and supply of transit service. The former can be further divided into those factors, discussed above, that influence the mode choice decision (this applies to those travelers who have the option of using their own automobiles—or another non-transit mode) versus those factors that more directly affect the need or market for transit service (e.g., population characteristics or changes in a region that have an impact on the number of transit-dependent travelers). The supply side refers to the ability to provide adequate transit service in a region; this is related to such factors as funding availability and land use/development patterns (e.g., can sufficient transit be provided to adequately serve dispersed employment and residential locations?).

Based on the industry review, the key external factors affecting transit ridership can be categorized as shown in Table 2-9. The type of impact (demand versus supply) is shown for each individual factor. As indicated, a number of factors apply to more than one of these classifications. As suggested above, while a transit agency may not be able to directly control such factors, it is important to understand their effect on demand and consider them in developing internal strategies. In fact, the appropriateness—and effectiveness—of specific types of agency actions will in many cases depend on the prevailing conditions and policies. An agency should thus monitor the prevailing trends within these factors and pursue strategies that take advantage of—or, if necessary, mitigate—them.

Table 2-9. Summary of external factors influencing transit ridership.

Type of Factor	Demand - Mode choice decision	Demand - Need/market for transit	Supply (i.e., ability to provide adequate transit)
Population characteristics/changes			
General growth in the region		X	X
High/increased immigration		X	
High/increased number of seniors		X	
High/increased tourism		X	
High number of college students		X	
Economic conditions			
Employment/unemployment levels	X	X	
Per capita income levels	X	X	
Household auto ownership levels	X	X	
Cost and availability of alternative modes			
Fuel and toll pricing	X		
Parking pricing and availability	X		
Taxi fares	X		
Fuel taxes	X		
Auto purchase and ownership costs	X		
Availability of commuter benefits programs by employers	X		
Land use/development patterns and policies			
Density of development		X	X
Relative locations of major employers and residential areas (e.g., increasing suburbanization)	X	X	X
Land use/zoning controls and incentives			X
Travel conditions			
Climate/weather patterns	X		
Traffic congestion levels/highway capacity	X		
Traffic disruptions (e.g., from major construction projects)	X	X	X
Public policy/funding initiatives			
Air quality mandates	X		X
Auto emission standards	X		
Federal/state transit funding levels (capital and operating)			X
Local transit funding (e.g., sales or other tax receipts)			X

Categorization of Internal Factors and Strategies/Initiatives
Factors Affecting Transit Demand

As indicated above, a transit agency can control key mode choice decision parameters in two basic areas: pricing/availability and service quality. Thus, the agency's goal in seeking to generate high ridership is essentially to influence mode choice by (1) maximizing the relative attractiveness of transit in those two areas, and (2) recognizing and addressing the full range of requirements imposed by travelers' personal and trip characteristics.

The basic factors comprising the pricing/availability mode choice considerations are as follows:

- Fare levels;
- Nature of subsidy programs (e.g., with employers, social service agencies, and educational institutions); and
- Amount (including service hours/days) and types of service available.

The basic factors constituting the service quality mode choice considerations include the following:

- Route design;
- Service schedules and frequency of service;
- Service reliability (perceived and actual);
- Accessibility features (for persons with disabilities);
- Parking availability (e.g., park-and-ride lots for rail and express services);
- Availability, ease of obtaining, and usefulness of information and customer assistance;

Table 2-10. Types of strategies/actions/initiatives.

Category/Subcategory	Type of Strategy	Examples of Specific Actions/Initiatives
Operating/Service Adjustments		
Routing/coverage adjustments		
	Increased route coverage	Service expansion; introduction of local circulators
	Route restructuring	Reallocation to most productive routes, new crosstown routes
	Improved schedule/route coordination	Feeder services; timed transfers; transit centers; regional integration
Scheduling/frequency adjustments		
	Increased service frequency	Increased frequency on specific routes
	Increased span of service	Longer service hours (e.g., late night/weekend)
	Improved reliability/on-time performance	Implementation of AVL, transit signal priority, transfer connection protection
New types of service		
	Improved travel speed/reduced stops	Introduction of express bus, BRT, rail
	Targeted services	University-oriented service, downtown circulator, special event shuttle
Improved amenities		
	Passenger facility improvements	Improved bus stop/station, transit center, park-and-ride amenities
	New/improved vehicles	Improved amenities, use of articulated buses
	Increased security	Increased agency security presence
	Increased safety	Promotion of safety features of vehicles
Partnerships/Coordination		
Partnerships		
	University/school pass programs	Reduced pass price or per trip reimbursement to university (or other school)
	Travel demand management strategies	Employer pass/voucher programs; vanpooling; ride-matching; parking cash-out
	Subsidized activity center service	Subsidized service to office parks or other activity centers
Coordination		
	Consistent regional (inter-agency) oper. policies	Transfer agreements
	Coordination with social service agencies	Mobility manager; user-side subsidy program
	Coordination with other transportation agencies	Roadway or parking management strategies
	Promotion of transit-supportive design/TOD	Requirements for bus stops/shelters at new developments
Marketing and Information Initiatives		
Marketing/promotional initiatives		
	Targeted marketing/promotions	New resident/college student/tourist promotion; individualized marketing
	General marketing/promotions	Agency image advertising, special promotions, cooperative advertising
Information improvements		
	Improved informational materials	Easier to read printed system and route maps/schedules, flyers/newsletters
	Improved customer information and assistance	Transit information center, in-station customer assistants
	Automated transit traveler information	Pre-trip planning and en-route information, including real-time information
Fare Collection/Structure Initiatives		
Fare collection improvements		
	Improved payment convenience	AFC, new prepaid fare options, expanded fare media distribution/reload options
	Regional payment integration	Regional smart card program
Fare structure changes		
	Fare structure simplification	Elimination of fare zones; elimination of express or rail surcharge
	Fare reduction	Deeply discounted options; reduced base fare; free transfers, free fare zone

- Nature of passenger amenities (i.e., related to cleanliness, aesthetics, and comfort of vehicles and stations/bus stops/shelters);
- Ease of fare payment (e.g., purchase of prepaid options and type and technology of payment);
- Nature of integration (e.g., service/schedules and fare policies and payment) with other agencies in the region;
- Perceptions of agency safety and security; and
- Public image of agency.

Finally, certain aspects of the agency's organizational structure and management approach may well affect the agency's ability to develop and implement the types of strategies needed to generate high ridership; these elements include:

- Agency labor practices,
- Governing board structure and vision, and
- Agency corporate culture.

Such elements have the potential to facilitate—or inhibit—the agency's ability to offer new types of service (such as flexibly routed community-oriented service), pursue new partnerships (with universities, employers, or social service agencies) or otherwise innovate or respond proactively to changing markets.

The next section identifies the specific types of strategies, actions, and initiatives transit agencies have utilized in addressing the above factors and generating and/or sustaining significant ridership increases.

Types of Strategies, Actions, and Initiatives

Based on the industry review, transit agency strategies, actions, and initiatives can be generally categorized as follows:

- Operating/Service Adjustments,
- Partnerships/Coordination,
- Marketing and Information Initiatives, and
- Fare Collection/Structure Initiatives.

Subcategories, as well as examples of more specific types of actions and initiatives, are shown in Table 2-10. Key considerations in identifying appropriate strategies are discussed in Chapter 3. Agency examples of use of the various types of strategies are discussed in Appendix A (provided on the accompanying CD-ROM) and Chapter 4, and details related to each strategy are provided in Chapters 5 through 8.

CHAPTER 3

Identification of Service Needs and Opportunities

Introduction

In addition to understanding the relative impacts of external and internal factors, selecting appropriate strategies aimed at attracting/retaining riders requires

- Identifying service needs and opportunities; this includes determining gaps/deficiencies in existing services, as well as assessing the nature of unmet needs and potential markets for transit service.
- Identifying strategies that efficiently and effectively address the needs of one or more market segments, address gaps in existing service, and are appropriate to particular service environments.

The first of these steps is discussed here; the second is addressed in Chapter 4.

Evaluation of Existing Services

The basic elements in identifying the nature of service needs and opportunities in a region are (1) evaluation of the existing service network—as well as the supporting marketing program, information system, and fare system—to identify gaps/deficiencies/opportunities; and (2) development of an understanding of the characteristics and service needs of different market segments.

Changes in a region's development patterns, population characteristics, and economic conditions can often result in significant gaps or inefficiencies in the existing transit network—and can also create new opportunities. The increasing dispersion of population and employment centers in particular has produced new travel patterns in most regions that are typically not well served by CBD-oriented transit routes. An agency's marketing, information, and/or fare systems may similarly be insufficient to effectively support the region's needs. The first step in seeking to boost ridership should therefore be to evaluate the current service design and route performance; the agency should then assess the effectiveness of the existing marketing, information, and/or fare collection programs.

Service Evaluation

An agency can follow one of several approaches to evaluating its service, including

- Ongoing or periodic monitoring of route performance, with detailed evaluation of individual routes deemed to fall below defined service standards;
- Evaluation of all routes (e.g., a comprehensive operational analysis or service restructuring study); and
- Evaluation of a particular type of service (e.g., express routes) or routes within a particular corridor (i.e., as part of an alternatives analysis or corridor study aimed at considering the need/potential for a higher capacity service such as rail or BRT).

A detailed service evaluation process typically includes the following steps:

Ridership Data Collection

There are several different methods and tools for collecting ridership data; the basic methods/tools are as follows:

- **Manual boarding/alighting counts or ridechecks**—Agency "checkers" (or outside contractors) observe and count riders on individual routes. Counts can either be done at stops (as riders get on or off vehicles), on board (which more easily allows load counts as well as boarding and alighting counts), or even in a trailing automobile. Ridership information may be recorded manually or via specially programmed handheld units. Counts are most often done on a sample of trips for each route, although in some cases an agency may opt for collecting data on all trips for a particular day or days.
- **Automated passenger counts**—Agencies are increasingly using automated passenger counters (APCs) installed on buses to collect ridership data. APCs can be integrated with automated vehicle location (AVL) systems to link counts to the location of the vehicle.
- **Farebox data**—Agencies that have electronic registering fareboxes can also use fare payment data for ridership information separated by type of fare payment (including incidence of transfers). However, this data tends to be less reliable than that collected by other means, as the quality of the data tends to vary somewhat depending on the conscientiousness of individual drivers. Automated fare collection can improve the reliability of the data, especially if no driver action is required to record each fare category.
- **Customer surveys**—Agencies also collect a range of types of usage data through surveys of riders. Besides information related to customer attitudes (see the *Conducting Market Research* section below), questionnaires distributed on board vehicles or at stops/stations are useful for compiling origin-destination patterns and data on frequency of use, fare paid, access mode, and so forth.

The particular method an agency uses will depend on the resources available (i.e., the existence of APCs and/or registering fareboxes, and the number of checkers or the budget available for hiring data collection contractors). The method chosen may also depend on the intended usage of the data (e.g., for evaluating route-level performance or for reporting systemwide ridership to the National Transit Database).

Classification of Routes

Because individual routes perform different functions and serve different geographic areas, it is generally inappropriate to apply one set of standards to all routes. Thus, the first step in developing a series of route evaluation measures is to create a system of route classification—recognizing that many routes will not fall neatly into one class because they serve dual or multiple functions. An example of a route classification scheme is as follows:[1]

- Radial line haul,
- Express,
- Commuter,
- Urban circulator,
- Urban crosstown,
- Urban feeder/distributor,
- Suburban local,
- Suburban circumferential, and
- Suburban feeder/distributor.

---

[1] TranSystems Corp. et al., *WMATA Regional Bus Study – Comprehensive Operational Analysis Summary Report* (February 2001), prepared for Washington Metropolitan Area Transit Authority, p. 3.

Development of Route Evaluation Measures

Route evaluation measures are often placed into two basic categories:

- **Design measures**—These measures concern where bus routes ought to be operated and what the service characteristics of those routes should be. Typical examples include
    - **Coverage**—This measure applies to the whole system, rather than to individual routes, and serves to set the recommended spacing between routes for varying densities. For example, for high-density residential areas with at least 3 households per acre, an agency could decide that 90% of households should be within one quarter mile of a bus route, while, for medium-density suburban areas (e.g., 2–3 households per acre), 80% of households should be within one-quarter mile of a bus route.
    - **Span of service**—This measure addresses how many days per week, and how long on each day, service should be provided. An example of proposed span of service guidelines for a transit system with the above route classification scheme is shown in Table 3-1.
    - **Frequency of service**—Frequency of service thresholds is set to ensure a basic level of service for the area served by a route. For dense areas, for instance, an agency could specify that service should be provided at least every 15 minutes in peak periods and at least every 30 minutes in off-peak periods. For less dense areas, the thresholds might be 30 minutes for peak periods and 60 minutes for off-peak periods. An example of proposed frequency of service guidelines for a transit system with the above route classification scheme is as follows (Table 3-2).
    - **Travel time**—This measure encompasses both route directness and travel speed, since it compares the in-vehicle travel time on a bus from point A to point B to the driving time from point A to point B. Bus routes that are indirect or that have an excessive number of stops would have more difficulty attaining the established threshold (e.g., of having a travel time not more than twice the driving time). An example of proposed travel time guidelines for a transit system with the above route classification scheme is as follows (Table 3-3).
- **Performance measures**—These measures, which are more directly applicable to an operational analysis, quantify how well existing bus routes are used and whether service is comfortable and reliable for the passengers. Typical examples include

Table 3-1. Example, span of service measures.

Type of Service	First AM arrival not later than	Last AM arrival not earlier than	First PM departure not later than	Last PM departure not earlier than
Radial line haul—Urban	7:00	N/A	N/A	22:00
Radial line haul—Suburban	7:00	N/A	N/A	20:00
Commuter	7:00	9:00	16:00	18:30
Express	7:00	9:00	16:00	18:30
Urban circulator	No specific threshold			
Urban cross-town	7:00	N/A	N/A	22:00
Urban feeder/distributor	7:00	N/A	N/A	19:00
Suburban circumferential	7:00	N/A	N/A	18:30
Suburban feeder/distributor	7:00	N/A	N/A	19:00
Suburban local	7:00	N/A	N/A	19:00

Table 3-2. Example, frequency of service measures.

Type of Service	Weekday Peak Period	Weekday Off-Peak and Weekend
Urban Classes: Headway not greater than	15 minutes	30 minutes
Suburban Classes: Headway not greater than	30 minutes	60 minutes
Express Routes: Peak period trips not fewer than	4 trips	0 trips

Table 3-3. Example, travel time measures.

Type of Service	Ratio of Scheduled End-to-End AM Peak Bus Running Time to Zone-to-Zone Auto Travel Time
All types other than Express	2.0
Express	1.5

- **Productivity**—Productivity measures the level of demand for the route. The demand can be quantified, for instance, in terms of the number of boardings per vehicle revenue hour or boardings per trip for express routes. The measure may have separate thresholds for peak period and off-peak period service and may also have a full-day threshold in case ridership and operational data are not available for peak and off-peak service separately. An example of proposed productivity measures for a transit system with the above route classification scheme is as follows (Table 3-4).
- **Crowding**—A passenger's perception of the *crowding* on a bus is most easily quantified by the load factor—the number of passengers on board at the peak load point divided by the number of seats. A load factor above 1.0 indicates that some people were forced to stand for a portion of the trip. Except for infrequent services (headway greater than 30 minutes) the load factor on one individual trip is typically not critical; thus, this measure may instead consider, for example, the average load over two consecutive trips for medium frequency services, and over all trips within the peak 30 minutes for frequent services. An example of proposed crowding measures for a transit system with the above route classification scheme is as follows (Table 3-5).
- **Reliability**—Measures of reliability/schedule adherence apply to the whole system, rather than to individual routes. An example of an assessment of reliability for a transit system is shown in Table 3-6.

Route-level Performance Assessment

Once evaluation measures have been established, each route is then evaluated in terms of how it compares to agency goals or thresholds for that class of routes. The overall system's performance may also be assessed for certain measures (e.g., coverage). Examples of the application of two of the above measures (span of service, by route class, and productivity, by area) are shown in Tables 3-7 and 3-8.[2]

Table 3-4. Example, productivity measures.

Type of Service		Weekday Peak Period	Weekday Whole Day	Weekday Off-Peak and Weekend
Radial Line Haul Routes:	Boardings per VRH	30	24	18
Urban Classes (buses ≥30 ft.):	Boardings per VRH	30	24	18
Suburban Classes (buses ≥30 ft.):	Boardings per VRH	15	12.5	10
Express Routes:	Boardings per trip	23	23	23
All Classes (buses <30 ft.):	Boardings per VRH	12	11	10

---

[2]In Tables 3-7 and 3-8, the percentage of passing routes is calculated in two ways: at the route level unweighted, and by route weighted by vehicle revenue hours (VRH) of service. The unweighted method treats each route in the region equally, while the weighted method counts routes in proportion to the vehicle revenue hours of service on that route. The second method gives a more accurate picture of the span of service or productivity in the region, since if a minor route with only a few trips a day is unable to meet the service span or productivity threshold, it would have only a minimal impact on regional mobility, but if a major route with many trips is unable to meet the threshold, more people would be affected.

Table 3-5. Example, crowding measures.

Type of Service	Weekday Peak Period Load Factor	Weekday Off-Peak and Weekend Load Factor
All Classes other than Urban Cross-town and Express	1.2	1.0
Urban Cross-town	1.1	1.0
Express Routes with premium fare	1.0	1.0

Table 3-6. Example, weekday schedule adherence results.

Allowances	Percent On Time	Percent Early	Percent Late
Departures			
0 min. early/5 min. late	90.5%	3.9%	5.7%
1 min. early/5 min. late	92.7%	1.6%	5.7%
Arrivals			
0 min. early/5 min. late	57.4%	25.2%	17.3%
1 min. early/5 min. late	66.5%	16.2%	17.3%
2 min. early/5 min. late	72.3%	10.4%	17.3%
2 min. early/6 min. late	75.9%	10.4%	13.7%
Departures and Arrivals			
0/5 Departure and 0/5 Arrival	55.1%		
-1/5 Departure and -2/6 Arrival	73.3%		
Number of trips in sample	14,617		

Table 3-7. Example, weekday span of service evaluation.

Route Classification	Number of Routes	% Meet Threshold, Routes	Total VRH	% Meet Threshold, VRH
Radial Line Haul	25	92%	3,477	96%
Express	32	19%	741	31%
Commuter	63	35%	969	53%
Urban Circulator	6	100%	192	100%
Urban Cross-town	10	100%	1,354	100%
Urban Feeder/Distributor	44	93%	2,443	94%
Suburban Local	25	64%	813	82%
Suburban Circumferential	6	83%	550	94%
Suburban Feeder/Distributor	83	77%	4,519	88%
TOTAL	294	66%	15,058	87%

Table 3-8. Example, weekday productivity evaluation.

Area	Period	Number of Routes	% Meet Threshold, Routes	Total VRH	% Meet Threshold, VRH
Urban	Peak	97	88%	7,176	94%
	Off-Peak	94	90%	7,135	96%
Suburban	Peak	167	74%	6,677	85%
	Off-Peak	171	70%	7,493	85%
TOTAL	Peak	264	79%	13,854	90%
	Off-Peak	265	77%	14,628	91%

Identification of Problem Routes

Based on the route-level assessment, "problem routes" (i.e., those with design and/or performance measures that fall below specified thresholds) can be identified. An example of a summary of an agency's route-level assessments for the above measures is shown in Table 3-9.

Identification of Actions to Address Problems

Based on the route-level assessment, the agency can then identify potential actions for improving the design and performance of problem routes. The types of service adjustments that might be considered are described in Chapter 5.

A route-level evaluation is thus an important element of an overall assessment of a transit system. When combined with market research and an assessment of unmet needs/latent demand, an agency can identify opportunities for attracting new riders or expanding usage by current riders. A comprehensive system evaluation may also include a peer analysis that compares the agency's services and systemwide performance to those of a set of comparable agencies.

The next section briefly discusses the evaluation of an agency's marketing, information, and fare systems.

Needs Assessment of Marketing/Information and Fare Systems

In addition to identifying service gaps or deficiencies, an agency seeking to maximize ridership should review its marketing and information programs, as well as its fare structure/system. With

Table 3-9. Example, summary of routes meeting design thresholds.

Route/Line	Classification	Span	Freq.	Travel Time	Productivity	Crowding	# Not Met	# Borderline
22A-F	Urban feeder/distributor	No	No	No	No	Yes	4	0
AT7	Urban feeder/distributor	No	No	No	No	Yes	4	0
24M,P	Urban feeder/distributor	No	No	Yes~	No	Yes	3	1
11P	Commuter	No	No	Yes	No	Yes	3	0
13A-G	Radial line haul	Yes	No	No	No	Yes	3	0
21A-F	Express	No	Yes	Yes	No	No	3	0
25A-R	Urban feeder/distributor	No	No	Yes	No	Yes	3	0
28C	Urban feeder/distributor	No	No	Yes	No	Yes	3	0
AT2	Radial line haul	No	No	No	Yes	Yes	3	0
AT3	Urban feeder/distributor	No	No	Yes	No	Yes	3	0
AT4	Urban feeder/distributor	No	No	Yes	No	Yes	3	0
AT5	Urban circulator	Yes	No	No	No	Yes	3	0
10B,C,D	Urban cross-town	No	No	No~	Yes	Yes	2	1
23A-T	Urban cross-town	No	No	No~	Yes	Yes	2	1
28A,B	Urban cross-town	Yes	No	No~	Yes	No	2	1
38B	Radial line haul	No	No	Yes~	Yes	Yes	2	1
25B	Urban feeder/distributor	No	No	Yes	Yes	Yes	2	0
3A-F	Radial line haul	Yes	Yes	No	No	Yes	2	0
AT8	Radial line haul	Yes	No	No	Yes	Yes	2	0
10A,E	Urban feeder/distributor	Yes	No	Yes	Yes	Yes	1	0
16A-J	Radial line haul	Yes	Yes	Yes	Yes	No	1	0
16L	Commuter	No	Yes	Yes	Yes	Yes	1	0
28F,G	Express	Yes	Yes	Yes	No	Yes	1	0
7A-X	Urban feeder/distributor	Yes	Yes	Yes~	Yes	Yes	0	1
16S, U, W, X	Commuter	Yes	Yes	Yes	Yes	Yes	0	0
4A-S	Urban feeder/distributor	Yes	Yes	Yes	Yes	Yes	0	0
8S-Z	Commuter	Yes	Yes	Yes	Yes	Yes	0	0
ART	Urban circulator	Yes	Yes	N/A	Yes	Yes	0	0
Shoppers Shuttle	Urban circulator	Yes	Yes	N/A	Yes	Yes	0	0
% of routes not meeting threshold		**52%**	**62%**	**24%**	**45%**	**10%**		

regard to marketing/information strategies, how effective are the existing programs/systems at informing riders about the transit service and how to use it? With regard to the fare structure and fare collection system, are there problem areas or opportunities for improvement? For both categories, are there new strategies that might improve the agency's ability to attract and retain riders? Considerations related to these areas are discussed in Chapters 7 (Marketing & Information Initiatives) and 8 (Fare Collection/Structure Initiatives).

Identification of Needs & Potential Markets

Traditionally, budgetary and other constraints (e.g., land use/roadway network limitations) have by and large forced transit agencies to focus their services on specific trip purposes (notably the work trip). In other words, the focus has been on serving the greatest number of people in the most cost-effective manner possible. However, the market for transit services is clearly not monolithic, but rather consists of a broad mix of types of users, with differing socioeconomic characteristics and trip purposes. Efforts to produce significant increases in overall ridership—or greater market share among particular user groups—may therefore require agencies to target specific market segments or niches. In any event, developing an understanding of the characteristics and travel needs of different groups is a key element in identifying the most appropriate ridership growth strategies/initiatives.

This section presents guidance on identifying unmet needs and potential markets for transit service. The key elements in identifying needs/markets include the following:

- Conducting analysis of demographics and travel patterns within the area or region; this analysis is used to identify
  - Gaps in transit service coverage, focusing on areas with the potential to support transit services (e.g., based on development density, activity centers, and concentrations of transit-dependent residents)
  - The size of the current and projected travel markets (e.g., based on travel volumes to major regional employment centers)
- Conducting market research, identifying (1) key market segments and (2) both current riders' and non-riders' service preferences and propensity to ride improved transit service.

These elements are discussed below.

Conducting Demographic and Travel Pattern Analysis

Several different types of analyses can be carried out in an effort to understand both the availability of transit services in a city or region and how well that transit service meets current and future travel needs. For example, transit coverage can be compared with current and future development patterns to contrast service availability with evidence of demand. In addition, travel patterns to major regional activity centers can be analyzed to identify potential transit markets. Then, within these potential markets, transit travel times can be compared with auto access times in order to examine the effectiveness of *transit accessibility*.

One approach that has been found to be invaluable in such analyses is to use geographic information systems (GIS) tools to map key indicators of potential demand (i.e., demographic characteristics, land use patterns, and key travel generators) as well as the existing transit services and ridership levels. Graphical displays of this information (see Exhibit 3-1 below for an example) can be quite helpful in identifying the nature of the existing market for transit service as well as areas of potential demand.

The GIS data can be used, for instance, to conduct a route coverage analysis. Service areas representing typical walking distance (¼ mile, or 1,300 feet) from the agency's route network as a whole, and from each individual route, can be produced and incorporated into the GIS database for display and analysis. These areas can then be used to calculate the total population, and the concentration of various transit-dependent segments, within walking distance of each route, and of the whole system. Unserved areas of moderate population density, or with a significant concentration of transit-dependent residents, can then be identified.

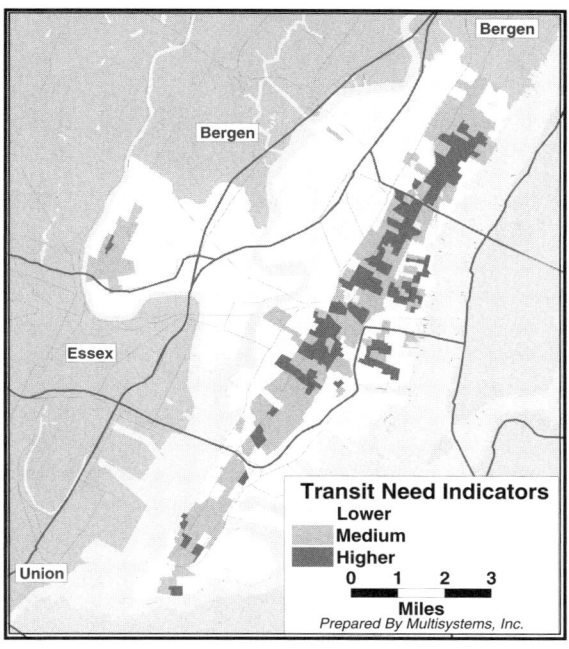

Exhibit 3-1. Example of GIS graphic.

Based on the evaluation of the existing service, coupled with the assessment of travel, development and demographic patterns—including anticipated future growth patterns—the agency can then identify (1) gaps in the existing service network and (2) specific travel markets in the service area which appear to be underserved. The results of this analysis should ultimately be combined with the findings of the market research (discussed in the next section) to identify the appropriate types of service changes to best address these unmet needs and future opportunities.

Conducting Market Research

Purpose/Goals of Market Research

Although demographic analyses are critical to making general assumptions about probable service gaps and the size of underserved market segments, these analyses can be enhanced significantly through the conduct of targeted market research. The purpose of this research is to specifically identify potential markets for increased transit ridership and to confirm the reasons for current mode choice decisions.

The most fertile markets for potential transit ridership increases are those where the actual rate of transit use falls below that group's expected level (e.g., based on Journey to Work Census statistics). Reasons for lower-than-expected transit usage include the lack of information availability, a mismatch between services provided and those desired (e.g., span of service or routing), pricing, and other operating environment issues (e.g., safety).

Trip characteristics, traveler characteristics, and travel needs and wants represent the primary pieces of information targeted by transit market research. Compiling responses to these travel characteristics-related questions with more precision than that afforded by a broad demographic analysis allows for a better understanding of why a transit provider is not reaching its full potential in market penetration.

In deciding on a market research methodology, a key initial question must be answered: is the agency attempting to learn more about riders or non-riders? Riders are easier to reach and their interaction with the system presents opportunities for a variety of market research methods, as well as providing for easier management of the research program. Non-riders present a host of challenges, not least of which is the large number of them (several times the number of transit riders in even the highest ridership metropolitan areas), and the costs inherent in reaching out to them.

Market Research Techniques

The next decisions are (1) whether to use quantitative or qualitative market research techniques and (2) which specific technique(s) to employ. These decisions are primarily governed by the nature of the desired information, as well as the resources—and amount of time—available. There is a wide variety of market research techniques, and each is suited to specific research needs and budgets. The basic market research approaches are as follows:

- Surveys and interviews,
- Travel diaries,
- Focus groups, and
- Customer panels and advisory committees.

The advantages and disadvantages of these are discussed below.

Although the above techniques vary in their applicability, all should strive to meet certain standard characteristics:[3]

- Sufficient detail to form the basis for agency decision-making,
- Statistically reliable,
- Fully inclusive and representative of target group,
- Justifies the costs of research,
- Replicable and understandable, and
- Usable in context with other techniques.

Surveys/interviews take many forms, including telephone, household/mailback, online, on board and intercept (e.g., in a station or at a bus stop). Some of these are suitable only for one target group (i.e., customer or non-customer) while others can be used for both. Telephone surveys targeting the broad population (both customers and non-customers) represent one of the more expensive market research techniques. However, this generally represents the best way of reaching non-riders and is particularly useful (for riders and non-riders) if the survey instrument is complex (e.g., a "stated preference" survey involving a series of trade-off questions). Other strategies for conducting a complex rider survey are to do in-person interviews or to hand out the questionnaires on board or at stops/stations and provide a mailback option; these approaches are also used to collect origin-destination and usage data, as described earlier in this chapter. Some of the key differences between telephone and on-board survey methods are compared in Table 3-10.

Travel diaries are another useful market research tool that is applicable to both customer and non-customer target groups. With this technique, participants log information on all aspects of their travel behavior (e.g., time of day, mode choice, and origin/destination) over a predetermined period. Once collected, this information provides a more comprehensive snapshot of participant travel needs and habits than could be obtained through surveys and other techniques. Travel diaries also provide the transit agency with enough information to determine the suitability of serving non-transit trips with existing or enhanced transit service.

Focus groups cost considerably less to administer than surveys or travel diaries, but have the drawback of being the least representative of the approaches.[4] Focus groups generally cannot be used to produce statistically significant information—or any quantitative information, for

---

[3]*NCHRP Report 487: Using Customer Needs to Drive Transportation Decisions* (2003).
[4]As discussed below, the relative cost of the different techniques to an agency ultimately depends on the nature of the resources available (e.g., whether there is any in-house market research staff and the specific capabilities of that staff).

Table 3-10. Comparison of telephone and on-board surveys.

	Telephone interviews	On-board surveys/personal interviews	On-board surveys with mailback
Data collection costs	Moderate to high	High	Low to moderate
Time for data collection	Short to moderate	Moderate to long	Moderate
Control over respondent selection	High	High	Low
Response rates	Moderate to high	High	Low to moderate
Ability to access hidden populations	Moderate	High	Low
Complexity of questions	Simple to moderate	Moderate to complex	Simple
Completion of boring/tedious questions	Moderate	High	Low
Completion of sensitive questions	Moderate to high	Low	Moderate
Interviewer bias and error	Low to moderate	Moderate to high	None
Ability to ask open-ended questions	Low to moderate	High	Moderate
Perceived respondent anonymity	Moderate to high	Low	Moderate to high

SOURCE: *TCRP Report 37: A Handbook: Integrating Market Research into Transit Management* (1998), p. 94

that matter. However, focus groups are useful for gauging levels of interest in new initiatives or getting input from different market groups on key issues or concepts. Agencies also sometimes use focus groups as a means of establishing or testing questions to be used in a survey.

Customer panels and advisory boards are typically more appropriate to monitoring an ongoing agency program than to identifying means for increasing ridership. *NCHRP Report 487* distinguishes between data-gathering techniques designed to solicit customer or public input and those that are aimed more at receiving *feedback* on a program that has already been implemented. While market research with the goal of increasing ridership falls into the first category of data gathering, customer panels and advisory boards are more suited to the second.

As suggested above, the availability of resources at an agency often governs the technique(s) utilized. The availability of resources—and the size of the agency—also affects an agency's organizational approach to market research. For example, large agencies that conduct ongoing market research programs may find it cost-effective to maintain a full-time, dedicated market research staff. However, this may mean that most of the agency's market research is limited to what can be directly undertaken by that staff. In such a case, for instance, an on-board survey is often the least expensive technique, as it can be carried out by agency staff. That same agency may find techniques such as focus groups prohibitively costly, given a limited budget for hiring outside contractors to do market research. Alternatively, for a smaller agency that conducts market research on more of an as-needed basis, contracting all survey efforts out to private firms may be the most cost-effective way to carry out the research. In such cases, the agency often assigns the responsibility for the research to the specific department in search of market information at that time. Even for agencies with in-house staff, though, contracting out large or particularly complex survey efforts to private firms is often necessary.

Examples of Agency Market Research Approaches

A number of agencies maintain regular comprehensive transit market research programs. In the San Francisco Bay Area, for instance, BART conducts bi-annual passenger surveys that gauge rider satisfaction with 44 BART service characteristics. BART compares the results with previous surveys to identify trends and measure improvement resulting from new service enhancements. This survey is augmented by follow-up telephone surveys conducted in the off year with a subset of the passenger survey respondents. BART also makes the results of this research available to the public through its website.

Depending on the desired information sought by the transit agency, a more focused research program targeting one submarket may be preferred. For instance, the City of Lowell (MA) was interested in attracting more city youths (a submarket with the potential for high ridership given the cost of automobile ownership and the minimum age requirements for a drivers license) to local transit service. The Lowell Regional Transportation Authority (LRTA) and the city's campus of the University of Massachusetts jointly conducted a survey of city high school and middle school students. The survey asked youths to identify gaps in service to popular recreational and employment destinations. The result of the research effort was a "Youth Loop" bus service serving 18 popular destinations and residential areas with high concentrations of young people.

Another approach is to conduct a survey focused on a particular aspect of the transit service. For example, agencies often conduct surveys related to fare payment preferences and concerns as part of fare system or policy studies. Similarly, an agency introducing a new type of service (e.g., BRT or LRT) may find it useful to survey area residents on desired attributes and potential usage of the new service.

Survey Analysis Methods

There is a broad range of survey analysis methods. The appropriate method depends on the nature of the questions and the intended use of the results (e.g., what type of market segmentation will be developed?). For straightforward questions (e.g., related to frequency of travel or demographic characteristics), simple frequencies are useful. Cross-tabulation is the simplest and most common method for analyzing the relationships between pairs of variables. Another useful technique for depicting the relationship between two variables is quadrant analysis; the relative ratings or performance of the two variables are plotted on a graph that clearly shows their relative importance. For analyzing the relationships among several variables or analyzing more complex questions (e.g., trade-off questions related to how respondents value alternative service or fare attributes), more sophisticated multivariate analysis techniques must be used; examples of such techniques include correlation analysis, multiple regression analysis, discriminant analysis, factor analysis, correspondence analysis and conjoint analysis.[5]

Regardless of the specific analysis methods employed, the ultimate goal of the market research should be to provide the agency with a better understanding of the attitudes, preferences, characteristics, and/or unmet needs of different service area market segments. These findings should then be combined with the service evaluation and the analysis of demographic data and trends to identify mobility needs and growth markets and opportunities for transit in the region. An important aspect of this process is the identification of the needs of key market segments; market segmentation is discussed in the next sections.

Identifying Market Segments

Market Segmentation Approaches

TCRP Report 36: A Handbook: Using Market Segmentation to Increase Transit Ridership notes the following:

- "Everyone is not a prospect for every product or service offered. It is evident to everyone in the transit industry that not everyone rides or will ride the bus, participate in a carpool or vanpool, ride a bike to work, or otherwise leave their car at home—even for a day.

---

[5]For a description of these techniques, as well as other details related to market research, the reader is directed to the following reports: *TCRP Report 37: A Handbook: Integrating Market Research into Transit Management* (1998); D. Aaker et. al., *Marketing Research* (1995); P. Alreck and R. Settle, *Survey Research Handbook* (1995); and G. Churchill, *Marketing Research: Methodological Foundations* (1995).

- An agency's product or service mix must be controlled for maximum efficiency. Recent cutbacks in funding make it increasingly important to understand customers' needs and wants in order to use these increasingly scarce resources most effectively.
- Since the product/service mix and customer pool are limited, it is most efficient to match your products and services to customer needs and wants." (p. 2)

Of course, there are a number of different ways to segment the market for transit (or any product or service). *TCRP Report 36* explains that there are two basic approaches:

- "Pre-determined (a priori) segmentation—selecting certain groups from a population based on known characteristics and declaring them 'segments.'
- Market-defined (post hoc) segmentation—identifies segments based on actual market investigations, notably analysis of answers to survey questions intended to predict marketplace responses." (p. 75)

The authors of *TCRP Report 36* suggest that "Bases used for pre-determined (a priori) segmentation vary widely depending on goals." (p. 13). They provide a number of examples, including

- "Riders versus nonriders, frequent riders versus infrequent riders versus occasional riders, or former riders versus current riders.
- Loyal riders versus vulnerable or nonloyal riders.
- Transit dependent riders versus choice riders.
- Residents of high-density areas versus suburban residents.
- Commuters to downtown CBDs versus suburb-to-suburb commuters.
- Student commuters versus work commuters.
- 'High' versus 'mid' versus 'low' income groups.
- Geographic location as defined by zip code, census tract, or transit analysis zone." (p. 13)

While a priori segmentation uses existing group definitions, post hoc segmentation requires new market research. A list of some of the types of classifications and variables often deployed in market-defined segmentation analyses is presented in Table 3-11. (*TCRP Report 36* describes and presents examples of various types of market segmentation that have been used by transit agencies.)

Table 3-11. Some common bases for post hoc segmentation.

Product Selection Behaviors	Mode Selection Behaviors
Usage rates and occasions (e.g., frequency of riding or trip purpose)	Favorite travel mode
Knowledge of and experience with product	Acceptable modes
	Disliked modes
Substitutability of related categories (e.g., availability of alternative modes)	Mode loyalty versus mode switching
Product Class-Related Attitudes	**Mode-Related Attitudes**
Benefits sought	Awareness and perceptions
Problems encountered using product/service	Mode user imagery
Attribute utilities of mode	Perceived appropriateness for use occasions
Person-Related Attitudes	**Other Bases**
Self-perceptions	Stage in life cycle
Values	Socioeconomic status
Life styles	Ethnicity
Other "psychographics"	Other demographics

SOURCE: *TCRP Report 36: A Handbook: Using Market Segmentation to Increase Transit Ridership* (1998), p. 20

Key Market Segments

With regard to identifying specific market segments, a report recently prepared for APTA (B. Hemily, *Trends Affecting Public Transit's Effectiveness: A Review and Proposed Actions*, November 2004) identifies four key segments for transit, based on an analysis of demographic, socioeconomic, and land use trends; these segments are (p. 27)

- Commuters;
- Immigrants (particularly in older inner suburbs);
- Serving the mobility needs of an aging population; and
- Access for customers with special needs (i.e., persons with disabilities and economically disadvantaged).

Hemily argues that these are the market segments most likely to yield significant ridership increases in future years and transit agencies must therefore recognize and understand the different needs of these markets in developing service and marketing strategies.

In a broader study of transit market segments, *TCRP Report 28: Transit Markets of the Future—The Challenge of Change* analyzed current and future transit market groups, based on use of transit as reported in the 1990 U.S. Census and 1990 Nationwide Personal Transportation Study (NPTS). Table 3-12 shows "transit use by various market niches indexed to average metropolitan transit use." In this table, groups with an "MSA Transit Index" higher than 1 were "more likely than average to commute using transit"; the higher the index, the higher the group's

Table 3-12. Transit use by various market niches indexed to average metropolitan transit use.

Market Niches	MSA Transit Index	Market Niches	MSA Transit Index
Sex		**Household Income**	
Men	0.85	<$5k	1.23
Women	1.18	$5 — 10k	1.24
		$10 — 15k	1.08
Race & Ethnicity		$15 — 20k	1.04
White	0.68	$20 — 25k	0.97
Black	2.72	$25 — 30k	0.90
Hispanic	1.73	$30 — 40k	0.78
Asian	1.74	$40 — 50k	0.77
		$50 — 60k	0.84
Vehicle Ownership		$60 — 70k	0.91
No car	5.76	$70k plus	0.95
One or more cars	0.68		
		Immigration Status	
Age of Worker		Non-immigrant	0.84
17 — 29	1.14	Immigrant	2.08
30 — 39	0.96	**Years in US**	
40 — 49	0.87	<5	3.01
50 — 59	0.92	5 — 10	2.25
60 — 64	1.07	10 — 15	1.74
65 — 69	1.10	15 — 20	1.89
		20 — 25	1.88
Education		25 — 30	1.49
No school	2.59	30 — 40	1.48
Elementary	2.08	40 plus	1.80
Junior High	1.69		
Some High School	1.25	**Limitations**	
High School	0.91	Work limitation	1.25
Some College	0.82	Mobility limitation	2.41
College	1.05		
Graduate School	1.06		

SOURCE: *TCRP Report 28: Transit Markets for the Future—The Challenge of Change* (1998), p. 8 — data from 1990 U.S. Census

reliance on transit. Based on this analysis, the authors identified the following groups of transit users as "... being more likely than average to use transit as their principal mode for commuting to work in U.S. metropolitan areas in 1990:

- Women,
- Blacks,
- Hispanics,
- Asians,
- Workers with no household cars,
- Workers age 17 to 29,
- Workers age 60 and over,
- Workers with less than high school education,
- Workers with some high school but no degree,
- Workers with college degree,
- Workers with graduate school education,
- Workers with household income below $20,000,
- Immigrants, and
- Workers with mobility or work limitations." (p. 8)

The report notes that "The data show that there are distinctly different markets among those riding transit—it is unlikely that they all could or would be well-served by the same services, routes, schedules, and marketing approaches." (p. 3)

There may also be distinct differences in the types of strategies an agency should consider in targeting existing riders versus new riders. For instance, surveys from the recent regional bus study in the Washington, DC, region identified the types of transit improvements desired by both existing riders and non-riders. The results of these survey efforts are shown in Exhibits 3-2 and 3-3. As indicated, there are significant differences between the most desired improvements for the two groups: riders rated service-related improvements most important, while non-riders considered better information and improved amenities (i.e., "better shelters") most important. Thus, targeting new riders would argue for a different set of actions/initiatives than would an attempt to influence the usage patterns of existing riders.

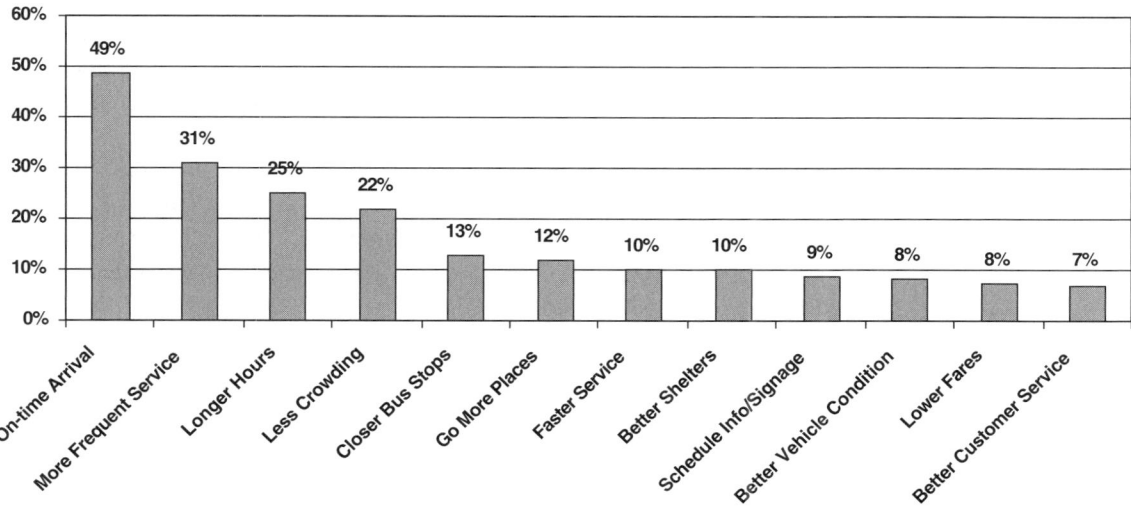

Exhibit 3-2. Results of rider survey (source: TranSystems et al., WMATA Regional Bus Study, 2003).

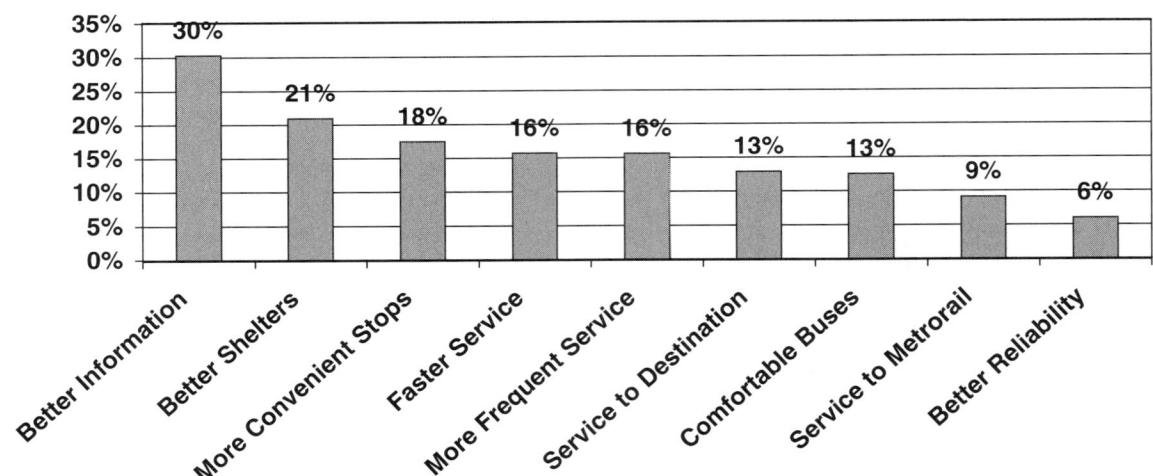

Exhibit 3-3. Results of non-rider survey (source: TranSystems et al., **WMATA Regional Bus Study, 2003**).

Along these same lines, a report prepared by the California Department of Transportation (*An Analysis of Public Transportation to Attract Non-Traditional Transit Riders in California*, April 2003) presents the results of market research conducted by a number of California transit agencies of rider and non-rider attitudes toward transit. The report notes that "Surveys across the state reveal that approximately one-half to two-thirds of current riders find the existing service in their area 'good' or 'excellent.' Their suggestions for improvement are overwhelmingly concentrated as follows:

- More frequent service (crosses all demographics);
- More 'on-time' service;
- Better timed transfers;
- Extended service (nights and weekends); and
- Additional routes (to a lesser extent)." (p. 14)

As for non-riders, the California DOT reports on two aspects of the market research: "why non-riders don't use the system now" and "what would entice non-riders to use the system." Regarding reasons for not using transit now, the most common reason cited was simply ownership of a car; many survey respondents claimed that they would only use transit if they had no alternative (e.g., if their car were broken). Regarding what could lure non-riders to transit, a survey from the Los Angeles area revealed that "To be attracted to transit, (these) non-riders would need the perceived value of transit to equal their current mode." (p. 20) These respondents considered "travel time compared to the auto" to be "of high importance" and also rated the local transit service as "unsafe."

Thus, given the different types of concerns and travel needs associated with different rider and non-rider groups, market segmentation can clearly be a useful component of any effort aimed at increasing ridership or market share; designing marketing plans—as well as types of service—that target specific market segments will often represent the best use of an agency's limited resources.

The remaining chapters provide guidelines on identification of appropriate strategies to address the service needs and potential markets identified through the above method.

CHAPTER 4

Selection of Strategies

Introduction

Identifying strategies, actions, and initiatives that can cost-effectively increase an agency's ridership thus require the agency to identify and understand (1) the nature of the external factors affecting demand, (2) gaps in existing service—and opportunities for improvements, and (3) the service requirements of key market segments. The agency can then select strategies that address the identified types of needs—and that are appropriate to the particular service environment. An agency may choose to focus on a specific market segment and select a single type of strategy/initiative—or alternatively may opt for a broader set of strategies that target multiple segments. Considerations in choosing individual types of strategies are addressed in Chapters 5 through 8; this chapter discusses the selection of appropriate strategies for different types of service environments, including a review of the characteristics and common elements of successful agency examples.

Service Environments and Strategies

Beyond targeting different market segments, one of the keys to developing transit strategies that maximize ridership is to identify the most appropriate type(s) of services for specific service environments. While transit service has typically focused on the urban core, for instance, the increasing dispersion of employment and residences throughout metropolitan areas has increased the need for suburban-oriented transit services. Exurban and rural areas obviously require different approaches as well, and more specialized environments (e.g., downtown areas, college campus areas, or major tourist attractions) may also merit consideration of specially designed services.

Identifying Types of Service Environments

Service environments can be defined in different ways. The FTA, on its *Innovative Practices for Increased Ridership* website, has categorized its entries by population, for instance:

- Rural area (under 50,000);
- Small urbanized (50,000—200,000);
- Medium urbanized (200,000—1 million); and
- Large urbanized (over 1 million in population).

For some types of strategies—service design considerations in particular—it is useful to define more specific environments, including different types of suburban settings as well as downtown areas and other specialized settings. While transit is provided in a broad range of environments, the following categories can be used to further define many agencies' services:

- **Metropolitan**—Service (often more than one mode) covers multiple types of settings within a metropolitan area; examples include agencies such as Chicago Transit Authority, Miami-Dade Transit Agency, and Denver Regional Transit District.
- **Suburban**—Service is focused on a suburban area or a stand-alone town/community within a metropolitan area served by multiple agencies; examples include the individual municipal services (e.g., Montebello Bus Lines, Culver CityBus, and Santa Clarita Transit) in the Los Angeles area, or local services outside of Washington, DC (e.g., the Fairfax, VA, Connector; Alexandria, VA, DASH; and Ride-On in Montgomery County, MD).
- **Downtown/Central Business District**—Service is focused on the urban core, either on the downtown/CBD area or one or more urban neighborhoods; examples include the LADOT's DASH intracommunity services in urban neighborhoods in Los Angeles.
- **Regional**—Service covers multiple jurisdictions in a region; examples include commuter rail services such as Metra (Chicago area), SCRRA (Los Angeles area) and VRE (Washington, DC, area).

Finally, service may operate within or have a special market focus, such as

- **Tourist centers**—Major tourist locations can be year-round (e.g., Las Vegas, NV, and Orlando, FL) or predominantly seasonal destinations (e.g., Cape Cod, MA). The service requirements for the latter areas obviously differ considerably from the former.
- **College area**—This includes large campuses within metropolitan areas (e.g., University of Washington in Seattle, University of Minnesota in Minneapolis, and Cleveland State University in Cleveland), as well as stand-alone "college towns" (e.g., Ann Arbor, MI; Chapel Hill, NC; and Davis, CA).

As discussed later in this chapter and in Appendix A, services designed to focus on such markets can be quite effective at generating ridership.

One of these types of environment that has proven particularly challenging to transit agencies is the suburban environment. Effectively serving the increasingly dispersed travel patterns in suburban settings represents perhaps the single greatest challenge facing the transit industry. Suburban population and jobs have both grown much faster than in the central city: the population increase in the suburbs between 1990 and 2000 was two and half times the growth rate in central cities, and nearly three-quarters of job growth during the 1990s occurred in suburban areas. The crux of the suburban transit issue is summarized in *TCRP Report 55: Guidelines for Enhancing Suburban Mobility Using Public Transportation* (1999):

> "Average residential and employment densities today are not only much lower than a decade or more ago, but trip origins and destinations are also far more spread out. Nationwide, the share of work trips both beginning and ending in the suburbs, for instance, increased from 38 percent in 1970 to 52 percent in 1990. Traditional commuting paths are being replaced by a patchwork of radial, crosstown, lateral and reverse-direction travel. Increasingly, there is a mismatch between the geometry of traditional highway, bus, and rail networks, which mostly follow a hub-and-spoke pattern, and the geography of commuting, which seemingly moves in all directions. This has led to more circuitous trip making and increased suburban congestion." (p. 4)

Complicating the challenge of adequately serving suburban areas is the fact that there are a number of different types of suburban environments, each requiring a somewhat different focus. *TCRP Report 55* identified six basic types of suburban land use environments:

- "*Residential suburbs*, which occupy much of suburbia's land mass, range from large-lot, single-family tract subdivisions to more compact settings, with a mixture of housing stock.

- *Balanced mixed use suburbs* typically feature a mixture of housing, employment and commercial land uses.
- *Suburban campuses*, which proliferated during the 1980's, mainly comprise office parks, industrial estates, and low-density business centers. Most are master planned projects configured like university campuses.
- *Edge cities*, the massive suburban downtowns that blossomed throughout metropolitan America in the 1980's, feature many of the same land use mixes and sometimes match the employment densities of traditional downtowns.
- *Suburban corridors* differ from many of the other operating settings in that they are linearly configured, often made up of an assemblage of land uses aligned along an axial thoroughfare or freeway.
- *Exurban corporate enclaves. . .* is largely a 1990's phenomenon. Research has documented the leapfrogging of new commercial developments into favored corridors and exurban frontiers in many growing parts of the country." (p. 8)

The authors note that each of these ". . . represents a distinct operating setting that poses unique challenges to America's public transit industry." (p. 2) Hemily (*Trends Affecting Public Transit's Effectiveness: A Review and Proposed Actions*) suggests that edge cities in particular actually offer ". . . a relative opportunity to transit systems. They do represent a concentration of office and retail that creates a generator for transit ridership, more so than dispersed office parks in 'Edgeless Cities' or strip shopping mall." (p. 11)

Considerations in identifying appropriate types of strategies for different types of settings are discussed in the next section.

Identifying Strategies for Different Service Environments

General Applicability

While most of the strategies aimed at increasing ridership are not tied to a specific type of setting or service environment, some will be more effective (or efficient) in certain environments. In particular, certain strategies (e.g., any involving fixed guideways or major capital investments) are unlikely to be cost-effective solutions in rural and small urban areas. Moreover, while most strategies are not mode-specific, several are either inappropriate or infeasible with rail services (i.e., those related to flexible service designs).

The particular types of strategies used in each type of service environment are discussed in the remainder of this chapter and in Appendix A.

Applicability for Suburban Environments

As suggested above, addressing the needs of suburban areas represents a particular challenge—and opportunity—to transit agencies. *TCRP Report 55* explains that there are ". . . two basic categories of actions used to improve existing suburban networks:" (p. 10)

- *Actions to modify and improve the overall suburban transit framework*—These represent the first step in mobility strategies of most suburban operators and are generally taken at a system level. They include the following:
  - Establishing a transit centers concept and timed transfer program and
  - Enhancing line haul services, express buses, and limited services.
- *Actions that create supporting/complementary services*—This group includes those activities undertaken by transit operators to enhance and complete their network. Featured among these actions are the following:
  - Internal local area circulators,
  - Shuttle links,

- Subscription buses, and
- Vanpools.

Table 4-1 identifies which of these types of actions are appropriate for each of the six suburban categories. (Examples of the different types of actions are identified in Appendix A and Chapters 5 through 8.)

Developing a Family of Services

In line with the above discussion regarding different suburban environments, transit agencies are increasingly recognizing the need for a mix of products/services. As suggested in Chapter 3, it is becoming more and more apparent that "one size does not fit all." Rather, a metropolitan area is likely to be best served with an integrated network of different types and levels of service—a family of services targeted to different market segments and service environments. Such an approach is exemplified in the basic elements defined as part of a service restructuring study undertaken by the Niagara Frontier Transportation Authority (NFTA) in the Buffalo (NY) region in the mid-1990s:[1]

- **Provide different services in the urban, suburban and rural areas designed to meet each area's specific needs.** The plan built on the existing bus and LRT network and existing transit hubs, adding innovative and more flexible services to enhance collection and distribution around an expanded group of hubs.
- **Establish transit hubs at key locations throughout the region.** It was suggested that the hubs include well-lit and weather-protected waiting areas, as well as parking and improved user information.
- **Strengthen fixed-route services along major corridors between hubs.** Performance of all routes was reviewed, and recommendations were developed for improving service in selected corridors and modifying poorly performing routes or replacing them with alternative services.
- **Develop local circulation and feeder services around hubs.** In low-density suburban and rural areas, flexible services using small vehicles were recommended. These included community-based circulators and services targeting specific activity centers such as shopping malls, employment centers, and college campuses.
- **Introduce services targeted to particular markets.** Recommended target markets included inner city reverse commuters, groups of workers to specific employment centers, and seniors and other transit-dependent people.

Table 4-1. Matrix of suburban transit service strategies and land use environments.

Type of Action	Residential suburbs	Balanced mix-use suburbs	Suburban campuses	Edge cities	Suburban corridors	Exurban enclaves
Modifications to overall framework						
Transit centers	■	■	■	■	■	
Express routes	■	■	■	■	■	■
Limited routes			■	■	■	■
Actions creating complementary or supporting services						
Fixed route circulators	■	■	■	■		
Route deviation circulators	■	■				
Demand response circulators	■	■				
Rail station to employment shuttles			■	■	■	■
Residence to bus/rail shuttle: fixed route	■	■				
Residence to bus/rail shuttle: route deviation	■					
Residence to bus/rail shuttle: demand response	■					
Midday employee shuttles			■	■		■
Subscription bus	■	■	■	■		■
Vanpools	■	■	■			

SOURCE: TCRP Report 55 (*Guidelines for Enhancing Suburban Mobility Using Public Transportation*, 1999), p. 18

---

[1](Multisystems, Inc. et al., *Transportation Restructuring Study for Western New York – Final Report,* December 1997, p. 6-1.)

- **Incorporate supporting/complementary elements.** Recommendations included expansion of the guaranteed-ride-home and employer-subsidized transit pass programs, as well as improvements for pedestrians and accommodations for bicycles.
- **Collaborate with private and non-profit organizations to enhance the effectiveness of the transportation network.** These recommendations focused on coordinating efforts with private and non-profit paratransit carriers and human services agency-funded transportation programs.

Of course, providing a mix of products/services also applies to other categories of strategies/actions. For example, most agencies offer a range of *fare payment* options, often including one or more discounted prepaid passes as well as multi-ride instruments (e.g., 10-ride tickets, stored-value farecards, or packs of tokens). With the properly designed mix of options and prices, sometimes incorporating strategies such as "deep discounting," many agencies have succeeded at generating increased ridership levels without losing revenue (or, alternatively, raising revenue without losing ridership).

Many agencies have also discovered the value of utilizing targeted *marketing* programs, and in fact, as mentioned earlier, FTA has sponsored a series of "individualized marketing" demonstrations. Finally, with regard to disseminating *information* to riders, agencies have begun to utilize a range of automated pre-trip and real-time transit information applications to supplement traditional information strategies. (Examples of the use of the various types of strategies are included in Appendix A and Chapters 5 through 8.)

Identifying Relative Cost-Effectiveness of Potential Strategies

Selecting appropriate strategies also requires identifying the relative costs and cost-effectiveness of the alternatives. *TCRP Report 28* reviewed the cost-effectiveness of various service concepts at contributing to ridership increases at approximately 60 U.S. transit agencies. Of the 40 concepts considered, the researchers determined that 13 were effective at increasing total system ridership (see Table 4-2). The researchers conducted a preliminary assessment of the cost-effectiveness of these concepts, estimating the capital and operating cost ". . . for each new trip gained for a transit system by each transit service concept, both initially and over time." (p. 45) The results of this assessment are shown in Table 4-2. The costs represented in the table are in comparison to average peak-period bus service unit costs: "low" costs are roughly equivalent to the average peak bus unit cost, "very low" costs are lower than the average unit cost, "moderate" costs are up to 50% higher than the average unit cost, "high" costs are up to twice the average unit cost, and "very high" translates to at least twice the average unit cost.

Based on this analysis, the authors concluded "The preliminary cost-effectiveness assessments suggest that some of the effective concepts are often relatively inexpensive to implement in many cases (e.g., travel training, vanpool incentives, reverse commute, and route restructuring). Others are very expensive per ride and should be carefully considered before being implemented as a way to target new markets." (p. 49)

Cost considerations for different types of service and fare collection strategies are discussed in Chapters 5 and 8, respectively. The next section reviews considerations in evaluating ridership impacts, including the tradeoffs with other goals and the types of measures used.

Evaluating Ridership Impacts

The first step in identifying successful examples of achieving and sustaining high ridership is defining how to measure "success." Achieving high ridership can be a significant challenge due simply to the various types of external factors discussed in Chapter 2. Moreover, transit agencies

Table 4-2. Preliminary cost-effectiveness of successful service concepts.

Successful Service Concepts	Estimated Cost per New Net Trip					
	Initially			Long Term		
	Capital	Operating	Total	Capital	Operating	Total
Feeder Services	None to low	Low to moderate	Low	Low	Low to Moderate	Low
Service to Large Employers	None to low	Low to moderate	Low to Moderate	Low	Low to Moderate	Low to moderate
Express Buses	None to low	Moderate	Low to Moderate	Low	Moderate	Moderate
Reverse Commute Services	None to low	Low	Low	Low	Low	Low
Vanpool Incentives	Low to moderate	Very low to low	Low	Low to moderate	Very low	Low
Fare Incentives	NA	None to low	Very low to low	NA	Very low to low	Low
Park-n-Ride	Moderate to high	Moderate	Moderate to high	Low	Moderate	Moderate
Travel Training	NA	Low to moderate	Low	NA	Low	Low
Route Restructuring	None to low	None to low	Low	Low	Low	Low
Community Buses	Moderate	Low to moderate	Moderate	Moderate	Low to moderate	Moderate
Special Events	Low to moderate	Low	Low	Low	Low	Low
Commuter Rail	Very high	High to very high	Very high	Low to moderate	High	Moderate to high
Light Rail	High to very high	High to very high	High to very high	Low to moderate	Moderate to high	Moderate to high

NOTE: costs compared to average peak period bus service unit costs
SOURCE: TCRP Report 28, *Transit Markets for the Future – The Challenge of Change,* 1998 (p. 48 – Table 20)

invariably face a certain level of natural attrition of ridership, losing regular riders who move to a new city, change jobs (and can no longer use transit to commute), graduate from school, buy cars, or otherwise stop using transit on a regular basis. Based on surveys, a number of agencies of varying sizes and modes have estimated on the order of 20 to 25% annual turnover of individual riders. This estimate is supported by the results of the 2003 APTA/FTA Transit Performance Monitoring System (TPMS) survey of riders at 30 agencies, which indicated that 27% of transit trips are made by riders who have been using transit for less than 6 months; another 11% are by riders who have been using transit for 7 to 12 months. Thus, in order to experience a net gain in ridership, an agency must attract enough new riders—and/or expand usage by existing riders—to more than offset the level of attrition. Conversely, an agency showing a net ridership loss may actually be successfully attracting new riders, but simply not enough to replace those leaving the system.

Considering Tradeoffs Related to Competing Goals

Evaluating ridership success is also complicated by the fact that transit agencies must deal with the reality of competing goals and constraints; in particular, every agency must inevitably make tradeoffs between trying to increase ridership and needing to (1) increase—or at least maintain—operating revenue and (2) control—if not reduce—costs. As explained in *TCRP Research Results Digest 4* (and reiterated in *TCRP Research Results Digest 29)*, "increasing absolute ridership levels is not the sole or even primary criterion for 'success' across the industry. Success can be and is defined in a variety of ways. Frequently, ridership is combined with or even subordinated to financial and budgetary objectives. Relatively few systems are free to pursue increased ridership with unconstrained resources; relatively few systems can sustain the quality and performance of expanded service without increased funding" (p. 5).

This tension between ridership and revenue goals often constrains consideration of fare-related initiatives, for example. While an agency may be tempted to reduce fares—or perhaps introduce a new low-priced pass—in an effort to attract riders, budget constraints may prohibit consideration of such an option. Similarly, the ridership growth resulting from a service expansion must be weighed against the increased costs. Other types of goals that may compete with increasing ridership include equity considerations (e.g., requiring or preventing certain types of service improvements or fare incentives that are targeted to certain markets) and political considerations (e.g., requiring the continuation of poorly utilized service on certain routes favored by board members or local policymakers).

It is important to consider the impacts of these types of tradeoffs in attempting to identify successful examples of achieving and sustaining high ridership. *TCRP Research Results Digest 4* further notes that, in light of competing goals, "success is often defined informally as minimizing the ridership losses from measures taken to increase revenues or constrain costs" (p. 5).

Identifying Ridership Evaluation Measures

Measures that can be used to evaluate the success of ridership strategies include changes/trends in the following:

- Systemwide ridership (e.g., increased from the previous year or continued growth—or at least sustained levels—over several consecutive years);
- Market share of particular target markets (e.g., increased ridership among market segments such as commuters, college students, or seniors);
- Per capita ridership (e.g., high level compared to other agencies within a similar type of service environment); and
- Productivity (e.g., increased passengers per hour from the previous year).

The most appropriate measure(s) in any particular instance will depend to some extent on the types of ridership strategies or initiatives an agency has implemented. In considering systemwide marketing or service restructuring programs, for example, broad measures such as systemwide ridership growth or high per capita ridership are appropriate. If an agency is expanding service only on certain routes, however, it may be more appropriate to consider *productivity* measures, rather than simply looking at the total change in ridership. For, if the number of passengers per hour declines on a targeted route, a particular action may not be considered "successful" in terms of cost-effectiveness, despite an increase in absolute ridership. Meanwhile, for strategies that are targeted to specific markets, a significant increase in that particular *market share* may represent the most useful indicator of the initiative's success.

The remainder of this chapter discusses the characteristics and common elements of successful agency examples of use of ridership strategies.

Elements of Successful Strategies

A key aspect of this study was the identification of examples of transit agency strategies, actions, and initiatives that have proven successful at generating—and in many cases sustaining—significant ridership increases. The results of this analysis are detailed in Appendix A; the key findings/conclusions of this effort are reviewed below.

Characteristics of Successful U.S. Examples

Sources of Examples

As explained in Appendix A (provided on the accompanying CD-ROM), a set of 236 individual strategies or projects recently utilized by 100 U.S. transit agencies to increase ridership was compiled and reviewed. These examples came from the following sources:

- Previous research—Ridership trends over the past several years were reviewed for the examples presented in earlier studies of ridership strategies. Just over a third of the agencies considered were able to produce at least as much ridership growth between 1999 and 2003 as they had in 1994–1996. These agencies, as well as several others that experienced ridership gains of 10% or more in 1999–2003, were included in our list of successful examples.
- FTA's *Innovative Practices for Increased Ridership* database—Many of the projects reported on this website were used in our list of successful examples.
- Other sources, including newsletter/magazine articles—Several examples were selected from recent articles detailing agencies' efforts and results.

For each of the examples selected, systemwide ridership impacts between 1999 and 2003, as well as population changes and productivity information, were provided. The review also considered, where available, the reported ridership impacts of the different types of strategies (e.g., the change in demand on a particular route or a change in market share for a particular segment). Most of the agencies experienced systemwide ridership growth between 1999 and 2003. However, also included were a number of agencies that did not see overall ridership gains but significantly increased demand or market share on a targeted route/corridor/market segment.

Nearly three-quarters of these agencies experienced systemwide ridership increases between 1999 and 2003; nearly half saw gains of 10% or more, while a third had growth of 20% or more. This level of growth is noteworthy, as the transit industry overall saw less than a 2.8% aggregate ridership gain during these 4 years—and a 2.3% aggregate loss between 2001 and 2003.

Types of Strategies/Actions/Initiatives Used

The agencies reviewed here reported using the full range of types of ridership strategies, and many agencies used more than one strategy:

- Over 40% (42 of 100) of the agencies identified a combination of two or more types of strategies (e.g., operating/service adjustments and fare collection); 16 of these agencies deployed strategies from three or more categories. Moreover, 10 of the agencies that used only one category deployed two or more projects within that category. Over half of the agencies therefore indicated use of more than one project in an effort to boost ridership. A total of 11 agencies each identified five or more individual projects. The overall average was just over two projects per agency.[2]
- All of the possible combinations of types of strategies were used, with operating/service adjustments and partnerships/coordination representing the most common pairing. Operating/service adjustments and marketing/promotional initiatives were the second most common pairing.
- Operating/service adjustments were the most common type of strategy, being deployed by nearly 60% of the agencies (58 agencies). Nearly 40% of the agencies used partnership/coordination initiatives (39 agencies) and about 30% used marketing/promotional initiatives (31 agencies), while a quarter deployed fare collection/structure initiatives (25 agencies).
  - Among the 43 large urban area agencies, the distribution of types of strategies was relatively even: 13—22 of each type. Operating/service adjustments were used by just over half of these agencies, while the other three were each deployed by 30 to 40% of the agencies.
  - Among the medium urban areas, operating/service adjustments were much more predominant: 76% of the agencies used operating/service adjustments, as opposed to 48%

---

[2] As noted in Appendix A, the list of strategies reviewed represented only those identified by the agencies as examples. Many of these agencies have actually utilized additional strategies in recent years in an effort to generate higher ridership. Thus, while it is useful to review the distribution of different categories of strategies identified by these agencies, it is important to remember that we have not assembled an exhaustive list of the ridership initiatives each agency has undertaken.

using partnership/coordination, 28% using marketing/promotional, and 21% using fare collection/structure projects.
- Among the small areas, operating/service adjustments and partnership/coordination initiatives were each utilized by roughly half of the agencies; 21% used partnership/coordination initiatives and only 11% deployed fare collection/structure initiatives.

The distribution of the specific types of projects reported by all of the agencies is summarized in Table 4-3. Key points include the following:

- The most widely used subcategories of actions were partnerships (47, or 20% of all projects) and routing/coverage adjustments (46 projects, or 19%). These were followed by marketing/promotion initiatives (35, or 15%). These were used considerably more than the next most common subcategory, information improvements (22, or 9%). The least used were scheduling/frequency adjustments (12, or 5%) and fare structure changes (13, or 6%).
- With regard to specific types of project, the most common were university/school pass programs (28 projects), general marketing/promotional campaigns (24 projects) and increased

Table 4-3. Frequency of use by type of project (all areas).

Category/Subcategory	Type of Strategy	Number of Projects
Operating/Service Adjustments		86
Routing/coverage adjustments		46
	Increased route coverage	22
	Route restructuring	16
	Improved schedule/route coordination	8
Scheduling/frequency adjustments		12
	Increased service frequency	4
	Increased span of service	4
	Improved reliability/on-time performance	4
New types of service		14
	Improved travel speed/reduced stops	9
	Targeted services	5
Improved amenities		14
	Passenger facility improvements	9
	New/improved vehicles	3
	Increased security	1
	Increased safety	1
Partnerships/Coordination		61
Partnerships		47
	University/school pass programs	28
	Travel demand management strategies	13
	Privately-subsidized activity center service	6
Coordination		14
	Consistent regional (inter-agency) operating policies	3
	Coordination with social service agencies	7
	Coordination with other transportation agencies	-
	Promotion of transit-supportive design/TOD	4
Marketing/Promotional and Information Initiatives		57
Marketing/promotional initiatives		35
	Targeted marketing/promotions	11
	General marketing/promotions	24
Information improvements		22
	Improved informational materials	9
	Improved customer information/assistance	6
	Automated transit traveler information	7
Fare Collection/Fare Structure Initiatives		32
Fare collection improvements		19
	Improved payment convenience	15
	Regional payment integration	4
Fare structure changes		13
	Fare structure simplification	2
	Fare reduction	11

route coverage (22 projects); these were followed by route restructuring (16 projects) and improved payment convenience initiatives (15 projects).
- Among the large urban area agencies, the most popular types of project were general marketing/promotional campaigns (14 projects), university/school pass programs (10), and improved payment convenience initiatives (10).
- Among the medium urban area agencies, the most common types of project were increased route coverage (9 projects) and general marketing/promotional campaigns (8).
- Among the small urban/rural area agencies, university/school pass programs (12 projects) and increased route coverage (8) were by far the most popular types of project.

Ridership and Productivity Impacts

Beyond absolute ridership changes, it is useful to examine the impact of ridership-enhancing strategies on service productivity.

- Two-thirds of these agencies (66 of 100) experienced reductions in productivity between 1999 and 2003; this includes 41 agencies that had gained ridership during the period. This resulted from the fact that, while most of these agencies had increased the amount of service provided, the growth in demand fell short of the increase in service (revenue-vehicle hours).
- Thus, while these agencies were successful at raising ridership, their service effectiveness—and hence their cost-effectiveness (cost per rider)—was reduced somewhat. This underscores the need for agencies to carefully consider the tradeoff between increasing ridership and controlling costs.

Relationship between Types of Strategies and Ridership

Those agencies that experienced the largest percentage systemwide ridership increases between 1999 and 2003 deployed strategies spread among all four categories of strategies, although operating/service adjustments were most common, followed by marketing/promotional and informational initiatives:

- Among the agencies in large urban areas, operating/service adjustments and/or marketing/promotional initiatives were utilized by the three agencies that experienced the highest ridership gains (Pasco County, FL; Los Angeles DOT; and Tempe Transit, AZ). Among the 21 agencies in this category that had ridership increases of 10% or more, 14 used operating/service adjustments, 8 marketing/promotional efforts, 5 fare collection/structure initiatives, and 2 partnership/coordination projects. (The types of strategies identified by the large urban area agencies with the 10 largest ridership increases are summarized in Table 4-4.)

Table 4-4. Large urban agencies with highest ridership growth ('99–'03).*

Agency	% Ridership change ('99-'03)	Rides per capita ('03)	Type of Strategies Identified			
			Oper. / service	Partner. / coord.	Mktng / prom. / info.	Fare collec. / struc.
Pasco Co. Public Transit (FL)	697%	1.2	X			
Los Angeles DOT (CA)	272%	2.8	X		X	
Tempe Transit (AZ)	156%	40.0			X	
Virginia Railway Express (VA/DC)	83%	4.7			X	
Fairfax Connector (VA)	59%	7.6	X			X
Montebello Bus Lines (CA)	48%	36.0	X			
Johnson Co. Transit (KS)	38%	1.4	X			
Ft. Worth Transportation Authority (TX)	36%	12.3			X	
Broward Co. Division of Transportation (FL)	36%	22.1	X			
Santa Clarita Transit (CA)	35%	19.4			X	X

* This list covers only those agencies reviewed in this study (see Appendix A).

- In the medium urban area category, the agency with the highest increase (PARTA in Kent, OH) reported operating/service adjustments only, while the agency with the second highest gain (CATA in Lansing, MI) utilized strategies in all four categories. Among the 13 agencies in this category that had ridership gains of 10% or more, 9 used operating/service adjustments, 7 marketing/promotional efforts, 5 partnership/coordination projects, and 5 fare collection/structure initiatives. (The types of strategies identified by the medium urban area agencies with the 10 largest ridership increases are summarized in Table 4-5.)
- The small urban/rural agency with the highest ridership increase (Advance Transit in Wilder, VT) used strategies in all four categories, while the agency with the next highest gain (CATA in State College, PA) reported a partnership/coordination project only. The other agency that experienced nearly 100% ridership growth (Bloomington Public Transit, IN) used strategies in three categories. The three agencies ranked next in terms of ridership increases (CityBus in Lafayette, IN; RTS in Gainesville, FL; and Fargo Metro Area Transit, ND) all had partnership/coordination projects, although one of them (CityBus) also deployed a fare collection/structure initiative. Among the 14 agencies in this category that had ridership gains of 10% or more, 8 used operating/service adjustments, 8 partnership/coordination projects, 5 fare collection/structure initiatives, and 4 marketing/promotional efforts. (The types of strategies identified by the small agencies with the 10 largest ridership increases are summarized in Table 4-6.)

Table 4-5. Medium urban agencies with highest ridership growth ('99–'03).*

Agency	% Ridership change ('99-'03)	Rides per capita ('03)	Oper. / service	Partner. / coord.	Mktng / prom. / info.	Fare collec. / struc.
Portage Area Regional Trans. Auth. (Kent, OH)	102%	0.8	X			
Capital Area Trans. Auth. (Lansing, MI)	79%	27.6	X	X	X	X
Ventura Intercity Service Transit (CA)	60%	2.8			X	X
Chapel Hill Transit (NC)	52%	92.2				X
Interurban Transit Partnership (Grand Rapids, MI)	39%	11.2	X		X	
Utah Transit Authority (Salt Lake City, UT)	33%	17.5	X	X	X	X
Connecticut DOT (Hartford, CT)	28%	1.5		X	X	
Salem-Keiser Transit (OR)	28%	24.9	X			
Lee Co. Transit (Ft. Myers, FL)	26%	8.3	X			
Cape Cod Regional Transit Auth. (Hyannis, MA)	22%	0.1	X			

* This list covers only those agencies reviewed in this study (see Appendix A).

Table 4-6. Small urban/rural agencies with highest ridership growth ('99–'03).*

Agency	% Ridership change ('99-'03)	Rides per capita ('03)	Oper. / service	Partner. / coord.	Mktng / prom. / info.	Fare collec. / struc.
Advance Transit (Wilder, VT)	170%	16.7	X	X	X	X
Centre Area Trans. Auth. (State College, PA)	101%	72.3		X		
Bloomington Public Transit Corporation (IN)	98%	30.0	X	X		X
CityBus of Greater Lafayette (IN)	84%	35.8		X		X
Regional Transit System (Gainesville, FL)	84%	56.2		X		
Fargo Metro Area Transit (ND)	45%	5.1		X		
Santa Maria Area Transit (CA)	44%	6.2	X		X	
Kalamazoo Transit Division (MI)	38%	15.9	X			
Logan Transit District (UT)	36%	18.5	X			
University Transport System (Davis, CA)	34%	47.6		X		

* This list covers only those agencies reviewed in this study (see Appendix A).

Relationship between Geography/Population Change and Ridership

The geographical distribution of the highest gaining agencies (i.e., 10% or greater growth over the 4-year period) differs markedly for the three area size categories:

- In the large urban areas, the high growth agencies are, as might be expected, concentrated in the West Coast, South, and mid-Atlantic regions: 9 of the 21 agencies are on the West Coast (primarily Southern California), 5 are in the mid-Atlantic region (in and around Washington, DC), and 3 are in Florida; only 1 is in the Northeast, and none are in the Midwest.
- In contrast, more of the highest ridership medium urban systems (6 agencies) are located in the Midwest and Northeast than in the South or West Coast (5 agencies).
- The majority (57%) of the highest ridership small urban/rural agencies are located in the Northeast and Midwest; only 3 are on the West Coast or South.

While population growth is clearly one of many factors contributing to ridership growth, there is no evidence among these examples of a strong correlation between the extent of the population change and the level of ridership change:

- For the large urban areas, there is significant variation in the rate of population growth among the highest ridership agencies; moreover, the two areas that experienced the greatest population increases (i.e., Las Vegas and San Juan) actually lost riders during the evaluation period. Conversely, the Los Angeles area, home of six of the agencies with the highest ridership gains, had the smallest population growth among all of these areas.
- The three medium urban area agencies with the highest ridership increases experienced relatively modest population growth—or in one case, a significant loss; meanwhile, three of the highest growth areas lost riders during the 4-year period.
- Among the small urban/rural agencies, there is even less of a correlation between population change and ridership: nearly half (8 of 15) of the areas with the largest population increases were not among the higher ridership gainers, while half (7 of the 14) of the agencies with the highest ridership gains were not among the areas showing the highest population increases.

Per Capita Usage

As indicated above, *per capita ridership* represents another means of comparing agencies' success at generating transit usage.[3] Key findings related to this measure are as follows:

- More than two-thirds (68) of the 100 agencies carry 10 or more riders per capita per year; 27 carry 25 or more; 11 carry 50 or more.
  - Among the large urban areas, there is no clear correlation between type of strategies used and per capita ridership levels. The agencies with per capita figures of 25 or higher identified using all four types of strategies in virtually equal numbers: 8 agencies used operating/service adjustments, 7 each used partnership/coordination and fare collection/structure initiatives; and 6 agencies used marketing/promotional initiatives; 6 of these 16 agencies deployed two or more types of strategies, and 5 each used three or more types. (Table 4-7 shows the types of strategies identified by the 10 highest per capita ridership large urban areas.)
  - Among the medium urban areas, operating/service adjustments were used by 14 of the 19 agencies with per capita ridership figures of 10 or higher. The other three categories

---

[3] As discussed in Appendix A (p. A-18), while per capita ridership is a useful measure, it is strongly affected by the definition of each agency's service area. The service area is determined by such factors as the types of modes operated by the agency (e.g., whether it includes commuter rail) and the existence of other agencies serving the same region or metropolitan area. Thus, two agencies located in cities of comparable sizes can have rather different service area populations. This should be kept in mind in reviewing per capita figures.

Table 4-7. Large urban agencies with highest per capita ridership.*

Agency	Rides per capita ('03)	% Ridership change ('99-'03)	Type of Strategies Identified			
			Oper. / service	Partner. / coord.	Mktng / prom. / info.	Fare collec. / struc.
Washington Metropolitan Area Transit Auth. (DC)	299.5	10%	X			X
MTA New York City Transit (NY)	146.8	8%				X
Chicago Transit Authority (IL)	127.5	2%	X	X	X	X
Southeastern Penn. Trans. Auth. (Philadelphia, PA)	95.8	4%			X	
Massachusetts Bay Trans. Auth. (Boston, MA)	85.6	10%	X			
Tri-Co. Metro. Transit District (Portland, OR)	77.8	20%	X	X	X	
King Co. Dept. of Transportation (Seattle, WA)	53.6	(1%)		X		
Miami-Dade Transit Agency (FL)	41.5	2%				X
Greater Cleveland Regional Trans. Auth. (OH)	42.0	(12%)	X	X	X	X
Tempe Transit (AZ)	40.0	156%			X	

* This list covers only those agencies reviewed in this study (see Appendix A).

saw lower levels of usage: 10 agencies used partnership/coordination initiatives, 7 used *marketing*/promotional initiatives, and 5 fare collection/structure initiatives; 10 of these agencies deployed two or more types of strategies, and 4 each used three or more types. While operating/service adjustments predominated in this group, however, the agency with by far the highest per capita ridership used only a fare collection strategy (the elimination of fares). (Table 4-8 shows the types of strategies identified by the medium urban areas with the 10 highest per capita ridership figures.)

– Among the small urban/rural areas, the agencies with per capita ridership figures of 10 or higher most often deployed partnership/coordination strategies (13) and operating/ service adjustments (10); fare collection/structure and marketing/promotional initiatives were used by 5 and 4 agencies, respectively. The agencies in this size category were more apt to use a single type of strategy than those in the larger areas: 7 agencies each deployed two or more types of strategies, while 3 each used three or more types. (Table 4-9 shows the types of strategies identified by the 10 highest per capita ridership small urban/rural areas.)

- As would be expected, the bulk of the highest usage agencies are located in large urban areas; 7 (64%) of the over 50 group, 17 (63%) of those over 25, and 30 (44%) of those over 10. However, the small urban/rural group has the next largest percentages of high usage agencies: 3 (27%) of the over 50 group, 7 (26%) of those over 25, and 19 (28%) of those over 10.
- The relatively high per capita ridership figures at a number of agencies in both the small urban/rural and medium urban categories can be attributed, at least in part, to their presence

Table 4-8. Medium urban agencies with highest per capita ridership.*

Agency	Rides per capita ('03)	% Ridership change ('99-'03)	Type of Strategies Identified			
			Oper. / service	Partner. / coord.	Mktng / prom. / info.	Fare collec. / struc.
Chapel Hill Transit (NC)	92.2	52%				X
Capital Area Transportation Authority (Lansing, MI)	27.6	79%	X			
Regional Transportation Commission (Reno, NV)	25.4	6%	X			
Salem-Keiser Transit (OR)	24.9	28%	X			
Ann Arbor Transportation Authority (MI)	19.8	0%	X	X		
Utah Transit Authority (Salt Lake City, UT)	17.5	33%	X	X	X	X
Corpus Christi Regional Transportation Authority (TX)	16.4	(8)	X	X		
South Bend Public Transportation Corp. (IN)	16.3	(4%)	X			
Norwalk Transit District (CT)	16.3	(5%)		X		
Greater Bridgeport Transit Authority (CT)	16.2	(9%)	X			

* This list covers only those agencies reviewed in this study (see Appendix A).

Table 4-9. Small urban/rural agencies with highest per capita ridership.*

Agency	Rides per capita ('03)	% Ridership change ('99-'03)	Type of Strategies Identified			
			Oper. / service	Partner. / coord.	Mktng / prom. / info.	Fare collec. / struc.
Champaign-Urbana Mass Transit District (IL)	74.6	8%		X		
Centre Area Trans. Auth. (State College, PA)	72.3	101%		X		
Regional Transit System (Gainesville, FL)	56.2	84%		X		
University Transport System (Davis, CA)	47.6	34%		X		
CityBus of Greater Lafayette (IN)	35.8	84%		X		X
Bloomington Public Transit Corporation (IN)	30.0	98%	X	X		X
Tompkins Consol. Area Transit (Ithaca, NY)	28.7	19%			X	X
Santa Cruz Metro Transit District (CA)	24.1	(3%)	X	X		
Chittenden Co. Trans. Authority (Burlington, VT)	19.0	7%		X		
Logan Transit District (UT)	18.5	36%	X			

* This list covers only those agencies reviewed in this study (see Appendix A).

in a particular service environment: 9 of the 10 highest levels among the small urban/rural agencies (see Table 4-9), as well as 3 of the 5 highest levels among medium urban agencies (see Table 4-8), occur at agencies in major university towns. In addition, four of the other small urban/rural agencies—as well as five of the medium urban agencies—with 10 or more rides per capita feature university-oriented strategies. The large urban group also includes substantial use of university-oriented strategies, as half of the agencies with per capita ridership levels of 25 or greater—and four of seven agencies carrying 50 or more—have deployed such strategies.

- Among those with per capita figures of 10 or more, 33 (49%) are located in the Northeast (18) or Midwest (15), and 10 are in California. The others are relatively evenly distributed among the other parts of the country. Among those with levels of 25 or higher, 12 of 27 (44%) are in the Midwest (7) or Northeast (5). Among those with levels over 50, four are in the Northeast.
- Among the large urban area agencies, the highest per capita usage levels are, as expected, by and large associated with the largest—and highest ridership—agencies, and these are predominantly older, more mature systems located in the Northeast, Midwest and mid-Atlantic regions (see Table 4-7).
- As can be seen in Tables 4-5 through 4-9, the agencies with the highest per capita ridership figures are not necessarily the agencies that have had the highest percentage ridership increases.
  - In the large urban group, only half of the agencies that experienced 20% or more ridership growth (1999–2003) are among the higher per capita ridership agencies.
  - For the medium and small groups, this figure is 55% and 71%, respectively. In each of these categories, though, there is considerable overlap among the agencies with the highest per capita levels: the two medium urban area agencies with the highest per capita usage levels also had among the four highest ridership increases; and six of the seven small urban/rural agencies with per capita usage levels over 25 also include the agencies with the four highest ridership increases.

Successful Examples from Abroad

Despite the much higher rates of transit usage outside of the United States, it was though that inclusion of examples from abroad would provide useful information for U.S. agencies. Thus, 28 selected ridership strategies, representing 17 agencies from Canada, Mexico, Europe, and South America were included in this review (see Appendix A). Key points from the review of examples from abroad are as follows.

Factors Influencing High Ridership

A range of elements contributes to the high transit mode share abroad, and certain factors relate to an underlying physical, economic, and political environment favoring transit that are simply not present in most U.S. cities. These factors include very high fuel prices and densely developed (and often physically constrained) towns and cities. However, certain practices and policies used in other countries could be given further consideration in U.S. cities. The key elements include

- Emphasis on convenient, reliable, and comfortable transit service (e.g., provision of transit priority in mixed traffic, long spacing between stops, advanced information systems, and improved passenger amenities);
- Policies/practices making transit competitive with the automobile (e.g., implementation of central city parking limits and restricted automobile use in certain areas); and
- Comprehensive integration of land use/development policies and transit planning (e.g., formal rules and guidelines on making development designs and street improvements conducive to transit service).

Types of Strategies

A set of examples of innovative transit efforts from these countries was developed. The key types of strategies represented were

- Bus rapid transit and other premium bus services,
- Real-time traveler information systems, and
- Smart-card-based regional payment systems.

The success of such strategies has led U.S. agencies to begin to adopt them in the past few years. While it is unlikely that most—if any—U.S. cities will ever be able to approach the levels of transit usage found in these countries, continued expansion of the types of approaches studied here will doubtless bolster the efforts of U.S. agencies to increase ridership.

Conclusions

The review of examples from both the U.S. and abroad has shown that transit agencies in all types of environment have successfully utilized a broad range of strategies to increase ridership—if not systemwide then at least within a targeted market segment, route or corridor. External factors, as discussed in Chapter 2, doubtless played major roles in producing ridership change in many of the locations studied here. Nevertheless, these agency strategies—often used in combination—have apparently been key factors in their own right.

While operating and service adjustments were the most frequently used type of strategy, these agencies have demonstrated the effective usage of various marketing and fare-related actions as well. Moreover, partnerships and coordination with entities such as universities, employers, and social services agencies have proven effective at tapping key markets; university/school pass programs actually represented the single most widely used strategy.

However, there is no clear evidence from this review that any particular type of strategy is significantly more effective at boosting demand than the others. These agencies identified an average of just over two strategies apiece, and the largest ridership gains were attributable to different types and combinations of strategies. What has become clear is the importance of each agency (1) identifying its own needs and opportunities and (2) selecting one or more strategies that it believes will address these needs/opportunities. As discussed in Chapter 3, this requires developing an understanding of the gaps and inefficiencies in the existing service network as well as characteristics and service needs of different market segments. The following chapters present guidance on selecting and implementing appropriate strategies.

CHAPTER 5

Operating/Service Adjustments

Introduction

The most widely used types of strategies, actions, and initiatives aimed at increasing ridership are operating/service adjustments. The types of strategies—and specific actions/examples—included this category are shown in Table 5-1. These types of strategies are generally intended to attract and retain riders by improving the quality of transit service—or by making use of transit feasible at all. Thus, each strategy should address one or more of the following mode choice factors:

- Travel time,
- Convenience,
- Comfort,
- Reliability,
- Perceived personal security/safety, and
- Perceived "image" of the system.

Guidance on the design and implementation of—and agency examples of—the different types of operating/service adjustment strategies are provided below.

Design/Implementation Guidelines

As explained in earlier chapters, selecting and implementing any of these ridership strategies requires analysis of an agency's service needs and opportunities. The basic planning activities and types of considerations for operating/service adjustments are described below. Table 5-2 presents a checklist of the recommended steps an agency should consider in identifying and developing strategies within this category.

Applicable Settings

As demonstrated via the examples reviewed in Appendix A, all types of operating/service adjustment strategies can be used in a range of service environments. However, some strategies or particular types of actions are not well-suited to certain settings or modes. Table 5-3 identifies which environments and modes are generally appropriate for each type of strategy; obviously, though, each specific action must be designed to reflect the needs and constraints of the agency's environment.

Planning/Research Activities

As discussed in Chapter 3, changes in a region's development patterns, population characteristics, and economic conditions can often result in gaps or inefficiencies in the existing transit

Table 5-1. Types of operating/service adjustments.

Type of Strategy	Specific Actions/Examples
Routing/coverage adjustments	
Increased route coverage	Service expansion; introduction of local circulators; expansion into rural areas
Route restructuring	Reallocation to most productive rtes; revising operating strategies
Improved schedule/route coordination	Feeder services; timed transfers; transit centers
Scheduling/frequency adjustments	
Increased service frequency	Increased frequency on specific route
Increased span of service	Longer service hours (e.g., late night/weekend)
Improved reliability/on-time performance	Implementation of AVL, transit signal priority, transfer connection protection
New types of service	
Improved travel speed/reduced stops	Introduction of express bus, BRT, rail
Targeted services	University-oriented service, downtown circulator, special event/other shuttles
Improved amenities	
Passenger facility improvements	Improved bus stop/station, transit center, park n' ride amenities
New/improved vehicles	Improved amenities, use of articulated buses
Increased security	Increased agency security presence
Increased safety	Promotion of safety features of vehicles

network—and can also create new service opportunities. Based on an evaluation of (1) the current service design and route performance and (2) service needs and potential market opportunities, an agency can thus identify appropriate operating and service adjustments that address any existing gaps and/or serve potential new markets. As indicated in Table 5-2, the types of planning/design activities that an agency should consider include the following (see Chapter 3 for descriptions of these methods):

- Evaluation of existing services (route- and/or system-level), to identify inefficient or problem routes; this might include a *peer agency analysis* to identify performance of and strategies used by comparable agencies;
- Analysis of markets and projected growth, to identify gaps in service coverage and the size of current and projected travel markets; and
- Market research and public outreach, to identify key market segments and the service preferences and propensity (of both riders and non-riders) to ride new or improved service.

Based on the findings of such efforts, an agency can then consider which types of operating/service adjustments to pursue. The types of design and performance measures that can be applied in evaluating service are reviewed below.

Design and Performance Measures

As described in Chapter 3, various route- or system-level measures can be used to guide the evaluation of existing services and design of service improvements or new services. Examples of measures that might be applied are shown in Table 5-4 (see Chapter 3 for a description of the usage of such measures).

The specific guidelines for each measure will depend on the nature of the agency's service network and environment—and the goals/thresholds the agency has established. However, the basic approach for increasing ridership in any system entails making adjustments to those routes—or in those areas—that do not meet the designated goal or threshold level for that type of route or service. The agency should select strategies that best address the specific service shortcoming or opportunity. The types of strategies and actions that could be considered with each type of service deficiency or problem area are shown in Table 5-5.

Table 5-2. Checklist—Developing and implementing operating/service adjustments.

	Key Steps/Activities	
	Evaluation of Existing Services	

	Conduct system-level evaluation
	    Examine service and ridership trends
	    Assess system-wide performance measures
	    Conduct peer agency review	

	Conduct route-level performance assessment
	    Identify design/performance measures and establish goals/thresholds
	    Evaluate route performance according to goals/thresholds
	    Identify deficiencies/problem areas
	    Identify potential strategies to address deficiencies	

	Analysis of Markets and Projected Growth	

	Conduct demographic and travel pattern analysis
	    Identify characteristics of key market segments (e.g., seniors, youth, low-income households)
	    Identify residential and employment densities
	    Identify locations of employment and other activity centers
	    Identify key travel patterns within area/region	

	Review growth projections
	    Identify projected development patterns (office, retail, residential, other)
	    Identify projected numbers/characteristics of households/residents
	    Identify projected employment levels and characteristics	

	Market Research and Public Outreach	

	Conduct surveys/focus groups
	    Conduct survey of current riders (e.g., on-board/in-station)
	    Conduct survey of non-riders or infrequent riders (e.g., telephone)
	    Conduct focus groups of riders and non-riders
	    Analyze results of market research	

	Conduct public outreach/input
	    Meet with stakeholder groups (e.g., civic, government, business, institutional interest groups)
	    Conduct public meetings or open house sessions	

	Development of Ridership Strategy(ies)	

	Select and design strategy(ies)
	    Identify range of potential strategies
	    Evaluate options and select most appropriate strategy or combination of strategies
	    Design service change or new service
	    Estimate ridership impact	

	Identify cost impacts
	    Estimate costs (capital, operating & maintenance) of strategy (design, implementation, operation)
	    Estimate revenue associated with additional riders
	    Identify net cost	

	Implementation of Strategy(ies)	
	Develop implementation plan	

	Implement service change, new service or amenity improvement
	    Conduct public hearings (if necessary)
	    Procure new equipment or locate/construct new facilities (if necessary)
	    Hire additional personnel (if necessary)
	    Develop informational/marketing materials regarding strategy(ies)
	    Put strategy(ies) in place	

	Monitor performance of strategy
	    Identify actual ridership impact
	    Make any necessary operational adjustments	

Table 5-3. Applicable modes/settings for types of operating/service adjustments.

Type of Strategy	Mode		Service Environment					
	Bus	Rail	Large Urban	Medium Urban	Small Urban	Rural	Suburb	CBD
Increased route coverage	+	+	+	+	+	+	+	+
Route restructuring	+	—	+	+	+	+	+	+
Improved schedule/route coordination	+	+	+	+	+	+	+	+
Increased service frequency	+	+	+	+	+	O	+	+
Increased span of service	+	+	+	+	+	O	+	+
Improved reliability/on-time performance	+	+	+	+	+	O	+	+
Improved travel speed/reduced stops	+	+	+	+	O	O	+	O
Targeted services	+	—	+	+	+	+	+	+
Passenger facility improvements	+	+	+	+	+	O	+	+
New/improved vehicles	+	+	+	+	+	O	+	+
Increased security	+	+	+	+	+	+	+	+
Increased safety	+	+	+	+	+	+	+	+

Key: — = not applicable or inappropriate; O = applicable, but may not be cost-effective; + = applicable and appropriate

Table 5-4. Sample service design/performance measures.

Type of Measure	Definition or Form of Measure	Example of Guideline or Threshold
Design Measures		
Coverage	Recommended spacing between routes	90% of households in high density area (>3 household/acre) should be within ¼ mi. of bus rte.
Span of service	Days/week, hours/day for each type of service	Service 7am-7pm, 5 days/week for Express Routes
Frequency of service	Maximum headway for each type of service	Headway not greater than 30 min. for local (non-express) routes
Travel time	Comparison of in-vehicle travel time to driving time (for same distance)	Ratio of end-to-end AM peak express bus running time to auto travel time 1.5 or less
Performance Measures		
Productivity	Boardings per vehicle-revenue hour (or boardings per trip)	30 boardings/VRH (local service, peak), 18 (local, off-peak)
Crowding	Load factor (no. of passengers at peak load pt. divided by no. of seats)	Weekday peak load factor (avg. for consecutive trips) no higher than 1.2
Reliability	Schedule adherence (i.e., percent on-time, as well as percent early and percent late)	At least 90% on-time departures for weekday trips

Table 5-5. Strategies associated with types of service problem areas.

Problem Area	Types of Strategy to Consider	Types of Specific Actions to Consider
Coverage	Increased route coverage, Improved schedule/route coordination, Targeted services	Service expansion; Introduction of local circulators, Feeder services; Timed transfers; Transit centers; Regional integration; Employer-sponsored/reverse commute service
Span of service	Increased span of service	Longer service hours (e.g., late night/weekend)
Frequency of service	Increased service frequency	Increased frequency on specific rtes.
Travel time	Improved schedule/route coordination, Improved travel speed/reduced stops, Route restructuring	Feeder services; Timed transfers; Transit centers; Introduction of express bus, BRT, rail; New crosstown rtes
Productivity	Route restructuring, Improved schedule/route coordination, Improved travel speed/reduced stops	Reallocation to most productive rtes, New crosstown rtes (eliminating the need to transfer), Introduction of express bus, BRT, rail
Crowding	Increased service frequency, Increased route coverage, Route restructuring, Improved travel speed/reduced stops	Comprehensive service expansion, Reallocation to most productive rtes; Introduction of express bus, BRT, rail
Reliability	Improved reliability/on-time performance, Improved schedule/route coordination	Implementation of AVL, transit signal priority, transfer connection protection; Feeder services; Timed transfers

Cost Estimation Considerations

Types of Cost Impacts

The cost of implementing and operating these strategies varies considerably, depending on the specific action(s) selected.[1] The key factors determining the net cost impact include the following:

- What types of capital expenditures, if any, are needed?
  - Some of these strategies involve physical improvements (e.g., establishment of transit centers or enclosure of bus shelters).
  - Some strategies may require additional vehicles (e.g., introduction of new types of service such as BRT) or other purchase (e.g., AVL or vehicle tracking system).
- What are the operating & maintenance (O&M) cost impacts associated with the strategy?
  - Strategies that involve provision of additional service will likely entail increased O&M costs (e.g., expansion of service or introduction of new services).
  - Some strategies may result in overall cost savings, or at least improved efficiency and/or effectiveness (e.g., reallocation of existing service or improved route/schedule coordination).
  - Strategies that involve replacement of low-productivity fixed-route service with flexible service using smaller vehicles may result in lower costs; in a few cases, agencies have negotiated lower wage rates for demand-responsive or small vehicle community-based services using small vehicles. Contracting out such service to a private operator may in some cases reduce costs as well.[2]
- Can a portion of the capital and/or operating costs be covered by partnerships or additional fare revenue?
  - Some strategies may be subsidized (all or in part) by partner entities (e.g., targeted services to major employment sites, tourist attraction, and college campus or airport).
  - Special service to sporting events or other special events typically allows the agency to charge higher fares than it does for regular transit service.
  - In some cases, a strategy may generate sufficient additional fare revenue (i.e., by increasing ridership) to offset much, if not all, of the additional O&M cost.

Methods for estimating costs are discussed below.

Cost Estimation Methods

Clearly, an agency planning for some type of operating/service adjustment will have to calculate the cost requirements of the specific strategy(ies) under consideration. The capital cost associated with a strategy can be estimated based on average industry unit costs (e.g., for new vehicles or bus shelters) or may require a full engineering analysis (e.g., for construction of transit centers).

The O&M costs associated with new or expanded services can be calculated in different ways, depending on the specific type and magnitude of the strategy in question. For instance, in estimating the O&M cost of a new type of service (e.g., BRT or a new light rail line), the FTA recommends using a *resource build-up* approach. Resource build-up models estimate staffing, utility, and materials resources needed for a specific unit of service supply (i.e., a "productivity ratio"), defines unit costs for these resources, and calculates resulting costs in each cost category. Essentially, the cost of each item or category is computed through an equation of the following form:

O&M Cost = Unit of Service ∗ Productivity Ratio ∗ Unit Cost

---

[1] An order of magnitude assessment of the cost-effectiveness of various strategies, conducted as part of a previous TCRP study, is discussed in Chapter 3; the results of this assessment are summarized in Table 3-5.
[2] The net cost impact of private contracting will depend on a number of factors, including (1) the amount of agency expense required to administer and monitor the contracted service, (2) the actual contract rate and payment basis (e.g., per hour versus per passenger), and (3) whether the contractor is providing and/or maintaining vehicles.

These factors are typically defined as follows:

- Unit of service is typically expressed in terms of vehicle-miles, vehicle-hours, peak vehicles, garages, passengers, stations, track-miles, and so forth.
- Productivity ratio is expressed as a resource-required-per-unit-of-service, e.g., operators per vehicle hour, mechanics per vehicle mile, or gallon of diesel fuel per vehicle mile. For new services, these ratios are typically based on figures from similar operations in other locations, although all figures must be adjusted to reflect unique local conditions, as appropriate.
- Unit costs are expressed in such terms as average annual wages and fringes per mechanic, average price per gallon of fuel, average cost per kwh of electricity, and so forth. These figures are based on local cost data to the extent possible, using national productivity data where local sources do not provide a reliable base.

The resource build-up approach will yield the most accurate cost estimates, but is more time-consuming and data-intensive than other approaches. Alternatively, the cost of expanding or increasing the span of existing service can be estimated more simply using some type of cost allocation or unit cost approach. The cost allocation method distributes all of the agency's O&M costs among a set of factors; the standard three-variable model typically assigns costs to vehicle hours, vehicle miles, or peak vehicles, based on the closest causal relationship. The aggregate cost in each category is divided by the quantity of that category to produce a unit cost. Given the unit costs per factor, systemwide O&M costs can be allocated to specific routes or groups of routes. Incremental costs associated with expanding existing service may also be estimated using fixed versus variable cost figures; the latter typically represents a blended unit cost, based on the agency's current costs per hour, mile, and peak vehicle. For any of these approaches, the agency will have to identify the requirements for annual revenue vehicle-hours and vehicle-miles, as well as the number (and type) of vehicles.

Expected Ridership Response

The most widely used indicator of the expected ridership response to a particular type of change (in level of service or price) is the elasticity measure.[3] As explained in Chapter 2, *TCRP Report 95: Traveler Response to Transportation System Changes* summarizes the results of analyses of the nature of the impacts of various types of transit actions on demand. Chapters 9 (*Transit Scheduling and Frequency*) and 10 (*Bus Routing and Coverage*) of that report review elasticity measures and other indicators for different types of operational/service adjustments. Key findings of these chapters include

- "The traveler response to service frequency changes varies substantially. Ridership increases proportionately exceeding the frequency increases they are related to have been observed, reflecting an elasticity in excess of +1.0, but not often. Circumstances where frequency improvements failed to attract new ridership at all are also reported. The average response to frequency changes, including both increases and decreases, approximates an elasticity of +0.5 as measured in terms of response to service quality" (p. 9-4).
- "Ridership is typically most sensitive to frequency changes when the prior service was infrequent, such as hourly or half-hourly, and when the transit line involved serves middle and upper income areas. Where transit headways are already short, and particularly when lower income service areas are involved, ridership tends to be less affected by frequency changes and

---

[3] For instance, a service elasticity of "+0.5" means that a 10% increase in service would be expected to result in a 5% ridership gain.

may be more sensitive to fare changes. Otherwise, ridership is typically more responsive to frequency changes than fares" (p. 9-4).
- "The mid-range of ridership response to expansions of bus transit, either acting alone or with fare changes, is bounded by service elasticities in the +0.6 to +1.0 range. Much broader variations have been reported, including instances of ridership increases in the elastic range (over +1.0)" (p. 10-5).
- "There is evidence suggestive that packages of improvements, not only better routes and schedules but also new buses and/or fare reductions, do particularly well in attracting increased ridership. Service expansion and restructuring, in conjunction with fare reductions or new unlimited travel pass partnerships have led to a tripling of systemwide ridership in instances of university towns, and to substantial ridership gains in larger cities with targeted universities" (p. 10-5).

Of course, it is important to keep in mind that these findings are based on analyses of individual systems, each having its own service and demographic characteristics. As noted in *TCRP Report 95, Chapter 9*, "The environment within which a transit service change takes place will affect the results, and this places a special burden on the analyst seeking to judge the transferability of traveler response findings from one situation to another" (p. 9-4). Thus, such guidelines should be considered order-of-magnitude indicators only, rather than hard and fast planning rules.

The types of operating/service adjustment strategies are described below.

Routing/Coverage Adjustments

Routing and coverage adjustments are intended to improve service efficiency, effectiveness, and/or accessibility through one or more of the following types of actions:

- Increased route coverage (e.g., service expansion, introduction of local circulators, and expansion into rural service areas);
- Route restructuring (e.g., reallocation to most productive routes and revising operating strategies); and
- Improved schedule/route coordination (e.g., introduction of feeder services, timed transfers, and/or transfer centers).

Descriptions and agency examples of these types of strategies are provided below.

Increased Route Coverage

In response to gaps in service coverage, crowding on certain routes, or the need to extend service to newly developing areas, an agency may be able to generate additional ridership through various forms of increased route coverage or route restructuring. The particular type of service expansion warranted will depend on such factors as the density of the area to be served, the proximity to major trip attractors, the predominant types of trips to be served, and the nature of the existing route structure in the area. Examples of specific types of increased route coverage include comprehensive service expansion and the introduction of local circulator service. For increasing coverage or expansion into rural service areas, a variety of types of service can be considered. The different approaches are discussed below.

Service Expansion

Expansion into unserved—or underserved—areas may involve extensions to existing routes, new routes, or route branching. Branching in particular may allow an agency to provide improved coverage in suburban areas while economizing on the number of buses required. While extensions to existing routes or route branching would presumably continue to utilize fixed-route service (local or express), new service may in some cases be more efficiently provided using some form of flexibly routed service; the different types of flexibly routed service are described below. Certain types of new services also fall under other operating/service adjustment categories or subcategories (e.g., Improved Schedule/Route Coordination and New Types of Service), and are discussed under these sections; these include, for instance, introduction of feeder services, BRT and employer-sponsored services, and other shuttles.

Introduction of Local Circulator Service

This represents one form of new service. Such services are designed to improve mobility within a local area or to provide connections to the urban and regional bus network—and rail lines, if present. Circulators can be designed to serve all types of riders and trip purposes, or they may target particular markets. In fact, services for the general public that operate in suburban areas typically serve senior citizens, youth, low-income travelers, and work trip commuters accessing regional services. Three basic types of circulator services can be considered: community circulator (fixed) route, flexible route, *and demand-responsive.*

- **Community circulator routes**—Community circulator routes are designed to serve local community trips, including stops at neighborhood commercial districts, employment centers, and shopping malls. These services can also provide connections to regional bus and rail networks. By using small buses or vans, they can travel along neighborhood streets and enter driveways and parking lots. In some communities, these circulators may be designed specifically to accommodate the travel needs of seniors and persons with disabilities, with connections to senior housing and health-care facilities; these specialized services are sometimes known as service routes. Such routes may in some cases be able to reduce some riders' dependency on more expensive ADA paratransit service and would offer these individuals service without requiring advance reservations. (Note that, while service routes may be effective at serving some of the ADA paratransit demand, the ADA requires that complementary paratransit be offered wherever fixed routes operate; this would include service routes.)
- **Flexible routes**—Flexible routes can enhance service on local circulators and have been used in a number of suburban settings around the country. There are several variations of this general concept. For example, *route deviation* services have a designated route and schedule, with specified stops and scheduled time points. The vehicles are allowed to leave the route a limited number of times to pick up or drop off passengers; the service is designed to ensure that the driver can return to the defined route with enough time to meet the schedule. Passengers may board the bus at the designated stops (or in some cases, anywhere) along the route, or they may call ahead to request a pick-up deviation off the route, which may require an incremental fare. Some systems direct passengers to call the dispatcher, while others equip the operators with cellular telephones so that passengers can contact the drivers en route; advance notice requirements vary. Passengers on board may request a drop-off deviation from the driver while on board. Other variations of flexible routes include *point deviation* and *checkpoint deviation.* Point deviation service offers a limited number of fixed stops, but there is no fixed route between them; this gives the driver more flexibility and reduces the time between designated stops. However, this system may encourage more deviation requests since it does not allow passengers to flag the vehicle between formal stops, which some route deviation services do. Checkpoint deviation service limits deviations to specific on-call stops rather than deviating all the way to the passenger's curbside; this reduces the impact of deviations on the schedule. Offering certain types of deviation on local circulators can help transit operators meet ADA requirements in a cost-effective manner, with less duplicative service.

> **Estuary Transit District (ETD)**
> **Shoreline Shuttle**
> *rural area (under 50,000)*
>
> The Estuary Transit District, based in Old Saybrook, CT, replaced a costly and underperforming leg of its fixed route service with a point deviation shuttle service in 1996. The shuttle has designated stops with fixed times, but also allows for off route stops to be scheduled up to the same day, within a reasonable distance of the route. This has proven to be a very effective way of providing transit for seniors and persons with disabilities in the area. Shuttle ridership is currently 2 to 3 times higher than that of the old fixed route, and sees an annual growth of 10%.

- **Demand-responsive services**—Demand-responsive curb-to-curb service is generally known as *dial-a-ride*. Such service typically provides greater coverage in an area of low density than does a fixed-route network, but operates at much lower productivities. Dial-a-ride for the general public has been most successful where it provides access to fixed-route bus and rail services. Other factors that contribute to success include well-defined service zones and operating rules that help create cost-effective services. Dial-a-ride does not require complementary ADA service, but it effectively substitutes for it by providing paratransit for all riders.

Expansion into Rural Service Areas

For rural areas, several different types of service might be considered. Rural service concepts include planned demand route, rural demand-responsive service, and volunteer ridesharing, described below. In addition to these services, vanpools and other ridesharing services would serve work trips, as described in separate sections. The basic concepts are as follows:

- **Planned demand routes**—Planned demand bus routes are designed to maximize service coverage given the scarce resources in low-density, rural areas. Since many of the users of rural public transportation are retired senior citizens, they can often plan their travel to match the service schedule. Planned demand routes—which can operate as fixed-route or route deviation services—are scheduled to serve selected towns and activity centers on different days of the week.
- **Rural demand-responsive service**—Because rural population tends to be distributed over a large area, demand-responsive service can be a more effective means than fixed-route service to meet local transportation needs. Demand-responsive or dial-a-ride service can be provided with a taxi, van, or small bus. Passengers are typically required to make reservations, although the advance notice requirements could vary from 20 to 30 minutes (like a taxi) to 24 hours or more (like many paratransit services). Dial-a-ride services can be designed to transport passengers curb-to-curb between origin and destination or to provide connections to regional fixed-route buses. Rural dial-a-ride would be similar to suburban dial-a-ride, but with some different characteristics, such as a longer advance notice requirement and a slower response time.
- **Volunteer ridesharing**—Volunteers have long been a resource in providing a variety of services, including transportation in rural areas. One option for expanding on volunteerism is to establish a pool of funds to be used for mileage reimbursement for volunteer drivers who use their own vehicles to transport passengers. Other program costs would be associated with administration, additional insurance coverage, and volunteer recognition. A key to the success of volunteer programs is providing organizational support, including training, enforcement of safety policies, coordination, supervision, and recognition of volunteer efforts. A volunteer program might be easily integrated with other mobility coordination and rideshare services. To capitalize on volunteerism, it may also be best to maintain a social services agency as a sponsor or co-sponsor.

City of Los Angeles, Department of Transportation (LADOT)
DASH - Intracommunity Transit Changing to Meet Changing Need
large urbanized (over 1,000,000)

In recent years, the L.A. Department of Transportation has seen the bulk of its ridership growth come from its community circulator program. The circulators provide a low-cost option for low-income, transit dependent residents. There is a process of routine monitoring of service in place, to ensure that changing travel needs are consistently met. This flexibility allows routes to be restructured as needed. Ridership increased 6.2% from 2002 to 2003.

Route Restructuring

Another type of routing/coverage adjustment is route restructuring, which might include, for instance, reallocation of service to most productive routes or revising operating strategies. As defined in *TCRP Report 95* (Chapter 10), "Restructuring is the strategy of reworking an existing bus network to rationalize or simplify service, accommodate new travel patterns, reduce route circuitry, ease or eliminate transfers required for bus travel, or otherwise alter the service configuration. Restructuring may include through routing of separate bus routes, realignment and recombination of routes, and the provision of trunkline, crosstown, express, and feeder services, generally in the context of a cohesive systemwide service plan." (p. 10-2)

Rationalization of bus services in specific areas should begin with a close examination of the ridership and operating statistics—specifically productivity, load profiles, span, and frequency by time of day (see Chapter 3). Using schematic maps and available stop-by-stop boarding and alighting data, relatively strong and weak segments of existing routes can be identified. Routes can be classified according to their broad function, such as line-haul, feeder-distributor, and local circulator. In some cases, routes serve multiple functions simultaneously or change their functions during the course of the day; these nuances need to be recognized.

An agency may wish to establish a set of principles or guidelines to apply to its routes in considering restructuring opportunities. An example of the types of principles that could be deployed is as follows:

- Line-haul routes ought to be as direct as possible while still serving areas that generate high numbers of transit trips.
- Line-haul routes should stay on arterials and other major streets to the extent possible.
- One-way travel times for line haul routes should generally be less than 60 minutes to make schedule adherence easier.
- Circulator routes may follow circuitous routings in order to provide maximum coverage; the area covered by the route should be small, however, so that total one-way travel time is less than 30 minutes.
- Circulator routes can penetrate deep into neighborhoods if small vehicles (less than 30 feet in length) are used.
- A single route should not attempt to serve too many markets or serve too many functions; routes operate more efficiently and effectively when they have an identifiable focused market and purpose.
- Flexible-service routes may be more appropriate for areas with household densities below the threshold of three households per acre identified in the *Transit Capacity and Quality of Service Manual*.

- Overlapping routes should be avoided, except in the following circumstances:
  - Two or more line-haul routes with moderate frequency and a common terminus share a common segment beginning at that terminus; in such a case, the schedules should be coordinated to provide an effective headway that is twice as good as the routes individually.
  - A line-haul route with limited-stop service is overlaid on a local service route.
  - The routes sharing the overlapping segment operate at different times of day or serve different functions and can meet productivity standards.
  - There is only a single feasible roadway connection between two points, or a secondary routing that would generate no ridership.
- Routes should have consistent and understandable patterns at all times of operation.
- Doubling back and retracing steps should be avoided whenever possible.
- Transit centers can increase mobility in suburban areas by facilitating transfers between higher frequency, shorter routes that would replace low-frequency direct routes.

Of course, principles such as these are general in nature and must be applied with care, taking into account any special or unusual features of the subject area. Application of such principles to an area may result in a range of restructuring service strategies, including

- Splitting long routes;
- Straightening line-haul routes;
- Shifting coverage from line-haul routes to circulator routes;
- Separating overlapping routes onto different streets;
- Removing instances of doubling back;
- Consolidating route patterns (or routes within a line);
- Consolidating service along a segment into one line where service is now split among two or more;
- Eliminating very low productivity routes (less than 10 boardings per vehicle revenue hour) and reallocating resources elsewhere; and
- Restructuring service around new transit centers (and extending routes to reach new activity centers and to improve overall connectivity).

Overlapping and/or duplicative services may offer opportunities for improving efficiency, making service less confusing for passengers, and freeing up resources that could be used more productively elsewhere in the service area.

Grand Rapids Interurban Transit Partnership - The Rapid (ITP)
Productivity Measures/Route Restructuring
'medium urbanized (200,000 - 1,000,000)

The Rapid, in Grand Rapids, Michigan, has developed a comprehensive route evaluation system that produces monthly statistics for each bus route, including farebox recovery ratios and passengers per mile, hour, and day. The measures are used in a formula that assigns scores to each route on a monthly, as well as an annual basis. Staff members monitor each route on a regular basis; thus, low-performing segments are continually reviewed and improved. System ridership increased more than 4% between 2002 and 2003.

Improved Schedule/Route Coordination

Another general approach to improving an area's service coverage and thereby increasing attractiveness to riders is *improved schedule/route coordination*. In a service area with dispersed origins and destinations—as characterizes most regions today—this may involve, for example, establishing an integrated service network featuring *feeder services* (to line-haul routes) and *timed transfers,* perhaps focused on a series of *transit centers*. Such a structure can help to address coverage, travel time, productivity, crowding, and reliability problems in an existing network. The key elements of this approach are discussed below.

Feeder Services

A key element of an integrated "hub and spoke" service design is local feeder routes that collect and deliver riders to a line-haul bus route or rail line. Such routes may also serve as community circulators, or they may simply provide a direct connection between a key residential or employment center and the bus transfer point or rail station. The latter strategy is often referred to as a shuttle service.

Housatonic Area Regional Transit District (HART)
Harlem Line Shuttle Services
small urbanized (50,000 - 200,000)

HART, based in Danbury, CT, operates two shuttle services that deliver riders to stations along MTA Metro-North rail lines. This service helps Connecticut commuters bypass limited parking to reach trains heading into New York City. The service is timed to meet the most popular trains and was planned jointly by the Connecticut and New York Departments of Transportation. The first shuttle consistently sees annual ridership increases of over 20%, and the second has enjoyed rapid success as well.

Timed Transfers

In an effort to minimize transfer wait times between connecting routes, agencies sometimes use timed transfers. Timed transfers are often designed to occur at transit centers, although this is not necessarily the case. Transfers may involve connections between a trunk route/line and local feeder routes at different stops or stations—or, especially in smaller cities, all routes may be scheduled to meet at a single transfer pulse point. As noted in *TCRP Report 95* (Chapter 9), "The connecting transit routes must be designed within route running time parameters that facilitate timed transfer scheduling. Route length, traffic conditions and passenger activity determine run time, and run time determines ability to make a complete bus trip and still maintain timed transfer meets and bus layover time requirements." (p. 9-17)

Transit Centers

Transit centers—also sometimes known as *hubs*—are designated locations where passengers can access transit or transfer conveniently between modes. These modes might include rail, local buses, express buses, private and not-for-profit buses and vans, local circulator services using small buses or vans, paratransit service, automobiles, and bicycles. Transit centers, in conjunction with timed transfer operating policies, can be used to facilitate route connectivity and improve the overall level of service in an area.

A transit center-based system has the advantage of accommodating multi-centered and dispersed population and employment concentrations by connecting a very large number of possible origin-destination pairs through transfers at a few convenient, comfortable, well-lit transit centers. These centers are typically connected by a network of direct, frequent principal routes. Other routes provide the remaining coverage of the service area and connect to one or more centers. Because routes are focused on the transit centers and transfers are convenient, there is less need for overlapping routes and the number of routes can be kept to a minimum allowing service to be more frequent than it could be with a system comprised of a larger number of routes. The frequency of service, in turn, makes transferring less onerous for riders.

Transit center functions range from facilitating operations by providing off-street layover space to supporting large numbers of transfers between automobiles and transit and between different transit services. A transit center serving local routes may have simple bus pull-outs, shelters, and detailed system information. Large-scale regional transit centers, in turn, can be regional focal points for the transit system and may include large-scale bus facilities, large-scale parking facilities, additional passenger services, and information and may also be foundations for joint development.

The ideal location and design concept for a transit center will vary as a function of its intended purpose. For example, transit centers that provide park-and-ride access to express commuter bus services must relate well to freeways and other major highways, especially those with HOV or bus-only lanes. Other transit centers exist primarily to facilitate transfers between different bus lines by providing a convenient, safe, secure, and attractive transfer environment. Having adequate space and good street and highway access and being at the focal point of many different services will be of paramount importance to this type of transit center. The criteria typically used to site transit centers are outlined below. The relative emphasis placed on the different criteria depends on the particular function of the transit center:

- **High activity location**—One of the keys to a transit center's success is being sited in a high activity location. These locations can provide a focal point for transit-oriented development and often generate their own transit trips. Examples of this type of location are regional shopping centers/edge cities, traditional downtowns, suburban commercial concentrations, hospitals, and inter-city rail and bus stations.
- **High transfer volumes**—Ultimately, a transit center is a transfer point of some kind, whether that transfer is between automobiles and a rail line, between buses and rail, among two or more bus lines, between local transit and intercity bus and/or rail, or between pedestrians and bus. A transit center should be located where high numbers of passengers currently transfer or are expected to transfer. This would be at the intersection of many routes and modes serving different markets and functions.
- **Accessibility to adjacent communities and the transportation system**—A successful transit center must be accessible to all modes, including pedestrians, bicycles, automobiles (especially for those centers that have a park-and-ride or kiss-and-ride element to them), and neighborhood circulators. For a transit center that will be predominantly serving automobile access trips, high visibility from, and easy access/egress to, major roadways is important.
- **Safety and security**—A sense of security both for passengers and for parked cars and bicycles is essential.
- **Transit center spacing**—The spacing of transit centers will be dependent on the type of service structure and markets they are meant to support. If the purpose is to support a system of timed transfers, two key factors will play a role in their location. The first is that the transit centers should be spaced at equal intervals, based on bus run times, ideally 30 minutes apart. A second factor is that its catchment area must have sufficient population and commercial development to support a reasonably high level of transit service through or originating at the center. General population standards would be a minimum of 25,000 residents within the location's catchment area. Closer spacing than that suggested by the above criteria may be appropriate where the arterial grid is more closely spaced together, where there is a regional medical facility or university or a mega activity center or edge city.
- **Relationship to congestion on the highway system**—A transit center that is also a park-and-ride facility should be located in an accessible environment outside the point where highway congestion in the peak direction starts. It should also have a catchment area that represents 10 to 15 minutes' drive time to the center, adequate population to support express commuter bus

services in the peak period (assuming a reasonable work mode share), and demand for off-peak service at policy headways.

Because of the different functions transit centers play and the wide range of physical characteristics at potential transit center sites, identifying a single set of design elements that should be applied throughout a region may not be feasible. However, it is possible to identify a range of possible facility elements that could be incorporated into each transit center based on the center's specific function and site capabilities. These elements may include, for example

- **Off-street bus bays**—If feasible at a proposed site, off-street bus bays can provide a more comfortable and efficient boarding area for riders and a layover space that does not negatively impact local traffic operations or create undue negative environmental impacts (e.g., noise and exhaust fumes) on adjacent land uses.
- **Sheltered waiting areas**—Sheltered waiting areas are an essential means of improving the riders' overall transit experience. The design of these shelters can contribute to making the transit center a focal point for the transit system and to the overall transit system identity.
- **Pedestrian and bicycle access**—A transit center, especially in an urbanized area, should be an integral part of the pedestrian and bicycle circulation system. Safe and convenient walk and bicycle access to the transit center, including bicycle parking, will be essential to the center's success.
- **Dynamic signage/information**—Detailed information on transit options, service frequencies, and scheduled arrival times should be provided. Real-time information is also recommended. At larger transit centers and park-and-ride facilities, a kiosk could be used to provide timetables, system maps, and pass sales.
- **Parking**—Whether parking should be included at a transit center is directly related to the function each center will be serving. Parking is not recommended at transit centers serving heavily developed urbanized areas, but is recommended at transit centers that would support high performance service, such as long distance express or BRT and generally would have a majority of riders who access the transit center via automobile.
- **Kiss-and-ride and taxi facilities**—These facility elements are another key component in supporting a transit center that is truly intermodal in nature.
- **Other amenities**—Depending on the scale and purpose of the proposed transit center, other amenities, such as public telephones, vending machines, newspaper machines, and in some instances, a small news and candy stand, may be considered.

Transit center-based systems can attract new riders in markets that have traditionally not been well served by transit. Such systems also can help develop new markets by providing access to jobs and other activities for transit-dependent populations that previously lacked such access. Such systems can improve service for some current transit users through improved frequency of service and by providing much more appealing environments for making transfers. Even for those current riders who would be faced with an additional transfer, that transfer would be made at a comfortable, well-lit transit center.

Scheduling/Frequency Adjustments

These types of revised operating strategies are typically deployed in an effort to seek a better balance between the demand for and the supply of service:

- Increased service frequency (e.g., increased frequency on specific routes) or increased span of service (e.g., longer service hours) and
- Improved reliability/on-time performance (e.g., implementation of AVL, transit signal priority, or transfer connection protection capability).

Descriptions and agency examples of these strategies are provided below.

Increased Service Frequency and Increased Span of Service

Adjusting headways (i.e., the amount of time between vehicles) to respond to differences in route productivity and passenger loading is a common response to routes with low productivity. Service frequencies may be increased to alleviate crowding or to fill in service gaps—or they may be decreased to boost productivity. The span of service may be adjusted by adding (or subtracting service hours) each day—or by introducing (or removing) service on a particular day of the week (e.g., Sunday). A typical service span change is to add late night service, sometimes called "Owl" service.

Increased Frequency

Based on an evaluation of routes against a set of measures and thresholds, an agency can determine the need for frequency improvements. For example, as discussed in Chapter 3, an agency may establish a goal of all routes operating every 15 minutes in the peak and every 30 minutes in the off-peak in the urban areas, and perhaps every 30 minutes in the peak and every 60 minutes in the off-peak in suburban areas. This will result in shortening headways on some routes; in some cases, though, reducing the headway will cause a route to have a lower-than-acceptable productivity. The agency may in that case decide not to change that route's frequency.

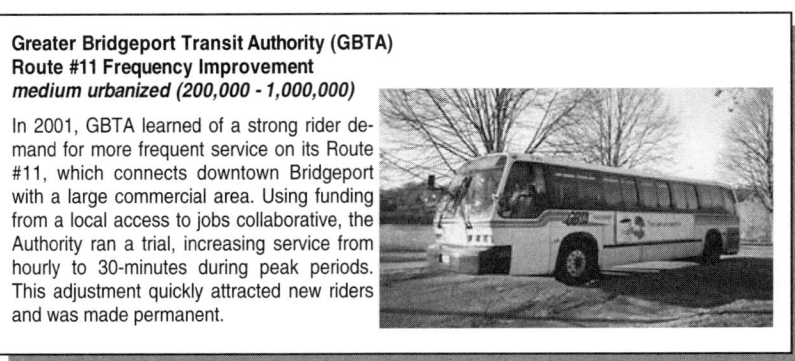

Greater Bridgeport Transit Authority (GBTA)
Route #11 Frequency Improvement
medium urbanized (200,000 - 1,000,000)

In 2001, GBTA learned of a strong rider demand for more frequent service on its Route #11, which connects downtown Bridgeport with a large commercial area. Using funding from a local access to jobs collaborative, the Authority ran a trial, increasing service from hourly to 30-minutes during peak periods. This adjustment quickly attracted new riders and was made permanent.

Portland TriMet designed an entire ridership program around increasing service frequency on major bus lines. The *Frequent Service* initiative was inaugurated in the late 1990's, and the frequency adjustments have been coupled with improved amenities (see Exhibit 5-1) and improved customer information systems; the initiative was also accompanied by an extensive marketing and promotional effort.

Extended Span of Service

Improvements to service span should also be identified based on an evaluation of routes against a set of measures and thresholds. An agency may decide, for instance, to extend service later into the evening, earlier in the morning, and/or on Saturdays and Sundays. Ridership potential associated with extensions can be estimated based on the productivity of the service in the nearest time period with service. As with frequency increases, though, in cases where an extension to a particular route would not meet the ridership or productivity threshold, the agency may decide against an extension to that route.

Exhibit 5-1. TriMet Frequent Service bus stop sign.

Washington Metropolitan Area Transit Authority (WMATA)
Extended Late Night Weekend Hours on Metrorail
large urbanized (over 1,000,000)

WMATA utilized funding from the District of Columbia to run a trial expansion of Metrorail hours, extending the closing hour from 2 to 3 AM on Saturday and Sunday mornings. The trial program, which ran for 18 months, was projected to draw an additional 3,000 riders to Metrorail during the extra hour. In reality, performance exceeded these expectations by 20%. The WMATA Board has proposed to make the extension permanent.

Improved Reliability/On-Time Performance

Reliability and on-time performance are clearly important aspects of transit scheduling and performance, as they affect passenger wait time, delay, and uncertainty. Reliability is measured in terms of schedule adherence (i.e., percentage of trips that are on time, as well as percentage early or late, compared to the scheduled arrival/departure times; missed vehicle trips are also included).

Transit reliability problems can stem from "environmental" factors such as traffic signals and changes in traffic conditions, as well as from fluctuations in boarding and alighting times. However, operator and vehicle availability can also affect reliability on any given route and day. Improving reliability and on-time performance may therefore require a combination of strategies; these may include improved scheduling (i.e., to ensure that there is sufficient running time for a route and account for fluctuations in both traffic and transit usage), as well as various technological enhancements. Technology-based strategies include the following:

- **Automated vehicle location (AVL)**—AVL is the backbone of several other types of strategies that can improve operations and customer service (e.g., transfer connection protection and real-time information system). Combined with specific design strategies, such as splitting routes, agencies that have deployed AVL systems have reported as much as a 25% increase in on-time performance.
- **Traffic signal priority (TSP)**—This technology can be deployed on specific streets or corridors to improve service reliability (i.e., by allowing the transit vehicle to extend or advance green light times or to allow left turn "swaps.") TSP also has the potential to improve travel times for BRT and other limited stop routes by ensuring that the vehicle stays on schedule. This strategy requires coordination with the city's traffic department, as intersections must have TSP-capable equipment.
- **Transfer connection protection (TCP) capability**—Once AVL is deployed on an agency's buses, TCP capability can be deployed to ensure that passenger transfers are protected; this

Saint Cloud Metropolitan Transit Commission - Metro Bus (SCMTC)
Transit Signal Priority Deployment
small urbanized (50,000 - 200,000)

Using funds from a Minnesota DOT ITS initiative, St. Cloud MTC explored transit signal priority technology as a solution to on-time performance and schedule adherence issues. The results of a one-route pilot study showed that TSP did indeed improve performance, as well as customer satisfaction. The study determined that buses with increased on-time schedule adherence produce a stronger likelihood of rider retention and potential growth through an increased competitiveness with the automobile.

will improve service reliability from the passenger's perspective. TCP also facilitates the splitting of routes, creating a more seamless environment for transferring passengers. Passengers may accept transfers more readily once TCP functionality is deployed. TCP might be considered in particular on routes with low frequency of service and a high number of transfers. In a multi-agency region, TCP capability can also be considered to include inter-agency trips.

In addition, other intelligent transportation system (ITS) applications that provide real-time information to passengers can minimize the uncertainty associated with on-time performance; these applications are discussed in Chapter 7.

New Types of Service

Several strategies involving the introduction of new types of service might be considered in an effort to improve service attractiveness and possibly cost-effectiveness; these strategies include

- Improved travel speed (e.g., introduction of express bus, BRT, and rail); and
- Targeted services (e.g., university campus-oriented service, downtown circulators, or other special purpose services).

Descriptions and agency examples of these types of strategies are provided below.

Improved Travel Speed

New types of service such as express bus, rail, or bus rapid transit (BRT) offer the potential to generate additional ridership by improving service coverage, reducing travel time, reducing crowding, and improving reliability. These strategies are discussed below.

Express Bus Services

Opportunities for new express bus service can be identified through a standard service evaluation process, including a review of changes in development patterns, demographics, and travel patterns within the area or region. In particular, travel patterns from suburban residential areas into the CBD or to major regional employment centers should be analyzed to identify potential markets for limited-stop, higher speed service.

One key to making express service cost-effective is to avoid empty deadheading of the vehicles back to the origin areas by identifying reverse commute markets that can use the services in the outbound direction. Express services can help meet the commuting needs of city residents working in suburban areas. An agency may therefore find it useful to work with employers and developers—both downtown and suburban—to develop express services; employer-sponsored services are discussed in Chapter 6, Partnership/Coordination Initiatives.

Rail Service

New rail services (i.e., heavy, light, and commuter rail) require sufficiently high demand within one or more well-defined corridors to be effective. Agencies typically consider the viability of high-capacity modes (i.e., rail and BRT) through an alternatives analysis or corridor study. There are a limited number of U.S. cities with the population densities and development/travel patterns to support heavy rail, and all of these cities already have such systems. Thus, while a number of the existing systems have expanded their rail lines in recent years, there have been only a couple of new heavy rail systems implemented in recent years (Los Angeles' Red Line and San Juan's Tren Urbano). The vast bulk of the new rail systems built over the past couple of decades—or now being developed—are either light rail or commuter rail. In fact, several cities (e.g., Dallas, Los Angeles, and Seattle) have introduced both light and commuter rail lines in recent years.

Several other forms of rail service have also been implemented in limited numbers; these include downtown people mover (i.e., Miami, Detroit, and Jacksonville), monorail (i.e., Las Vegas and

Seattle), cable car (i.e., San Francisco) and inclined plane (i.e., Pittsburgh). However, these modes are typically focused on a specific limited area (e.g., downtown) and tend to be relatively short in length. An exception is the new monorail currently being developed in Seattle; the first line of what is envisioned as a larger regional system is planned to be approximately 14 miles long and is seen as carrying the full range of types of passengers, including commuters as well as visitors to the city.

New light rail systems have been shown to be capable of generating significant ridership growth. While a certain portion of their demand is simply shifted from bus service (i.e., routes that have been restructured, truncated, or eliminated in favor of the new rail line), there is widespread agreement within the transit industry that rail attracts certain discretionary riders who would not ride a regular bus; this rail preference is attributed to characteristics such as a clearly identifiable route and stops (and these are typically protected to a greater extent than are bus stops), as well as larger (and often more comfortable) vehicles. In fact, BRT, described below, represents an effort to create a bus service mode that has many of the characteristics typically associated with rail.

Bus Rapid Transit

BRT, also sometimes known as *rapid bus*, is a flexible, rubber-tired form of rapid transit that combines stations, vehicles, services, running way, and ITS elements into an integrated system with a unique identity. BRT includes a variety of features to minimize travel time and maximize convenience for passengers. These features may include signal priority, dedicated right-of-way, automated and off-vehicle fare collection, automated information systems, level boarding, modern vehicles, and stations/bus shelters with enhanced amenities. Buses can be painted with special graphics to provide a system identity consistent with the rest of the given line's stations, running ways, etc. The concept of a unique identity is an important element of BRT, just as a rail line has an identity that makes it stand out from the local bus network. Physical improvements to help provide this identity include unique bus shelters (see Exhibit 5-2), special markings in the street such as a painted traffic lane or bus pad area, unique vehicles, unique signage, and detailed schedule/route information (including real-time information) at the station/stop.

Exhibit 5-2. Los Angeles' RapidBus BRT station.

Running way improvements for BRT applications may include exclusive right-of-way (see Exhibit 5-3) or improvements to enhance roadway operations where exclusive right-of-way is not available. BRT applications are designed to be appropriate to the market they serve and their physical surroundings and can be incrementally implemented in a variety of environments, from rights-of-way totally dedicated to transit (surface, elevated, underground) to mixed traffic rights-of-way on streets and highways. Guided rubber-tired systems—which require less lane-width—make exclusive lanes more feasible and have been implemented overseas.

Exhibit 5-3. Exclusive lane for BRT in Rouen, France.

In virtually every fully integrated, full-feature BRT application to date, customer, community, and developer acceptance is comparable to that of any high-quality rapid transit mode such as light rail. As indicated in the description below, for instance, implementation of *Metro Rapid* in Los Angeles has resulted in substantial increases in total corridor bus ridership.[4]

---

[4] For extensive description of BRT characteristics and examples, see the following recent reports: *TCRP Report 90, Volume I: Case Studies in Bus Rapid Transit* (2003) and *Vol. II: Bus Rapid Transit – Implementation Guidelines* (2003); and FTA, *Characteristics of Bus Rapid Transit for Decision-Making* (2004).

> **Los Angeles County Metropolitan Transportation Authority (LACMTA)**
> **Metro Rapid**
> *large urbanized (over 1,000,000)*
>
> In 2000, LACMTA implemented the Metro Rapid Program, which placed bus rapid transit (BRT) service in several of the Los Angeles area's busiest corridors. The new buses used traffic signal priority, reduced stops, and headway-based (rather than timetable-based) schedules to reduce passengers travel times by up to 29%. In the Wilshire-Whittier and Ventura Blvd. corridors, bus ridership has increased by 20% and 50%, respectively, since the implementation of BRT. Significantly, up to one third of BRT riders were previously not transit users.
>
>

Targeted Services

Services targeted to specific market segments or service areas can be effective at generating additional ridership. There is a wide range of targeted services, including employer-sponsored shuttles and reverse commute services, university campus services, downtown circulators, airport shuttles, and special event shuttles. As these services are often subsidized—all or in part—by partner entities, this category overlaps with the Partnership/Coordination Initiatives category. Employer-sponsored services are discussed in that chapter; examples of other targeted services are described below.

University Campus-Oriented Service

Transit agencies in a number of locations provide services that focus on major university campuses. In fact, as noted in Chapter 4 and Appendix A, agencies that serve major universities tend to have significantly higher per capita ridership figures than do other comparably sized areas. In some cases, the campus service dominates the overall system, while in others, the campus routes represent one element of a larger transit system. Examples of the former type of arrangement include agencies operating in Chapel Hill (NC), Gainesville (FL), State College (PA), and Champaign-Urbana (IL). Examples of the latter approach include agencies in Lansing (MI), Grand Rapids (MI), Lancaster (PA), Lafayette (IN), and Portage (OH).[5] In some systems, the transit agency operates the campus-oriented service under contract to the university; in Lansing, for instance, CATA entered into a contract with Michigan State University in 1999 under which the agency took over the formerly independently run MSU campus service; see Exhibit 5-4. (Of course, many transit agencies also have fare agreements with local universities; in fact, university pass-type arrangements represent the single

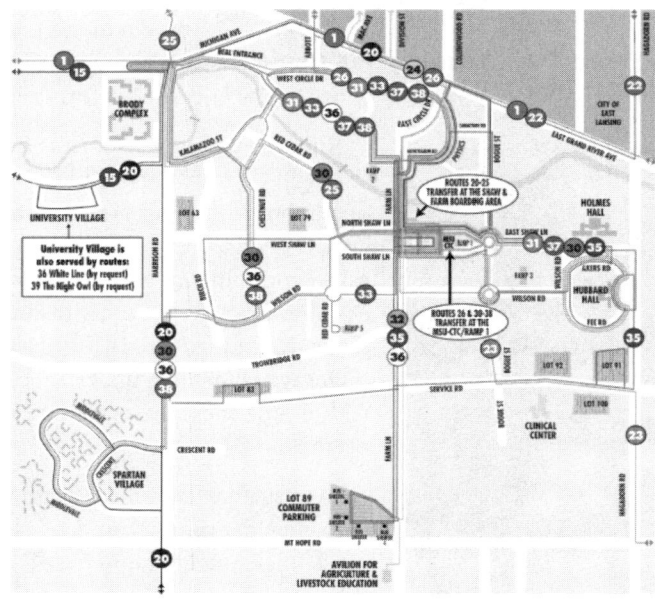

Exhibit 5-4. CATA MSU campus route.

---

[5]These examples are all included in our database of examples, discussed in Appendix A and Chapter 4.

most common type of initiative instituted by the agencies reviewed in this study. These programs are discussed in Chapters 6 and 8, Partnership/Coordination Initiatives and Fare Collection/Structure Initiatives.)

Downtown Circulators

While transit service is often focused on downtown areas, the existing routes are typically designed to get people in and out of these areas; many cities lack an efficient circulator system for moving people around *within* the downtown. A well-designed and appropriately priced downtown circulator service can address a number of travel needs, including improving both visitor and downtown worker mobility. Such a service can also reduce traffic congestion, improve air quality, and support economic development in the downtown. An examination of downtown circulators in nine U.S. cities conducted as part of a feasibility study for a new service in Washington, D.C., led to several conclusions regarding the design and implementation of circulators:[6]

- Direct, fast, and reliable service is an important factor in attracting the downtown worker market. Several circulators offer peak service every 5 minutes and the majority operate at least every 10 minutes.
- Circulators should be low cost. Four of the nine circulator services reviewed are provided free of charge. The remainder charge much less than a regular transit trip, with the highest at $0.50.
- Unique-looking vehicles are important in attracting the visitor market. Some operators have opted for the unique look of diesel-powered trolleys, while the rest have gone with compressed natural gas (CNG), electric, or hybrid engines on low-floor buses that have a more innovative look. None use conventional diesel buses.
- The public must be provided with adequate information about the service.

The downtown circulators included in the above study were in Austin, TX ('Dillo routes); Chattanooga, TN (Downtown Electric Shuttle); Dallas, TX (M-Line Trolley Bus); Denver, CO (16th Street Mall Shuttle); Los Angeles (Downtown DASH routes); Miami Beach (Electrowave); Milwaukee, WI (Transit Trolley); Oklahoma City (Spirit Trolley); and Orlando (Lynx Lymmo). The number of circulator routes varies among these systems: four have a single route, while the greatest number of routes is six (Los Angeles and Oklahoma City). All routes are less than 8.5 miles in length, with most around 3 miles round trip. Most of these agencies reported that their ridership is a mix of downtown workers, conventioneers, residents and visitors. The agencies invariably expressed the belief that different service characteristics are important to different market segments. The most important service characteristics for attracting the two major segments, based on that review, are shown in Table 5-6.

Table 5-6. Service characteristics for downtown circulator markets.

Downtown Workers	Tourists and Visitors
Most Important • Frequency • Directness of service • Travel time • Reliability • Simple schedule	Most Important • Information/signage • Uniqueness of the vehicles • Serve tourist attractions
Also Important • Cleanliness • Low Fare • Perimeter seating	Also Important • Friendliness of drivers • Knowledgeable drivers • Availability of a day pass

SOURCE: *District of Columbia Downtown Circulator Implementation Plan*, p. 38.

---

[6]TranSystems Corp., *District of Columbia Downtown Circulator Implementation Plan*, prepared for National Capital Planning Commission and others, July 2003 (p. 3).

Other Targeted Services

Other targeted or special purpose services include airport shuttles, shuttles serving special events (e.g., sporting events), and tourist-oriented services (i.e., other than downtown circulators). Airport and special events services typically have premium fares. In contrast, tourist-oriented services often have the same fares as the rest of the system—or in some cases are free or have lower fares than the rest of the system. In some locations, the entire transit systems are essentially tourist-oriented services. Systems such as Cape Cod (MA) RTA, Lake Tahoe (CA-NV) Regional Transit, and Island Explorer (serving Acadia National Park in Maine), for example, serve what are principally tourist areas—although such services may well carry area workers and other local residents as well as tourists. Funding for tourist services comes from a variety of sources, including local attractions and hotels, local governments, fares, the state, and the federal government (e.g., for systems serving national parks).

Delaware Transit Corporation - DART Wilmington Trolley Investment
large urbanized (over 1,000,000)

In 2002, DART implemented the new Wilmington Trolley to serve both residents and tourists in downtown Wilmington. The trolley replaced an existing fixed route that had served the same area in a loop pattern. The new service was heavily marketed towards business visitors, lunchtime downtown workers, and tourists. Successful partnerships with downtown businesses and convention organizers have helped to increase ridership and tourism in the area. Trolley ridership is 14% higher than that of the fixed route it replaced.

Based on a review of 20 U.S. tourist-oriented transit services, the keys to success in establishing such services include the following:[7]

- Free or minimal fare ($1 or less);
- Frequent, reliable service;
- Convenient/easy access to attractions;
- Service span coordinated with hours of attractions;
- Service perceived as tourist amenity (e.g., drivers act as regional "ambassadors");
- Disincentives to automobile use (e.g., constrained parking, traffic congestion); and
- Cooperation of resorts, hotels, and attractions in marketing and/or funding.

Moreover, it is important to provide adequate marketing of these services; possible marketing strategies include branding of vehicles, providing brochures and schedules at all lodgings in the area, advertising in local media, bundling of transit access (and information) in package tours, and encouraging participation of local businesses and Chambers of Commerce.

Improved Amenities

Passenger amenities in the following areas can play a key role in attracting and retaining riders:

- Passenger facility improvements (e.g., improved bus stop, station, and transit center or park-and-ride amenities);

---

[7]TranSystems Corp. et al., *Southeast Connecticut Intermodal Connections Study*, prepared for Southeast Connecticut Council of Governments, 2005.

- New/improved vehicles (e.g., improved amenities and use of articulated buses); and
- Increased security (e.g., increased agency security presence) and increased safety (e.g., promotion of safety features of vehicles).

Descriptions and agency examples of these types of strategies are provided below.

Passenger Facility Improvements

Facilities such as bus stops, stations, transit centers, and park-and-ride lots play an essential role in enhancing the waiting experience of passengers and supporting efficient bus operations. They also play a key role in facilitating convenient transfers between different bus lines as well as between bus services and other modes, providing access to the entire multimodal transit system through the provision of parking capacity, inducing and supporting transit-friendly development, and establishing an identity for different services. Thus, the chief objectives of passenger facility improvements might include

- Safe and secure access and facilities;
- Improved access for pedestrians and bicyclists;
- Real-time service information;
- Basic customer amenities, including improved comfort;
- Improved bus system image and visibility; and
- Improved transfer environment.

Some agencies may wish to consider possible passenger facility improvements in a hierarchical fashion based on facility scale. For instance, bus stop amenities would be at the first level. This would be followed by intermodal transfer facilities, including transit centers and park-and-ride lots. The latter group of facilities encompasses a wide range of facility type, from small on-street transfer facilities to large off-street transit centers that include layover facilities and potentially additional passenger amenities such as small retail centers, transit pass sales outlets, and detailed transit information. Often these large off-street facilities will also be supported by park-and-ride facilities. Transit center amenities are discussed above, under Improved Schedule/Route Coordination.

Bus Stops and Shelters

Bus stops are the entry point to the transit system for the large majority of transit riders, but often these stops are of poor design, are inadequate for the number of passengers using them, have poor and sometimes misleading information, and are often not well maintained. A comprehensive and consistent set of standards, based on daily boardings, can be applied regionwide as a means of upgrading this important element of the bus system. An example of such a set of standards is presented in Table 5-7. As indicated in Table 5-7, these standards suggest that all bus stops regardless of passenger volume should have

- A level concrete pad for waiting passengers.
- Reasonable pedestrian access, including a paved access path to the concrete waiting pad and slope that does not exceed 6% over 100 feet. If reasonable access cannot be provided, the stop should be removed.
- Adequate lighting, based on existing lighting standards.
- Up-to-date and accurate bus stop signs, including an accurate listing of routes using the stop and an accurate information telephone number.

The standards suggest that stops with more than 50 boardings per day (including transfers) should also have a standard shelter and a trash receptacle. Stops with more than 100 boardings per day (including transfers) should also have

Table 5-7. Example of bus stop/shelter amenities standards.

Amenity	Customer Boarding Activity per Day				
	< 50	50-100	100-300	300-500	Over 500
Level concrete pad	✓	✓	✓	✓	✓
Safe access	✓	✓	✓	✓	✓
Adequate lighting	✓	✓	✓	✓	✓
Bus stop signs	✓	✓	✓	✓	✓
Route map and schedules	✓	✓	✓	✓	✓
Standard shelter		✓	✓	✓	✓
Trash receptacle		✓	✓	✓	✓
Detailed schedule			✓	✓	✓
Larger/Multiple shelter(s)			✓	✓	✓
Benches in shelter			✓	✓	✓
System map				✓	✓
Real time travel information				✓	✓
Potential conversion to transit center					✓

Source: *WMATA Regional Bus Study*

- Detailed schedule information, including scheduled times of arrival for each line serving the stop;
- A larger shelter, or alternatively, two standard shelters; and
- One or more benches in the shelter.

Stops with more than 300 daily boardings (including transfers) should also have

- A system map and
- Real-time travel information in the longer term.

Finally, the standards indicate that stops serving multiple routes with over 500 boardings per day (including transfers) should be examined in greater detail for conversion to a transit center.

A consistent design for bus stops across a region can help provide an improved regional transit identity. There should be a consistent shelter design theme for the entire system (see Exhibit 5-5) and there should be safety standards that address shelter and stop location and pedestrian access. Depending on the number of shelters in question, it can prove most cost-effective for the agency to pursue a regional franchise approach in which a contractor installs and maintains all shelters.

Beyond the types of amenities mentioned above, shelters should also offer protection from inclement weather for waiting passengers. At a minimum, a shelter should provide shade and protection from rain or snow. However, a new generation of shelters is being designed to enhance waiting passengers' comfort in particularly hot environments. In Phoenix, for example, a consulting firm has collaborated with a local university architecture program to design a modular shelter for the region's bus system specifically intended to maximize protection from the intense heat and the hot breezes that characterize local weather. The shelter design reduces heat buildup by minimizing the use of metal, relying instead on materials such as fiberglass that stay cooler.

Exhibit 5-5. *TriMet bus shelter.*

**City of Fort Collins Transfort
Transit Centers**
medium urbanized (200,000 - 1,000,000)

In 2002, Transfort created a new transit center in downtown Fort Collins, Colorado. The new facility helped to improve transfers between routes, created a convenient location where passengers could obtain information, and served as an intermodal link to airport shuttles, taxis, and regional bus routes. The following year, a similar center was created at Colorado State University. System ridership increased 1.8% between 2002 and 2003.

New/Improved Vehicles

The vehicle environment also plays an essential role affecting the rider's transit experience. As explained above, one of the reasons some people prefer railcars to buses is the greater amount of room and, in some cases, the greater comfort level of the rail vehicle. While railcars do not always possess the clear advantage in these areas (e.g., a crush load on either type of vehicle is likely to feel similarly uncomfortable to a rider), the message is clear: a more appealing vehicle environment helps to attract and retain riders.

Improved Amenities

The vehicle environment includes the space and facilities on board (e.g., seating and circulation), but also how people board and alight the vehicle (including how they pay the fare and obtain information about upcoming stops). *TCRP Report 46: The Role of Transit Amenities and Vehicle Characteristics in Building Transit Ridership*, 1999) notes that "Among the features and approaches to consider regarding vehicle environment are

- Circulation into and through the vehicle, including arrangement of doors and seating
- Types of seating (degree of padding, height of the seat back, provision of armrest, type of fabric or material)
- On-vehicle passenger information displays (visual and audible information about route number and name, next stop, key destination, upcoming stops and connecting route announcements, sometimes performed by a 'talking bus,' route maps and schedules)
- Better vehicle access using low-floor technology
- Lighting (including the type of lighting as well as the ability of passengers to have individual reading lamps)
- Climate control and ventilation
- Security cameras
- A quieter and smoother ride resulting from enhanced insulation, particularly of the engine
- Multi-modal features, such as bike racks
- Driver courtesy and assistance." (p. 6)

Among the key lessons learned from *TCRP Report 46* are that

- "*People react positively to amenities designed to improve their transit experience, both at the stop and on-board vehicles.* Passengers especially appreciate these when they are well-placed and well-designed, particularly when such basic service characteristics as frequency, efficiency, safety and reliability are perceived by passengers to be well under control. Amenities can help to instill rider confidence in a transit agency, as well as raise passenger optimism regarding the quality of future transit improvements and service.
- *Amenities impact a broad range of passenger experience and the ridership decisions of passengers.* Infrequent or 'transit choice' riders, a major target audience for increasing ridership, showed significant interest in amenities in the case study cities surveyed. Amenities do not just help make

transit more comfortable, but safer (with lighting and security cameras, for example) and more efficient (with features such as low-floor buses that are shown to reduce dwell time). Amenities may also impact new riders' perception of transit as a mobility option for themselves." (p. 2)

Thus, improved vehicle improvements amenities are an important consideration in any effort to raise ridership.

Use of Articulated Buses

Another potential bus-related improvement is the use of articulated buses to increase capacity on certain routes. These vehicles offer the potential to (1) alleviate crowding on heavily utilized bus lines without increasing frequency or (2) reduce the number of buses needed on the most heavily utilized lines where frequency has already been increased to address crowding. This is a cost-effective way to address crowding in certain circumstances, particularly on bus lines that have very high frequencies. Articulated buses are also sometimes used in BRT corridors.

Bangor Area Comprehensive Transportation System (BACTS)
New Improved Community Connections: "Try Our New Buses"
small urbanized (50,000 - 200,000)

As part of a larger effort to increase transit ridership, BACTS, serving Bangor, Maine, introduced a new fleet of low-floor buses. These buses provide for quicker and easier boardings and alightings, which in turn allow for more efficient service. The new vehicles serve the dual purposes of improving the passenger experience and attracting new riders to transit through distinctive branding. System ridership increased 8% between 2003 and 2004.

Increased Security and Safety

Perceived personal security (i.e., protection from crime and terrorism) and safety (i.e., protection from vehicle-related injury) are both important mode choice decision factors. Thus, increased security and increased safety are both elements that must be considered in an effort to increase—or even maintain—transit usage levels.

Increased Security

Promoting a sense of adequate security in transit systems (e.g., in stations/transit centers, in vehicles, at bus stops and in park-and-ride lots) has always been considered important. This has been accomplished in facilities such as stations/transit centers primarily through the presence of clearly identified agency personnel, complemented by security cameras where feasible. Providing a sense of security at bus stops has been more problematic, but a key strategy is ensuring sufficient street lighting at and around stops. Location of bus stops in close proximity to other "active" land uses (e.g., retail, office, and residential sites) also helps, although this is not always feasible.

Prior to September 11, 2001, rider concerns primarily focused on the possibility of assault or theft in facilities, or perhaps damage to cars in parking lots. However, these concerns have now been joined by broader concerns about the potential for terrorist attacks on transit systems. Indeed, terrorist acts in transit systems in London, Tokyo, Madrid, and throughout Israel have heightened the need for all transit agencies to be able to assure riders—and would-be riders—that improved security measures are in place. Such measures should include, for instance, a clear evacuation plan (particularly for subway systems and other systems with enclosed stations or transit centers). Increased security measures can be particularly important for attracting choice riders, including tourists.

University of Connecticut Transportation Services (UTS)
Quick Reaction Checklists
rural area (under 50,000)

As part of an overall effort to increase safety and security, UConn Transportation Services created a "Quick Reaction Checklist" for dispatchers. The checklist provides concise step-by-step instructions to help dispatchers figure out what to do in an emergency (such as a bomb threat, a bus breakdown, or a hijacking). In addition, bus drivers are awarded "safe driving" pins for each year of operation without any preventable accidents. The agency has determined that the sense of security which riders have about the system has contributed significantly to its ridership success. Ridership has increased 30 – 55% over the past five years.

A number of agencies have begun to improve the quality of their security monitoring procedures by upgrading to digital security cameras systems that record—and transmit—highly-detailed color images, rather than the blurry black and white images common to most existing security systems. These new systems greatly enhance the ability of the agencies to monitor—and later review—activity within rail stations and on buses. For example, SEPTA in Philadelphia has installed such a camera system in its first "Smart Station." The Smart Station concept is designed to coordinate all security and safety functions, including fire alarms and intrusion alarms; the agency plans to implement 21 additional Smart Stations by 2007. WMATA in Washington has installed digital cameras in all of its rail stations; these transmit images to both a central control room and to a monitoring kiosk located in each station. WMATA has also placed digital cameras on 100 buses and plans to do so on another 125 buses. The MBTA in Boston is also in the process of converting to digital security cameras as part of a major project to renovate its rail stations. In its major "hub" stations, the MBTA is installing glass-enclosed booths that will allow passengers to observe the surveillance images from the station.

Finally, *TCRP Report 46* notes that "Amenities can also impact security indirectly. People often perceive a station as more dangerous than it really is because of a poor general appearance or lack of maintenance, or because it lacks the presence of official people, like ticket agents or retail vendors. These signs of deterioration are often equated with signs that a place is unsafe or 'out of control.'" (p. 23)

Increased Safety

A sense of safety on board transit vehicles—and while boarding and alighting—is also important to riders and potential riders. Certain security measures such as evacuation plans also pertain to personal safety. Otherwise, an agency should promote its safety record (i.e., related to incidence of vehicle accidents) as well as the safety features of its vehicles and any operator training programs in place.

South Bend Public Transportation Corporation (TRANSPO)
TRANSPO System Safety Program
small urbanized (50,000 - 200,000)

TRANSPO recently implemented a comprehensive operator training and safety program for its bus drivers. The program included safety awareness training as well as training on a bus operating simulator. The program served the dual goals of reducing vehicle accidents and insurance costs and increasing passenger satisfaction. System ridership increased 10.6% between 1999 and 2001.

CHAPTER 6

Partnerships/Coordination Initiatives

Introduction

An increasingly important category of strategies, actions, and initiatives aimed at increasing ridership is partnerships and coordination initiatives. The types of strategies—and specific actions/examples—included this category are shown in Table 6-1. These types of strategies are generally intended to attract and retain riders by improving the availability and/or affordability of transit service—or by making use of transit feasible at all. Thus, each strategy should address one or more of the following mode choice factors:

- Availability of service,
- Convenience,
- Cost of using transit—and ease of fare payment, and
- Perceived "image" of the system.

Descriptions and examples of the various types of partnership and coordination strategies are provided below.

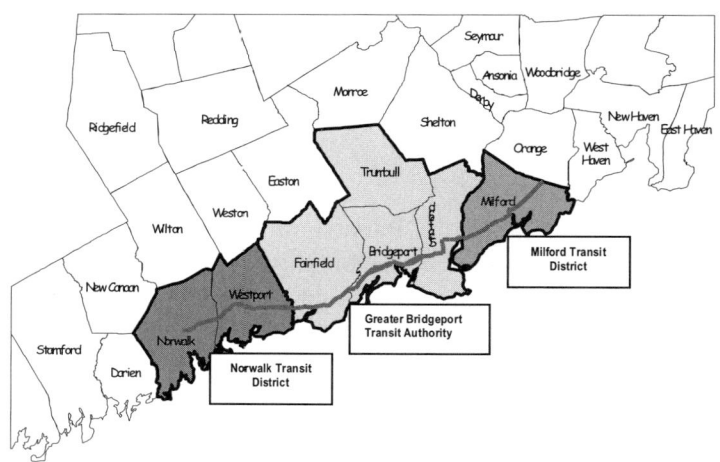

Guidelines and Examples

As demonstrated via the examples in Chapter 4, various types of partnership/coordination strategies can be used in a range of service environments. However, some strategies or particular types of initiatives are not well suited to certain settings or modes. Table 6-2 identifies which environments and modes are generally appropriate for each type of strategy; obviously, though, each specific type of initiative must be designed to reflect the needs and opportunities that exist within the agency's environment.

The different types of partnerships and coordination initiatives are described on the following pages, including examples of each type of strategy.

Partnerships

Transit agencies are increasingly entering into partnerships with other entities that effectively promote the use of transit by the partner entities' constituents. While there may be various part-

Table 6-1. Types of partnerships and coordination initiatives.

Type of Strategy	Specific Actions/Examples
Partnerships	
University/school pass programs	Reduced pass price or per trip reimbursement to university (or other school)
Travel demand management strategies	Employer pass/voucher programs; vanpooling; ride-matching; parking cash-out
Subsidized activity center service	Subsidized service to office parks or other activity centers
Coordination Initiatives	
Consistent regional operating policies	Transfer agreements
Coordination with social service agencies	Mobility manager; access-to-jobs programs
Coordination with other transportation agencies	Roadway or parking management strategies
Promotion of transit-supportive design/TOD	Requirements for bus stops/shelters at new developments

Table 6-2. Applicable modes/settings for types of partnership/coordination initiatives.

Type of Strategy	Mode		Service Environment					
	Bus	Rail	Large Urban	Medium Urban	Small Urban	Rural	Suburb	CBD
University/school pass programs	+	+	+	+	+	+	+	+
Travel demand management strategies	+	+	+	+	+	+	+	+
Subsidized activity center service	+	−	+	+	+	+	+	+
Consistent regional (inter-agency) operating policies	+	+	+	+	+	+	+	+
Coordination with social service agencies	+	+	+	+	+	+	+	+
Coordination with other transportation agencies	+	+	+	O	−	+	+	+
Promotion of transit-supportive design/TOD	+	+	+	+	+	O	+	+

Key: − = not applicable or inappropriate; O = applicable, but may not be cost-effective; + = applicable and appropriate

nership opportunities in a given area, the major types of partnerships transit agencies have developed are as follows:[1]

- University/school pass programs (e.g., reduced pass price or per trip reimbursement for university or other school);
- Travel demand management strategies (e.g., employer pass/voucher programs, vanpooling, rideshare matching, flex-time, and parking cash-out); and
- Subsidized activity center service (e.g., subsidized service to office parks or other activity centers).

These types of arrangements/programs are described below, including agency examples of each.

University/School Pass Programs

Some universities provide their own campus area transit services, but many campuses are served by the local transit operator. Where the latter is the case, many universities have established

---

[1] Certain other types of ridership strategies, though assigned in this report to other categories, can also clearly involve development of partnerships. Examples include introduction or expansion of a route serving a campus, or a cooperative marketing arrangement with a university.

partnerships with the local transit agencies to provide specially priced passes or other payment options to students. As discussed in Chapter 4 and Appendix A, such arrangements represent the single most common type of initiative instituted by the agencies reviewed in this study. By providing a low-cost and convenient form of transit payment to the university community, the transit agency typically sees increased ridership. Agencies that serve—and have some type of payment arrangement with—major universities, by and large, have significantly higher per capita ridership figures than do other comparably sized areas. Meanwhile, the university benefits by improving access for its students, faculty, and staff, and may ultimately be able to ease on-campus parking requirements by shifting some students and others to transit.[2]

The university pass/reduced fare arrangement represents one of the oldest types of fare-related transit partnership, with some (e.g., University of Massachusetts-Amherst, University of California-San Diego) dating back several decades. The pass programs, often called "U-Pass" or something similar, feature various formats, including the following:[3]

- The university pays the transit agency an annual lump sum per student in return for unlimited transit use for each participating student, faculty, and staff member; this type of arrangement has been given the generic name "Unlimited Access."[4] In this option, the student typically need only present his/her campus ID card to board a transit vehicle.
- The university purchases monthly (or perhaps semester or even full school year) passes from the transit agency, either at the regular price or at a reduced price, and then sells them to interested students—usually at a significant price reduction. These may be specially designed passes (either electronic or flash passes) issued by the agency or special stickers affixed to campus ID cards. (Exhibit 6-1 shows an example of a Upass issued by CT TRANSIT in Hartford.)
- The transit agency actually reads the university's student/faculty/staff ID cards directly in the fare collection equipment. A predetermined cost per ride is then billed to the university, based on the total uses of the cards during a month (or semester). Examples of this arrangement include OCTA (Orange Co., CA), which has agreements with University of California-Irvine and California State University-Fullerton; and Big Blue Bus (Santa Monica, CA), which has a partnership with UCLA.

Exhibit 6-1. Example of Upass.

In some cases, arrangements involve a single university or college, while in others, the transit agency provides the same basic deal to any interested institution. In Chicago, for instance, the CTA's U-PASS program is available to any university/college in the area; 22 universities or colleges are participating. In Atlanta, the MARTA U-Pass program has expanded from 4 colleges/universities when it was introduced in 1998 to 25.

Where implemented, university pass programs have typically proven quite successful at increasing transit ridership, while also providing guaranteed revenue to the transit agency.[5] Examples of the impacts are as follows:

- An analysis of unlimited access programs by researchers at UCLA's Institute of Transportation Studies found that such programs seem to have resulted in a net average ridership increase of

---

[2] For additional discussion of university pass arrangements, see *TCRP Report 94: Fare Policies, Structures and Technologies* (Update), 2003.
[3] Another strategy that has been introduced by some agencies whose service is focused on the university community is to offer low (or free) fares on the entire system (i.e., rather than just to university students, faculty and staff). This strategy is discussed in Chapter 8, Fare Collection/Structure Initiatives.
[4] J. Brown et al. "Unlimited Access," *Transportation* (vol. 28, pp. 233–267), 2001.
[5] Ibid.

over 7% per year at 13 transit agencies with university programs for the 2 years immediately following introduction of the program.[6] At five universities that collected ridership data before the initiation of the pass program, in the first year, student transit ridership increased between 71% and 200%; in subsequent years, there were annual increases of 2–10%.
- In Chicago, more than 40,000 eligible college students are using the CTA's U-PASS program, accounting for over 10 million rides per year; a quarter to a third of these are considered to be new transit rides, and half of total U-PASS ridership is thought to take place in midday/evening hours.[7]
- In Seattle, 86% of eligible university students, faculty, and staff participate in the U-PASS program, accounting for over 8 million rides per year (more than 10% of all Metro and Community Transit rides); 45% of these are estimated to be new transit rides.[8]

Moreover, these programs can build "brand loyalty" to the transit system. In Chicago, for example, the vast majority of survey respondents said that they would continue to use CTA after graduation.

Santa Cruz Metropolitan Transit District - Metro Student Pass Program
small urbanized (50,000 - 200,000)

The University of California at Santa Cruz worked with Santa Cruz METRO to establish a university transit pass program. A student ID entitles the holder to unlimited free rides on any METRO route, which encourages students to ride transit whenever possible. For UCSC staff and faculty, a quarterly bus pass provides the same benefit. The university makes payments to METRO on a per-student basis, the funds for which come from a transportation fee added to each student's tuition. Ridership has increased on routes serving the university.

Thus, university-transit agency partnerships are capable of generating significant increases in ridership, while also building interest in continuing to use transit after graduation. However, it is important to recognize the cost and revenue implications of such programs; key concerns are as follows:

- Agencies must carefully design the pricing parameters of university pass programs so as to minimize the potential negative revenue impact. In particular, the agreement should be structured so that it allows the agency to increase the amount paid per person so as to reflect actual usage rates.
- Depending on the success of the program (i.e., at attracting riders), there may be added costs to the agency (i.e., due to the need to provide additional service to meet the increased demand). In Seattle, Metro's costs have risen considerably with the provision of additional service to the UW campus; however, UW pays a portion of the increased costs, and Metro's revenue recovery rate for the new services has been comparable to its systemwide average.

Travel Demand Management Strategies

Travel demand management (TDM) comprises a range of strategies aimed at reducing single-occupant-vehicle (SOV) commuting and peak-period traffic congestion. Some of these strategies focus on encouraging transit use (e.g., pass/voucher programs) while others involve facilitating ridesharing (i.e., vanpool programs or rideshare matching in private automobiles) or simply spreading out the commuting period (e.g., through allowing flex-time); finally, some

---
[6]Ibid.
[7]TCRP Report 94.
[8]Ibid.

TDM strategies (e.g., parking "cash-out" arrangements or dedicated transit or high-occupancy-vehicle lanes) are generally intended to provide incentives to use some form of high-occupancy mode. Transit agencies can promote TDM in general (both transit and non-transit aspects), often through coordination with other public agencies, and can also play a key role through partnerships with employers to facilitate—and possibly subsidize—employees' use of transit to commute to/from work. Strategies involving coordination with other agencies are discussed below, under Coordination Initiatives. This section focuses on employer-oriented transit benefit programs.

Transit/employer programs were originally limited to the distribution of monthly passes by employers to their employees, often with at least a partial subsidy of the pass price. The programs subsequently became more flexible with the introduction of transit vouchers that the employees could use to acquire the transit payment option of their choice. In the last decade, these basic approaches have evolved and broadened, fueled both by a steady increase in the tax-free transit benefit employees could receive and the emergence of electronic payment technologies. Key types of employer-oriented transit benefit programs and strategies now in place include the following:

- Pass programs—In these programs, employers buy passes for employees and distribute them at worksites. The passes are often subsidized, all or in part. In addition to monthly pass programs, a number of agencies have adopted annual pass programs in which employers purchase annual passes for employees (at significantly less than the normal monthly cost of passes) based on a predetermined formula set by the transit agency.
- Transit voucher programs—In these programs, employees receive vouchers that can then be redeemed for transit passes or other payment options. In some cases, the vouchers are in the form of stored-value farecards that can be used directly for fare payment (see Exhibit 6-2).
- Automated benefits distribution programs—Other strategies for distributing transit benefits to employees are emerging as well, including the ability to automatically download the value of the benefit to an employee's smartcard.

Such programs are greatly facilitated by the existence of the "commuter choice" benefits program.[9] Commuter Choice allows employers to let their employees set aside up to $105 a month, or $1,260 a year, of their pre-tax salary to pay for transit or vanpool commuting, and $200 a month ($2,400 a year) for qualified parking expenses. Prior to TEA-21, commuter benefits had been allowed only in the form of a direct employer subsidy to an employee. A number of states have also introduced their own legislation providing state tax credits to employers who offer Commuter Choice benefits to their employees; these states include Maryland, Delaware, Oregon, and Georgia.

Exhibit 6-2. Example of stored-value vouchers.

The aforementioned approaches through which employers have worked with transit agencies to provide transit benefits are reviewed below.

Annual Pass Programs

Annual pass programs are offered by several agencies, including Denver RTD (Eco Pass), Dallas Area Rapid Transit (E Pass), Metro (Minneapolis) Transit (MetroPass), King County Metro (FlexPass), and Portland Tri-Met (PASSport). Such programs make participation convenient for both employers and employees. However, it is important in establishing these programs that

---

[9]*Commuter Choice* is a provision of the Transportation Equity Act for the 21st Century (TEA-21) that was signed into law in June 1998. TEA-21, along with the Taxpayer Relief Act of 1997, amended Internal Revenue Code Section 132(f) that already provided certain commuter program tax benefits. This tax code amendment significantly improved the status of employer-sponsored commute incentive programs.

transit agencies structure pricing in such a way that they protect themselves against losing revenue; the pricing should be able to capture at least some revenue from the new trips being generated. Since all employees at a company receive an unlimited-use pass, the transit agency can expect to see an increase in commuter ridership. However, since initial pass prices are normally based on pre-program transit mode share, the pass may become under-priced if mode share assumptions are not updated regularly. Denver RTD's announced intention to discontinue its Eco Pass program due to excessive revenue loss demonstrates the danger of failing to adequately update the pricing assumptions and formula.

Transit Voucher Programs

Beyond the direct distribution of passes, employers can provide transit benefits for employees through strategies such as *voucher programs*. In programs such as TransitCheck (New York City area), CommuterCheck (San Francisco, Denver, Boston, elsewhere), and Metrochek (Washington, DC), employees are given vouchers that can be redeemed for transit passes or other payment options. In some cases (e.g., New York City and Washington), the vouchers are in the form of stored-value farecards and can thus be used directly for fare payment where accepted—or redeemed for fare options for other agencies in the applicable region.

Automated Benefits Distribution Programs

The emergence of electronic payment media such as smartcards has created new strategies for distributing transit benefits to employees. One approach, mentioned above, is the direct provision of stored-value farecards, as is done in Washington, New York, and Chicago. A variation introduced in 2000 in New York City is the Premium TransitChek designed for city employees and other large employers. In this program, TransitCenter issues employees special MetroCards once a year. The City or employer deducts the cost of a 30-day pass from the employees' paychecks each month and transfers these funds—along with an active list—to TransitCenter; as long as an employee's payment status remains active, his/her card will remain active.

The use of smartcards further expands the ability to automatically distribute transit benefits. The existing examples of such a strategy are WMATA's "SmartBenefits" program (launched in September 2000), the CTA's Chicago Card Plus (introduced in 2004), and the TransLink card in the San Francisco Bay Area (pilot tested in 2002 and now being rolled out in the region). In the WMATA program, an employer establishes an account for each participating employee (and subsequently identifies any changes to an employee's status) via a WMATA website. Each month, the employee can then automatically download the value of the benefit to his/her SmarTrip smartcard at any WMATA farecard vending machine. As of 2003, over 550 employers and 17,000 employees were participating in the SmartBenefits program; while participation was growing at a slower pace than the agency had anticipated, the concept should take greater hold as the number of employees at each company using the SmarTrip card increases—and once SmarTrip is expanded to other services in the region over the next few years. The Chicago Card Plus and TransLink programs also involve automated downloading of transit benefits. Chicago Card Plus is an account-based card system; those cardholders not receiving transit benefits directly from their employers must establish a credit card-backed account with the CTA to use the card.

The combination of commuter choice legislation and the emergence of electronic payment technologies has resulted in a range of distribution strategies that facilitate the provision of transit benefits to employees. The major impacts on and benefits to transit agencies, employees, and employers from these types of strategies include the following:

- Annual pass programs, provision of vouchers in the form of electronic farecards, and automated download options (like SmartBenefits) are particularly convenient for employees, since they do not require them to go out of their way to purchase separate fare instruments.

- These programs also represent convenient mechanisms for employers to manage the distribution of commute benefits to employees. Besides providing a tangible benefit to their employees, employers benefit from such programs through payroll tax savings, as well as the potential to reduce parking requirements.
- Such programs help employers address state or local trip reduction ordinances; the existence of such requirements was a key factor leading to the establishment of both King County Metro's and Tri-Met's annual pass programs.
- Such programs typically result in increased transit usage. For instance, in Seattle, FlexPass has resulted in an average increase in employees' transit use in the first year of the company's participation of over 90%. In Portland, the average employee increase has been measured at 57% during the first year; PASSport passes account for over 7% of Tri-Met's overall system ridership. In New York, a 1994 survey indicated an average of over 240 additional transit rides per year per TransitChek recipient.

Thus, employer pass and voucher programs have been shown to benefit employees, employers, and transit agencies. Clearly, the simpler—and less costly—it is for employers to administer these programs, the more likely they will be to participate. Similarly, the more convenient it is for employees to take advantage of commuter benefits, the more likely they will be to use transit to get to and from work.

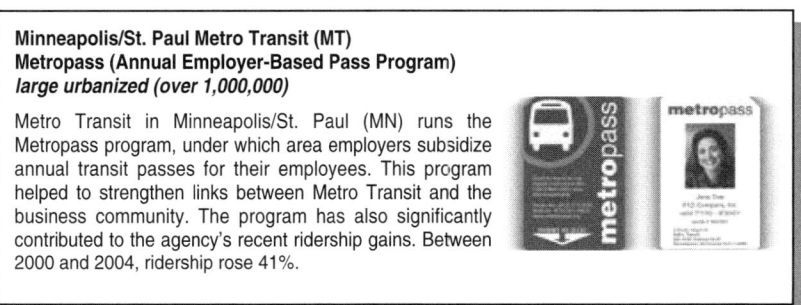

Minneapolis/St. Paul Metro Transit (MT)
Metropass (Annual Employer-Based Pass Program)
large urbanized (over 1,000,000)

Metro Transit in Minneapolis/St. Paul (MN) runs the Metropass program, under which area employers subsidize annual transit passes for their employees. This program helped to strengthen links between Metro Transit and the business community. The program has also significantly contributed to the agency's recent ridership gains. Between 2000 and 2004, ridership rose 41%.

Subsidized Activity Center Service

As indicated in Chapter 5, employers (private or public), developers, or other entities may also be involved in partnerships with transit agencies through subsidizing transit service to/from key activity centers. The most common form of such an arrangement is a shuttle service that provides a link between a transit hub (e.g., a commuter rail station or an intermodal center) and an office park or other large employment site. In order to help attract and retain employees—and possibly to minimize the amount of parking necessary—employers may be willing to sponsor such services or at least participate in their funding. Some type of fare subsidy may be involved as well; for example, fares may be waived with an employee identification card or the employer may provide a transit pass or voucher, as discussed in the previous section.

As noted in *TCRP Report 55*, such shuttle services "by their nature serve niche markets; that is, a small portion of the total travel market commuting to any one location. Thus, on a regional basis, the number of trips as a percentage of all trips is rather small; the key is to capture a reasonable mode share of the trips that originate within the corridor served by regional bus or rail." (p. 54) *TCRP Report 55* further points out that "Shuttle programs have to be carefully designed and tailored to the markets they serve in order to be effective. Given their relatively small markets, they have to have hours and headways tailored to the travel patterns of the local market and cannot overextend schedules." (p. 55)

Examples of privately sponsored shuttle services include the Metra "Shuttle Bug" (summarized in the inset) and the following, both operated by Central Contra Costa County (CA) Transit Authority outside of San Francisco:[10]

- Route 960 connects Walnut Creek BART station and Bishop Ranch Business Park. Bishop Ranch is basically an "edge city," with more than 60,000 employees. The developer, Subset Development, jointly sponsors the service with the California Department of Transportation. Bishop Ranch workers ride free, while the general public can ride for $1.25. The design and marketing of the service have apparently been quite successful, as evidenced by the fact that Route 960's productivity has been nearly 16 passengers per hour—compared to a productivity of under 7 passengers per hour for the regular transit route that had served the corridor prior to the implementation of Route 960. As of the late 1990s, ridership was over 270 per day.
- Route 991 connects the BART Concord station to three business parks. Employers at these business parks agreed to help subsidize the route as a condition of their receipt of building permits. As is the case with Route 960, employees can ride for free (by presenting their employee ID card or a special farecard); the general public must pay the normal transit fare. The route is relatively lightly used, about 80 passengers per day, but the employers are apparently satisfied with the service.

Of course, such services can also be subsidized solely by public agencies, typically for employees traveling to/from a particular local, state, or federal agency location. For example, the Nashville MTA operates two shuttles under contract to the State of Tennessee. The MTA bills the State for vehicle hours of service at a specified contract rate. State employees ride the shuttles for free, by presenting their state ID cards—and have priority access to the buses. However, the contract allows the MTA to carry paying passengers on a space-available basis; non-state employees wishing to ride these buses currently pay a fare of $0.25, and this represents additional revenue for the transit agency.

> **Northeast Illinois Regional Commuter Railroad Corporation – Metra (NIRCRC)**
> **Shuttle Bug & Other Linking Services**
> *large urbanized (over 1,000,000)*
>
> In order to better serve the reverse commute and suburb-to-suburb commute markets of the Chicago area, Metra runs a program that seeks to link corporate campuses with suburban rail stations. Through public-private partnerships, over 30 employers help subsidize more than 17 shuttle routes. Employers have a large say in determining the schedule and routing of each shuttle, and on-going monitoring of service ensures that the shuttles continue to meet the needs of the employees. Between 2003 and 2004, ridership in this program rose 12%.

Coordination Initiatives

Other types of strategies involve coordination with other entities—either other transit agencies in the region or non-transit entities—to better facilitate or promote the use of transit. Key types of strategies in this area include

- Consistent regional (inter-agency) operating policies (e.g., transfer agreements);
- Coordination with social service agencies (e.g., mobility manager and access-to-jobs programs);

---

[10] The two CCCTA examples come from *TCRP Report 55: Guidelines for Enhancing Suburban Mobility Using Public Transportation*, 1999 (p. 55).

- Coordination with other transportation agencies (e.g., roadway or parking management strategies); and
- Promotion of transit-supportive design (e.g., requirements for bus stops/shelters at new developments) and transit-oriented development (e.g., creation of a "transit village" around a rail station).

These types of initiatives are described below, including agency examples.

Consistent Regional Operating Policies

Many regions in the United States are served by multiple transit agencies operating in adjacent—and sometimes overlapping—service areas. Within these multi-agency regions, the extent of consistent operating policies varies significantly. In some areas, agencies have made concerted efforts to integrate one or more types of functions or policies with neighboring agencies, while in others, the agencies each continue to operate independently and make unilateral decisions.

The most common functional area of regional integration to date has been fare policy and payments. With travel patterns increasingly requiring transferring between adjoining transit agencies' services, there has been a growing emphasis on the development of multi-agency agreements and integrated regional payment arrangements. In fact, agencies are moving from simple inter-agency transfer agreements to more comprehensive integrated regional payment options. A number of agencies currently have some type of joint pass arrangement with at least one other agency. In other cases, agencies have transfer—or fare upgrade—provisions with agencies with which they intersect.[11] For example, in the Washington, DC, area, WMATA and eight neighboring bus agencies offer a joint 1-day pass that can be used on WMATA's Metrobus and the other services; WMATA and all but one of these agencies also has a regional bus transfer agreement. In the Los Angeles area, a regional pass—EZ Transit Pass—is accepted by LACMTA and 17 other agencies; there is also an inter-agency transfer agreement in the region. In the Central Puget Sound Region (Seattle, WA), a regional pass—the Puget Pass—is accepted by seven agencies (including the Washington State Ferry); five of these agencies also accept each other's transfers.

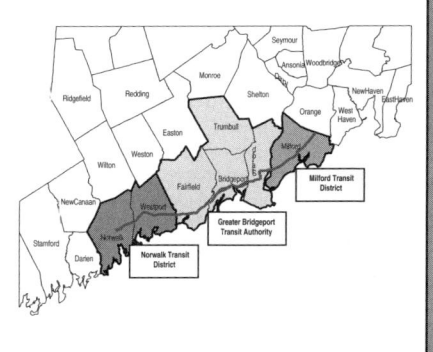

Norwalk Transit District—Wheels (NTD)
Coastal Link Service
medium urbanized (200,000—1,000,000)

The Norwalk (CT) Transit District partnered with two neighboring transit agencies (Greater Bridgeport Transit Authority and Milford Transit District) to create the "Coastal Link" bus route, which travels along the U.S. 1 corridor through 6 different municipalities. The agencies agreed to operate in each other's districts and accept each other's fares in order to provide a seamless service for the rider. This trip previously would have required two uncoordinated transfers among three different systems with three different fares. Ridership along this corridor has increased by more than 200% since introduction of the Coastal Link.

Of course, inter-agency integration can cover several other functional areas as well. A recent study completed by the California PATH Program, *Transit Service Integration Practices: An Assessment of U.S. Experiences* (2005), identified the following basic types of inter-agency integration:

---

[11]The emergence of electronic payment options, particularly smartcards, has facilitated an increasing focus on integrated multi-agency payment systems—i.e., introducing a regional farecard that is accepted at any participating agency. This strategy is discussed in Chapter 8, Fare Collection/Structure Initiatives.

- Infrastructure integration (i.e., shared stops/stations, inter-agency joint operation of routes, coordinated route restructuring, or inter-agency joint equipment purchases);
- Schedule integration (i.e., inter-agency schedule coordination or timed transfers);
- Fare integration (i.e., inter-agency free/reduced price transfers or regional pass);
- Information integration (i.e., inter-agency trip itinerary planning, inter-agency real-time trip information dissemination, inter-agency dissemination of maps/schedules, inter-agency marketing, or inter-agency sharing of operational/planning data); and
- Special events/emergency conditions integration (i.e., inter-agency planning for events or emergency conditions).

The PATH report identifies and discusses examples of each of these types of integration, based on a literature review, survey, and case studies. Fifty-six of the sixty agencies that responded to the survey indicated that they had put in place—or were in the process of implementing—one or more of these types of integration; moreover, nearly 75% of the respondents indicated some level of involvement (past or present) in at least four of the areas. (Strategies associated with these functional areas are described further—and examples are provided—in other chapters of this report.)

Coordination with Social Services Agencies

Coordination between transit agencies and social services programs can benefit both parties, by increasing transit ridership and maximizing the effective use of ever tighter social services agency resources. Examples of such coordination include

- Mobility manager programs—A transit agency might act as the central manager or coordinator of a range of publicly and privately operated services.
- Access-to-jobs programs—Transit agencies can play a key role in providing access to jobs for former welfare recipients.

These types of strategies are discussed below.

Mobility Manager Programs

Given that most areas feature a range of publicly and privately operated transportation services, there may well be opportunities to improve the overall cost-effectiveness and efficiency of service delivery. One approach to minimize duplication and gaps in services within a region is to establish a single entity to manage multiple services and/or to serve as an information clearinghouse. This type of structure is commonly known as a Mobility Manager or Coordinator. In many communities, the transit agency may well be the most appropriate entity to carry out that function.

One of the general objectives of the Mobility Manager should be to continually look for ways to provide more cost-effective and appropriate types of transportation for each trip, on behalf of the sponsoring agencies. For example, vanpools and dedicated shuttle services offer lower cost alternatives to advance-reservation, demand-responsive paratransit services. This is especially true where (1) a certain critical mass of riders makes roughly the same trip every day, and (2) where the users can either cover the cost of the service in a cooperative cost-sharing arrangement or have a sponsor (e.g., developer, employer, college, or human services agency) fund some or all of the cost. Such shifts are easier to effect, in terms of both administration and operations, if a single entity has centralized oversight of a broad family of services. The Mobility Manager should be able to assemble the critical mass of programs to generate savings worthy of the effort associated with coordination and would reduce the marginal efforts needed to achieve efficiencies in each program. The Mobility Manager should provide oversight and arrange for the provision of a variety of transportation services, including for example, local circulation services and other more specialized services, which may be operated by a mix of private for-profit, not-for-profit, and/or public carriers.

Access-to-Jobs Programs

Federal welfare reform legislation, passed in 1996, radically changed the American welfare system, emphasizing the move of individuals from welfare to work.[12] In implementing the resulting welfare reform programs, states and localities quickly realized the importance of ensuring access to reliable and affordable transportation services for those residents attempting to make this transition.

MTA Long Island Bus (LIB)
Transit and Social Service Agency Collaboration
   to Enhance Access to Jobs
large urbanized (over 1,000,000)

New York's Long Island Bus worked with the Department of Social Services and other state agencies to identify transit needs relating to reverse commuters and the welfare-to-work program. Through joint collaboration on grants, the agencies were able to fund new routes, as well as service extensions on existing routes. To date, over 1.5 million passenger trips have been generated through these efforts. System ridership increased nearly 3% from 2002 to 2003.

Addressing welfare to work transportation issues has required creation of new collaborations among public agencies and private organizations, establishment of new transportation services, and development of innovative funding strategies. However, an important element of all access-to-jobs programs has been the provision of a mechanism for individuals to pay for these services, in terms of both subsidization of travel and furnishing the actual payment media. This has resulted in various types of special transit payment arrangements. In some cases, welfare recipients are directly provided with transit passes (or other fare media) for specified periods of time. In other cases, recipients must purchase their own fare media and then may be reimbursed (e.g., by the responsible social services agency). Finally, where new services are created specifically to address access-to-jobs needs, the service may be free to eligible users—whereas members of the general public using the service would have to pay a fare.

Access-to-jobs partnerships have been shown to increase transit ridership and to benefit eligible riders by providing affordable access to employment and training sites. However, since these programs often involve participation by a number of different entities, it is important that the participants clearly understand—and be sensitive to—each other's goals and concerns in developing and implementing the program.

Coordination with Other Transportation Agencies

As discussed in Chapter 2, existing transportation conditions related to factors such as parking availability/pricing and traffic levels can have a major impact on transit demand. Conversely, transit can play a key role in controlling congestion. Therefore, it should be of mutual benefit for transit agencies to coordinate wherever possible with local, regional, or state agencies (e.g., city or county traffic/highway departments, MPOs, or state DOTs) in the planning/development of the following types of efforts:[13]

---

[12] The Personal Responsibility and Work Opportunity Reconciliation Act (1996) replaced the Aid for Families with Dependent Children program with block grant funding and mandatory work requirements. The new welfare program imposed a 5-year lifetime limit on welfare benefits and a 2-year deadline for placing most recipients in jobs, job training, or vocational education programs.

[13] Other types of strategies requiring such coordination include transit-supportive design (discussed in the next section) and transit signal priority systems (discussed in Chapter 5).

- Roadway management strategies include establishment of various types of dedicated HOV/transit lanes or rights-of-way.
- Parking management strategies tend to focus on the establishment of downtown parking restrictions and/or parking surcharges.

Such efforts are discussed below.

Roadway Management Strategies

Specific forms of these strategies that should contribute to increased demand for transit include

- Downtown transit malls and bus lanes,
- Exclusive busways and BRT rights-of-way, and
- Dedicated HOV lanes (for buses as well as carpools and vanpools).

There has been considerable coordination of transit and other transportation agency efforts in the roadway management area. For instance, transit malls have been established in a number of U.S. cities, including Denver, Minneapolis, Dallas, and Portland (OR). Exclusive busways have been implemented in Pittsburgh, Miami, and northern New Jersey, while BRT systems with dedicated rights-of-way (for at least a portion of the total system) are in place or under development in such locations as Boston, Orlando, and Las Vegas. Finally, many highways have dedicated HOV lanes; examples include major arterials in Washington (DC), Houston, and Seattle. While HOV lanes can also be used by carpools and vanpools, all of these types of efforts offer transit users distinct travel time advantages over driving alone and thus serve to enhance the relative attractiveness of transit service.

Parking Management Strategies

Examples of possible forms of parking-related initiatives that should contribute to increased demand for transit include

- Establishment of a cap on downtown parking spaces;
- Allowance of maximum parking ratios for new commercial developments;
- Prohibition of construction of new freestanding garages;
- Increase in parking meter rates, reduction in maximum allowable meter stay, or expansion of short-term metering; and
- Establishment of a residential parking permit program (i.e., with substantial fines for parking without a permit).

While a number of U.S. cities have at one time or another implemented one or more of these strategies—typically in an effort to control downtown traffic congestion—the actual coordination of transit agency and other transportation agency efforts in their development has been limited. The most notable example of parking-transit policy coordination is in Portland, OR, where combined transit and parking initiatives have been in place for over 30 years; transit measures developed in combination with a range of parking restrictions include the aforementioned transit mall and a fare-free zone (Fareless Square). Another notable example is in Bellevue, WA, where the city has initiated a series of transit, parking, and other demand management initiatives in response to growing downtown traffic congestion.

Thus, while traffic levels and parking availability/pricing are generally considered external factors affecting transit usage, transit agencies should seek to coordinate with other transportation agencies that are developing approaches to manage local transportation conditions. Strategies such as dedicated bus lanes or parking restrictions combined with transit improvements can help to control traffic congestion while generating increased demand for transit.

Promotion of Transit-Supportive Design and TOD

The integration of transit and land use/development planning represents another form of coordination intended to promote transit usage. Two related types of strategies have been employed by transit agencies and local governments in an effort to ensure that new developments are conducive to the use of transit:

- Transit-supportive design guidelines are promulgated by transit agencies to guide developers in designing and constructing "transit-friendly" buildings and sites.
- Transit-oriented development (TOD) generally refers to compact mixed-use development in the vicinity of a transit station or transfer center that has been designed to facilitate transit usage.

These strategies are discussed briefly below.

Transit-Supportive Design

As many as a quarter of U.S. transit agencies have developed or adopted some form of transit-supportive design guidelines.[14] *TCRP Report 55* says of these guidelines, "Beside imparting technical design information, guidelines promote coordination among stakeholders, encourage long-range planning for transit, emphasize the importance of transit design considerations during project review, and educate the general public about transit issues. Some of the more effective guidelines provide examples of 'good design practices' that developers can emulate." (p. 19) Such guidelines typically suggest and describe design features that will (1) help to make development sites conducive to pedestrian access to transit facilities or bus stops, and (2) facilitate efficient bus operations within or approaching the site. Notable examples of comprehensive design guidelines documents include the following:

- Snohomish County (WA) Transit—*A Guide to Land Use and Public Transportation;* there is also an accompanying videotape;
- Portland Tri-Met—*Planning and Design for Transit;* and
- Central Contra Costa County Transit Authority—*Coordination of Property Development and Improvements* (this was one of the first such documents, produced in 1982).

Transit-Oriented Development

Transit-oriented development is defined differently in different locations. Indeed, as noted in *TCRP Report 102: Transit-Oriented Development in the United States: Experiences, Challenges and Prospects*, "There is no universally accepted definition of TOD, because development that would be considered dense, pedestrian-friendly, and transit-supportive in a middle-size city in the Midwest would be viewed quite differently in the heart of Manhattan or the District of Columbia." (p. 5) *TCRP Report 102* presents the definitions of TOD adopted by 10 different transit agencies; they vary in their details, although ". . . most focus on the design characteristics of transit-supportive environments." (p. 7) The most frequently cited characteristics among these definitions are high-quality walking environments and mixed land uses; moreover, several definitions link TOD to increased transit ridership. As noted in the TCRP report, there is general ". . . agreement within the professional transit community as to what constitutes a TOD: a pattern of dense, diverse, pedestrian-friendly land uses near transit nodes that, under the right conditions, translates into higher patronage." (p. 7)

---

[14]TCRP Report 55, p. 19

**CityBus of Greater Lafayette
Transit-Oriented Development for Small Cities**
small urbanized (50,000 - 200,000)

The City of Lafayette, Indiana, created the James Riehle Plaza as an intermodal station serving trains as well as local and regional bus service. Since it opened in 1995, a significant amount of transit-oriented development has emerged in the area, including a childcare center, retail, offices, and residential development. Ridership on the system has increased 117% in four years.

There are many examples of TOD around the United States. While most examples are focused on rail stations, a considerable number are associated with bus service. *TCRP Report 102* identified more than 100 TODs, based primarily on a survey of transit agencies. The regions responding to the survey featuring the largest numbers of examples are San Francisco, Washington (DC), Portland (OR), Atlanta, and Dallas.[15]

While TOD can have a variety of benefits to a community or a region, *TCRP Report 102* points out that "The most direct benefit of TOD is increased ridership and the associated revenue gains. Research shows that residents living near stations are five to six times more likely to commute via transit than are other residents in a region." (p. S-6) The mixed-use aspects of many TODs are also important in their potential to generate transit trips during off-peak periods (i.e., for restaurants, stores, and entertainment attractions), as well as during the peak commute periods.

---

[15] *TCRP Report 102: Transit-Oriented Development in the United States: Experiences, Challenges and Prospects* (2004)

CHAPTER 7

Marketing & Information Initiatives

Introduction

A widely used set of strategies and projects aimed at increasing ridership is marketing/promotional and information initiatives. The types of strategies—and specific actions/examples—included in this category are shown in Table 7-1. These types of strategies are generally intended to attract and retain riders by (1) informing them of the availability and benefits of using transit, (2) offering special incentives to try transit, and/or (3) informing them of service schedules and changes (both in advance and in real time). Thus, these strategies should address one or more of the following mode choice factors:

- Cost of using transit,
- Convenience,
- Service reliability,
- Perceived personal security/safety, and
- Perceived "image" of the system.

Guidance on the selection, design, and implementation of appropriate marketing/promotional and information strategies is provided below. This is followed by a section describing each type of strategy, including agency examples.

Design/Implementation Guidelines

Marketing, promotion, and information dissemination strategies are important in attracting riders to transit, educating them as to how to use it, and keeping them informed of any changes to the service. Thus, in addition to their role in promoting the usage of transit in general, these strategies should be key elements of all efforts to implement any other types of ridership strategy (e.g., introducing new service, adjusting existing service, changing fare levels, or introducing new payment options). Table 7-2 presents a checklist of the recommended steps an agency should consider in identifying and developing marketing, promotional, and information strategies.

Applicable Settings

As shown in the examples in Appendix A, various types of marketing/promotional and information strategies can be used in a range of service environments. However, some strategies or

Table 7-1. Types of marketing/promotional & information initiatives.

Type of Strategy	Specific Actions/Examples
Marketing/promotional initiatives	
Targeted marketing/promotions	New resident promotion; college student promotion, individualized marketing, tourist-oriented marketing
General marketing/promotions	agency image advertising, special promotions, cooperative advertising
Information improvements	
Improved printed informational materials	Easier to read printed system and route maps/schedules, newsletters/brochures
Improved customer information and assistance	Transit information center, in-station customer assistants
Automated transit traveler information	Pre-trip planning and en-route information, including real-time information

Table 7-2. Checklist—developing and implementing marketing/promotional/information initiatives.

	Key Steps/Activities to Consider	
	Evaluation of Existing Programs/Systems	

	Evaluate current marketing and information materials and programs
	   Identify goals, issues and constraints
	   Assess effectiveness of existing materials (e.g., maps/schedules, brochures)
	   Assess effectiveness of existing programs (e.g., campaigns, promotions, fare incentives)
	   Conduct peer agency review
	   Identify areas/opportunities for improvement	

	Evaluate current information dissemination systems/procedures
	   Identify goals, issues and constraints
	   Conduct peer agency review
	   Identify areas/opportunities for improvement	

	Identification of Strategy Options	

	Identify potential improvements to materials and programs
	   Identify market segments for potential targeted marketing campaigns and promotions
	   Identify types of improvements to printed materials (e.g., re ease of understanding)
	   Identify potential for cooperative advertising (e.g., with local media outlets)	

	Identify potential information improvements
	   Identify new methods/technologies (e.g., Internet-based trip planning, real time info at stops)
	   Identify other distribution options (e.g., on-board, in-station)
	   Identify customer service/assistance improvements	

	Market Research and Public Outreach	

	Conduct surveys/focus groups
	   Conduct survey of current riders (e.g., on-board/in-station)
	   Conduct survey of non-riders or infrequent riders (e.g., telephone)
	   Conduct focus groups of riders and non-riders
	   Analyze results of market research	

	Conduct public outreach/input
	   Meet with stakeholder groups (e.g., civic, government, business, institutional interest groups)
	   Conduct public meetings or open house sessions	

	Selection of Strategy(ies)	

	Select and design strategy(ies)
	   Evaluate options and select most appropriate strategy or combination of strategies
	   Design new materials or programs	

	Identify costs Estimate costs (capital, operating & maintenance) of strategies (design, implementation, operation)	
	Implementation of Strategy(ies)	
	Develop implementation plan	

	Implement strategy(ies)
	   Procure/install new software or equipment (if necessary)
	   Hire additional personnel (if necessary)
	   Develop new materials (do in-house or contract out)
	   Put strategy(ies) in place	

	Monitor effectiveness of strategy(ies)
	   Identify actual ridership impact
	   Conduct follow-up market research	

particular types of initiatives may not prove cost-effective in certain settings. Table 7-3 identifies which environments and modes are generally appropriate for each type of strategy; obviously, though, each specific type of initiative must be designed to reflect the needs, opportunities, and constraints that exist within the agency's environment.

Planning Activities

When thinking about any marketing or promotional initiative, it is important to develop a comprehensive plan. The plan should, at a minimum, include the following elements:

- The message and goals,
- The intended audience,
- The method of delivery, and
- A process for evaluating the success of the initiative.

The last element, though often neglected, is important. Knowing what works for its audience and what does not will save an agency time and money in future marketing efforts. As *TCRP Report 50: A Handbook of Proven Marketing Strategies for Public Transit* points out, even small agencies with few resources can follow some very basic evaluation procedures that greatly increase the value of the marketing effort. The agency should examine changes in ridership—and revenue—before, during, and following, the marketing campaign. For existing services, agencies can compare campaign-time ridership levels to those during the same time in the previous year. For a new service, ridership and revenue can be evaluated against the projected levels. If possible, the success of the campaign should also be evaluated based on changes in public perception of the agency. Through consistent surveying, changes in the perceived image of the agency can be detected.

Expected Ridership Response

As explained earlier in Chapter 2 of this report, *TCRP Report 95: Traveler Response to Transportation System Changes* summarizes the results of analyses of the nature of the impacts of various types of transit actions on demand. Chapter 11 of that report (*Transit Information and Promotion*) discusses the nature of the impacts on demand of marketing, information, and promotion efforts. The report notes, first of all, the limited data available on the ridership impact of specific marketing programs; despite the aforementioned importance of evaluating such initiatives, few agencies actually undertake comprehensive consumer tracking efforts, and "it is also difficult to monitor, measure and take into account the impact of other system changes and

Table 7-3. Applicable modes/settings for types of marketing/promotional and information initiatives.

Type of Strategy	Mode		Service Environment					
	Bus	Rail	Large Urban	Medium Urban	Small Urban	Rural	Suburb	CBD
Targeted marketing/promotions	+	+	+	+	+	o	+	+
General marketing/promotions	+	+	+	+	+	+	+	+
Improved printed informational materials	+	+	+	+	+	+	+	+
Improved customer information/assistance	+	+	+	+	+	o	+	+
Automated transit traveler information	+	+	+	+	o	o	+	+

Key: — = not applicable or inappropriate; o = applicable, but may not be cost-effective; + = applicable and appropriate

external events that may be occurring at the same time as the transit information and promotion programs" (p. 11-5).

Based on studies that have been conducted, the authors conclude that "the traveler response to transit information and promotion varies widely, both in extent and duration of ridership gains. Results are influenced by the utility and quality of the transit service product being marketed, by external circumstances, and by the type of promotion. While all types of transit information and promotion activities may help raise awareness of public transportation services, increases in ridership are most likely to occur within specific populations as the result of targeted programs, especially individualized efforts designed on the basis of market research findings, delineating particular needs and opportunities" (p. 11-5).

The different types of marketing, promotional, and information strategies are described in the following pages.

Marketing/Promotional Initiatives

Transit agencies use a range of types of marketing and promotional strategies in an effort to attract—and retain—riders; the basic types of efforts include the following:

- Targeted marketing/promotions (e.g., new resident promotion, college student promotion, individualized marketing, tourist-oriented marketing)
- General marketing/promotions (e.g., agency image advertising, special promotions, cooperative advertising)

The success of either of these types of initiatives can be enhanced by combining them with special fare incentives. These types of initiatives are described below, including agency examples of each.

Targeted Marketing/Promotions

Targeted marketing and promotions focus on a specific customer audience. The message or promotion is packaged to appeal to a particular market or market segment. The intended market might be defined by location of work or residence, occupation, leisure activity, age, and so forth. College students, new residents, seniors, employees at a particular worksite, shoppers, users of a particular transit service, and non-users of transit are common subjects for targeted marketing. Common methods of disseminating targeted messages include direct mailings and one-on-one promotions at work sites, events, and college campuses.

New Resident Promotions

New residents represent a great opportunity for transit agencies to increase ridership. When a person has just moved to a new area, he/she has neither established commuting patterns nor developed a perception of the local transit agency. Transit agencies can seize this potential by targeting new residents with a targeted marketing campaign. Agencies use direct mail to reach individuals at their new homes. Packets often include information about the transit system, and, typically, coupons for free rides that encourage people to try transit. Depending on the resources available, the agency can also tailor the information to focus on services available in the recipient's particular area. For example, Tri Delta Transit, in the San Francisco Bay area, took advantage of the rapid pace of local development to ensure that transit was automatically introduced to new residents. The agency convinced local government staff to require developers to provide new homeowners with a welcome packet that includes tailored transit information. The agency also distributes the packets to new renters in the area. Relocation packets distributed in San Jose (pictured in Exhibit 7-1) feature transit information along with other items.

Several transit agencies have also implemented a different type of strategy targeted to home buyers, by participating in Fannie Mae's "Smart Commute Initiative." This strategy, which can also be categorized as a partnership, involves the provision of financial incentives for the purchase of houses located in close proximity to transit service. Cities such as Nashville (TN), Columbus (OH), and Charlotte (NC) are participating in the program, which was initiated in July 2003. Essentially, a portion of the prospective home buyer's potential transportation savings can be added to his/her qualifying income; this allows the borrower to qualify for a higher mortgage. The transit agencies in each city offer different types of additional incentives as well; for instance, COTA (Columbus) provides free passes to participating home buyers.

Exhibit 7-1. San Jose relocation packet.

Chicago Transit Authority
New Mover program
large urbanized (over 1,000,000)

Chicago Transit Authority implemented a program to encourage new residents to use CTA's services. Each new resident receives a package containing a guide to CTA, timetables for the nearest rail station, and a transit card preloaded with fares for a roundtrip. CTA estimates that approximately 1 to 3 % of new ridership results from this program.

College Student Promotions

College students are a great potential market for transit agencies for a variety of reasons. Many students do not have private automobiles and are thus dependent on alternative means of transportation. Students are also more likely to use transit at under-utilized times (e.g., non-commuting daytime hours or late evening hours). In addition, college students typically have very limited budgets and find free or discounted services very appealing. Finally, students are young and may not have formed the same attitudes toward transit that older generations have. By getting college students "hooked" on transit, there is a great potential to create lifetime transit users. Many agencies recognize these facts and engage in targeted marketing campaigns directed at college students.

If the transit agency has established a relationship with a university, it can seek the university's help in marketing transit to the students. As discussed in other chapters, many agencies provide service specifically targeted to the university community, as well as reduced fare or pass arrangements. If a transit agency redesigns an existing route to better serve a university campus, for instance, it should take advantage of the university's pre-existing information dissemination network to market that service. Through e-mail, bulletin boards, and school papers, the new service can be marketed directly to the target audience at little cost to the transit agency. Obviously, any special promotional materials should highlight the availability of transit to students. Some agencies therefore provide a rider's guide and transit service information for distribution to freshmen at orientation. (The cover of UCLA's commuting guide for students, which alerts them to the many available transportation alternatives, is pictured in Exhibit 7-2).

Exhibit 7-2. UCLA Commuter Guide.

> **Greater Portland Transit District**
> **University of Southern Maine Student Awareness Program**
> *small urbanized (50,000 - 200,000)*
>
> In 2000, the Greater Portland Transit District launched an awareness campaign to introduce the students of the University of Southern Maine to transit. The campaign featured an 8-month introductory period of free rides, advertisements in the campus paper, and a substantial on-campus presence at events throughout the period. The University contributed substantially to the cost of advertising and promoting the program. After the introductory period, a 50-cent student fare was introduced, and ridership remained high. Ridership continues to increase on the University routes by 2 to 3% annually.

Individualized Marketing

A technique that can be used to target transit non-users is individualized marketing. This method takes a personalized approach and informs individuals of what their alternative transportation options are for the trips that they typically make. While this technique may require more resources than others described here, it has the potential to be very effective. The FTA conducted a pilot project in Portland, OR, and found that as a result of the effort, use of transit and other "environmentally friendly" modes in the targeted area increased by 27%. The FTA is now sponsoring four more individualized marketing demonstrations: WTA in Bellingham, WA; TTA in Durham, NC; Sacramento (CA) RTD; and GCRTA in Cleveland, OH. This basic technique has been applied more widely in Europe and Australia; *TCRP Report 95* notes that participating transit operators in Germany saw ridership transit increases between 10 and 30% among the targeted market segments.

Tourist-Oriented Marketing

In many locations, tourists represent a key potential market segment. Transit can be an attractive local travel option for out-of-town visitors: it is generally less costly than rental cars or taxis and may well offer easier access to local attractions. The tourist market also represents a great opportunity for partnerships. Many local businesses, such as restaurants, hotels, and retail outlets are seeking business from tourists as well. If transit can bring more tourists to these destinations, the businesses may be willing to share the costs of promotion.

When DART introduced the downtown trolley to Wilmington (mentioned in Chapter 5), it perceived that a key segment of the market for this service would be tourists. In anticipation of this, DART created the "Trolley Ambassador" relationship with forty local businesses. Tourists can pick up the credit card-sized route maps (pictured in Exhibit 7-3) at any of these locations. The route maps display both the trolley route and the tourist destinations along the route. Local hotels feature the trolley in the area guides they provide to guests, and convention venues pass out the trolley guide to attendees. This partnership promotion has proven very successful in drawing tourists to the downtown area.

Exhibit 7-3. Credit card-size route map.

General Marketing/Promotions

General marketing and promotions are designed to appeal to a broad audience, rather than any particular market segment. Goals may include providing information about transit, improving the public image of the transit agency, encouraging non-riders to try transit, and building public support for transit. A wide variety of methods may be used to disseminate general marketing messages, including mass mailings, newspapers (inserts or ads), television ads, radio ads, and the internet (e.g., the agency's website, as well as links to other sites such as local government or chambers of commerce). Examples of types of general marketing initiatives are described below.

> **Corpus Christi Regional Transportation Authority**
> **Harbor Ferry Ridership Sponsorship Program**
> *medium urbanized (200,000 - 1,000,000)*
>
> Corpus Christi RTA launched a creative promotional partnership with local businesses to sponsor its Harbor Ferry service. During the summer tourist season, the ferry shuttles passengers between the downtown and the tourist area. Local businesses agree to sponsor free ferry services on a particular day or weekend. In exchange, they can place advertisements on the ferry and at the ferry stops, and the RTA incorporates the business into their marketing efforts. During the first year of this program, ferry ridership increased by 42%.

Image Advertising

A transit agency can use image advertising to improve the perception of the agency, and transit in general, within the community. This type of marketing is typically directed at both transit users and non-users, although the real focus may well be on non-users. The hope is that image advertising can entice non-users to try transit. It can also help develop a positive attitude toward transit among the tax-paying public.

> **Chautauqua Area Regional Transit System**
> **Marketing To Increase Name Recognition**
> *rural area (Under 50,000)*
>
> In 2003, CARTS began a marketing campaign designed to improve its visibility and image. As part of this effort, CARTS held a system logo re-design contest at local area high schools. It also coordinated an educational outreach program to better inform other agencies and county departments about CARTS services. The transit agency also developed distinct flyers that specifically targeted college students, seniors, and hotel guests. The initiative was implemented at very little cost to the agency, and has served to increase awareness and ridership.

Transit agencies often promote their public image through *newsletters* such as Greater Cleveland RTA's "Riders Digest," Chicago Transit Authority's "Going Places," VIA Metro's (San Antonio) "Rider Reader," or OCTA's Transit Talk (see Exhibit 7-4). Newsletters are an excellent tool because they can be simultaneously informational and promotional. They can help inform riders of route or fare changes, while also promoting new or underutilized services. Newsletters also serve to personalize the connection between the public and the transit agency; through feature articles and human interest stories, the transit agency can project itself in a friendlier light.

Branding is another method of image advertising. A transit agency can update its image with a new logo, a new name, new slogans, new colors on the vehicles, and so forth. This strategy can also help to create a unified perception of a system that may contain many distinct elements. A recent example of an image advertising effort is CTA's comprehensive marketing campaign to reinforce its brand identity. One element of the campaign was a new slogan: "CTA – Take it Everywhere." The agency used this slogan to remind the public that CTA (bus and rail) is a "convenient and reliable way to get everywhere." Agencies often choose to engage the public in the branding effort, by holding a logo or slogan design.

Exhibit 7-4. OCTA newsletter.

> **Connecticut Department of Transportation**
> **Statewide Transit Branding Project (Unified Paint Scheme)**
> *medium urbanized (200,000 - 1,000,000)*
>
>
>
> In the late 1990s, the Connecticut Department of Transportation launched a branding campaign to unify services statewide under the name CTTRANSIT. As part of this effort, all new buses were painted with the CTTRANSIT logo and distinctive colors. As a result of the unified look, system identity and visibility has improved dramatically. This is an ongoing effort that will eventually incorporate other public transportation modes and enhanced customer service.

Special Promotions

Transit agencies often use special promotional efforts to get non-riders to try their services. On the national level, for instance, the American Public Transportation Association (APTA) has promoted "Try Transit Week," which encourages people to use transit at least once during the week, instead of driving alone in a car. Agencies across the country use such opportunities to raise awareness about the benefits of transit in their own communities. Agencies often offer special promotions (such as reduced or free fares) during these events to encourage non-users to try transit. More recently, APTA has encouraged the celebration of "Communities in Motion Day" (see Exhibit 7-5). This effort was designed to build support for public transportation by promoting the benefits transit provides for communities. On this day, agencies held information sessions, community discussions, raffles, fare-free days, and other promotional activities to raise transit awareness.

Exhibit 7-5. APTA promotional ad.

> **Utah Transit Authority**
> **Five Free Rides Campaign**
> *medium urbanized (200,000 – 1,000,000)*
>
> In an effort to boost summer ridership, the Utah Transit Authority introduced the "Five Free Rides" promotion. By contacting a call center or visiting the transit agency's website, citizens could request five free all-day passes to ride the system's buses. This promotion was successful in getting non-users of transit to try the buses; over 1/3 of coupon requests came from citizens who were not regular bus riders. Overall bus ridership rose by more than 2%

Independent of such events, agencies have successfully advertised the overall benefits (particularly economic and environmental) of using transit in their own promotional efforts. Recently, agencies have found that rising gas prices have produced "free" marketing for transit. Media coverage of the high cost of private automobile usage has naturally turned the spotlight on the public transportation alternative. As reported in a recent *Passenger Transport* article, many agencies have used this to their advantage in attracting new riders.[1] For example, the Greater Cleveland RTA (see Exhibit 7-6) has launched a marketing campaign entitled

Exhibit 7-6. GCRTA ad.

---

[1] Michael Salmon, "As Fuel Prices Climb, Transit Ridership Grows," *Passenger Transport*, April 25, 2005, p. 1.

"Fuel Crisis '05: Take a Stand. Take RTA," which "humorously depicts the desperate behavior of commuters pushed over the edge by high gas prices."[2] GCRTA has added commuter cost savings calculations to its website, to show how economical it is to use transit. The agency's ridership in early 2005 was reportedly 6% higher than ridership in the same period of the previous year.

> **Northeast Illinois Railroad Corporation (Metra)**
> **Transit Awareness Outreach**
> *large urbanized (over 1,000,000)*
>
> Metra recently launched a program to raise awareness of Metra services in the Chicago area. Metra hosted Transit Events at corporations throughout the region. Staff from Metra and other transit agencies were made available to answer questions and provide information to employees in the lobbies and cafeterias of workplaces. This program has helped to boost Metra's reverse commute ridership and improve its public image.

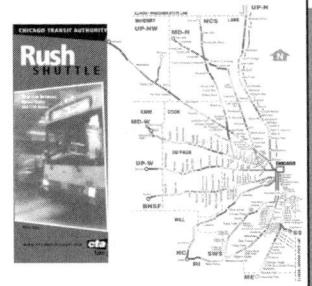

Cooperative Advertising

Given the scarcity of funds for marketing efforts, transit agencies should do everything they can to take advantage of "free" or shared-cost advertising. Developing solid relationships with various media outlets can be an extremely effective and low-cost way of getting out the message. In *TCRP Report 50: A Handbook of Proven Marketing Strategies for Public Transit*, the authors discuss the importance of dealing with the media in a consistent, coordinated way. Designating staff to handle media relations is important, even for a small agency. Personal relationships between an agency and reporters can often lead to more positive coverage. The authors also suggest taking a proactive approach. Agencies should send materials to media outlets and call them with story ideas, instead of waiting for them to call. When backed by a solid relationship, the media can serve as an excellent partner in promoting transit.

> **Greater Cleveland Regional Transit Authority**
> **Shop Tops, Ride Home for Free**
> *large urbanized (over 1,000,000)*
>
> In 2001, the GCRTA began an innovative promotional partnership with Tops Friendly markets. Under the program, customers who travel to Tops on GCRTA's Community Circulators and purchase $15 in groceries on a Tops Bonus Card receive a free ride home. Shoppers display their RTA transfer at the checkout and are presented with a one-ride farecard for their return trip. This initiative has increased ridership on the circulators and boosted revenues for the grocery stores. The program is marketed via advertisements, route timetables, in-store signs, and public address announcements.

Partnering with private entities in marketing campaigns and promotions is another economically efficient method of advertising. Cooperative advertising is particularly appropriate for special events. For example, an agency might partner with a sports team to encourage people to attend games and travel there via transit. This could potentially alleviate pressure for parking availability (good for the team) and get more people to ride transit (good for the agency). Transit agencies can also use transit-friendly events, such as Earth Day and bike fairs, to promote their services.

Another type of cooperative effort seeks to join transit agencies with retail destinations. In partnership with the transit agency, a local merchant might offer discounted merchandise

---
[2] Ibid.

Exhibit 7-7.   EATRAN ad.

Exhibit 7-8.   Guaranteed ride home guide.

to holders of a transit pass or ticket. For example, when Eaton County Transportation Authority in Michigan launched its Summer Fun Pass program (see Exhibit 7-7) for youth, it sought out partnerships with 14 local businesses. These businesses agreed to offer discounts or giveaways to pass holders and, in exchange, the names of the businesses were printed on the pass. The businesses also contributed funds toward advertising the program. This type of program is beneficial to both parties, as it simultaneously encourages people to use transit and draws them into the destination retail area.

Finally, employers can be valuable promotional partners. Employers have built-in information distribution systems (such as e-mail and company newsletters) that can be very effective means of informing employees about transit services—as well as other TDM strategies (see Chapter 6). An example of a marketing program tailored to the commuter market is a Guaranteed-Ride-Home program (the cover to a guide for such a program is shown in Exhibit 7-8).

Information Improvements

Transit agencies use a range of types of informational materials and dissemination methods; the basic types of strategies include the following:

- Improved printed informational materials (e.g., printed system and route maps/schedules and on-board flyers or newsletters);
- Improved customer information and assistance (e.g., transit information center and in-station customer assistants); and
- Automated transit traveler information (e.g., pre-trip planning and en-route information, including real-time information).

These types of initiatives are described below, including agency examples.

Exhibit 7-9.   HART information center.

Improved Printed Informational Materials

Printed informational materials are designed to inform and educate the public about the availability of transit services and how to use them. The information can be very specific (i.e., route maps and schedules) or more general (e.g., on-board flyers or newsletters as described above). Materials can be posted or distributed at information or customer centers (such as HART's information center, shown in Exhibit 7-9) or distributed to passengers on board or in stations.

There are many ways to improve printed informational materials. Agencies can make the information usable by a wider range of potential riders by printing in multiple languages and using recognizable symbols. Agencies must also ensure that materials are accessible to individuals who have visual impairment, by providing (on request) Braille, large print, and even audio tape versions.[3] Materials can also be improved to show connections between different modes of service (even when that service comes from a different provider). This allows riders to more easily see how to make many potential trips using transit.

Printed materials are useful on their own, but are also needed to provide information about other types of strategies, including service changes or fare-related initiatives. Obviously, many of the above types of marketing and promotional strategies also involve some type of printed material.

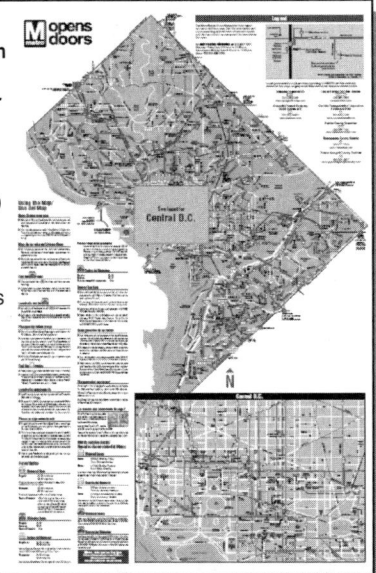

District of Columbia, Department of Transportation Bus Route Maps
medium urbanized (200,000 - 1,000,000)

In 2004, Washington D.C.'s Department of Transportation began installing more than 300 new maps at bus shelters throughout the city. The new large scale maps are customized for each individual shelter's location. The maps display all the routes serving that particular stop, as well as city-wide bus routes. Passengers can easily see the many destinations that can be reached by bus. It is hoped that the maps will also encourage transit non-users to try riding the buses.

Santa Maria Area Transit Bi-lingual Route Brochures
medium urbanized (200,000 - 1,000,000)

Santa Maria Area Transit recently revised its informational materials to encourage more ridership among the Spanish-speaking population. The three elements of this initiative were: revised route brochures featuring bilingual information, a comprehensive new bilingual Bus Book containing all route maps and timetables as well as rider information, and saturation of the Spanish mass media market including TV, radio, and print media.

---

[3] In fact, U.S. DOT's *Transportation for Individuals with Disabilities (Final Rule)*, Part 37, states that "The entity shall make available to individuals with disabilities adequate information concerning transportation services. This obligation includes making adequate communications capacity available, through accessible formats and technology, to enable users to obtain information and schedule service." Federal Register, Vol. 56, No. 173, p. 45640.

Improved Customer Information and Assistance

In addition to printed materials and automated information distribution methods (see the next section), the provision of "live" customer information and assistance services continues to be an important strategy. Typically, an individual can call a customer service line or visit an information center to inquire about service availability, schedules, and fares. Many transit agencies, when creating new transit centers or updating old ones, have sought to incorporate customer service operations into the design.

Exhibit 7-10. MBTA customer information agent.

Some agencies, particularly those with rail stations, also provide in-station (or transit center) customer assistants. In cities such as New York City and Chicago, for example, the transit agencies have taken advantage of the introduction of automated fare collection to improve in-station customer assistance. Since both the NYMTA and the CTA have eliminated tokens in favor of automated farecards, many of the former token clerks have been converted to station customer assistance agents. They wear distinctive uniforms and assist passengers by answering questions and helping with the automated fare machines. (An in-station customer information agent for the MBTA in Boston, which is in the process of installing an AFC system, is pictured in Exhibit 7-10).

> **Orange County Transportation Authority**
> **OCTA: Putting Customers First - Customer Service Changes**
> *large urbanized (over 1,000,000)*
>
> In 2003, the Orange County Transportation Authority launched a comprehensive campaign to improve customer service. Many elements of the initiative focused on improving the personal interactions between riders and customer information assistants. The improvements included expanding Customer Information Center hours and advertising information staff employment opportunities to transit riders, to increase the number of staff who are regular transit users.
> The agency also provided hands-on transit route training for customer information staff, to ensure that staff could successfully advise customers in the event that the automated trip planning system was unavailable. These improvements have contributed to an overall system ridership increase of 8.6% in the past year.
>
>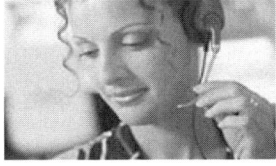

Automated Transit Traveler Information

Transit agencies' ability to deliver transit information has improved significantly over the past decade with the advent of (1) new technologies, such as automatic vehicle location (AVL) and advanced communications; and (2) new/improved dissemination mechanisms and media, such as the Internet, wireless application protocol (WAP), mobile telephones, and personal digital assistants (PDAs). The various automated forms of transit information are collectively referred to as transit traveler information or simply TTI. TTI can provide riders—and those considering using transit—comprehensive information about multiple modes (including traffic information) in one place or from one source and on a variety of media.[4]

---

[4] Additional information on TTI is available in several recent reports, including: *TCRP Report 92: Strategies for Improved Traveler Information* (2003) and *TCRP Synthesis Report 48: Real Time Bus Arrival Information Systems* (2003), and *TCRP Project J-09— eTransit: Electronic Business Strategies for Public Transportation—Advanced Features of Transit Web Sites* (2003).

The information provided via TTI can either be *static* (i.e., information on routes, schedules, or fares that may be updated periodically, but does not represent current service operating status) or *real-time* (i.e., depicting the current operational status of service). There are different ways to categorize TTI, including the type of information or the particular communication medium. However, the most common classification scheme is one that simply groups TTI services according to the stage of the journey at which the information is received: pre-trip versus en-route; in-vehicle strategies are also often categorized separately. Strategies of each type are delivered via technologies such as the Internet, dynamic message signs (DMS), and wireless mobile devices.

Pre-Trip Transit Information

Pre-trip information is accessed by riders before embarking on their trips. It covers an array of areas such as route alignments, schedules, arrival times, delays, itinerary planning (i.e., trip planning), and multi-modal information. This information includes timetables for individual train and bus routes and system maps and schematics. Hence, pre-trip transit information plays a critical role in the user's decision on which mode to take, what route(s) to take, when to make the trip, and how to get to his/her destination.

Automated pre-trip information can be accessed in a number of ways, including personal computer (i.e., to access the Internet), telephones (either land line or mobile), pagers, PDAs, and kiosks (i.e., in transit facilities or elsewhere; these can either contain pre-installed information or can be used to access the Internet). Websites accessible by customers using screen reader software facilitates transit usage by individuals with visual impairments.[5] Examples of web pages from two agencies' trip planning websites are shown in Exhibits 7-11 and 7-12.

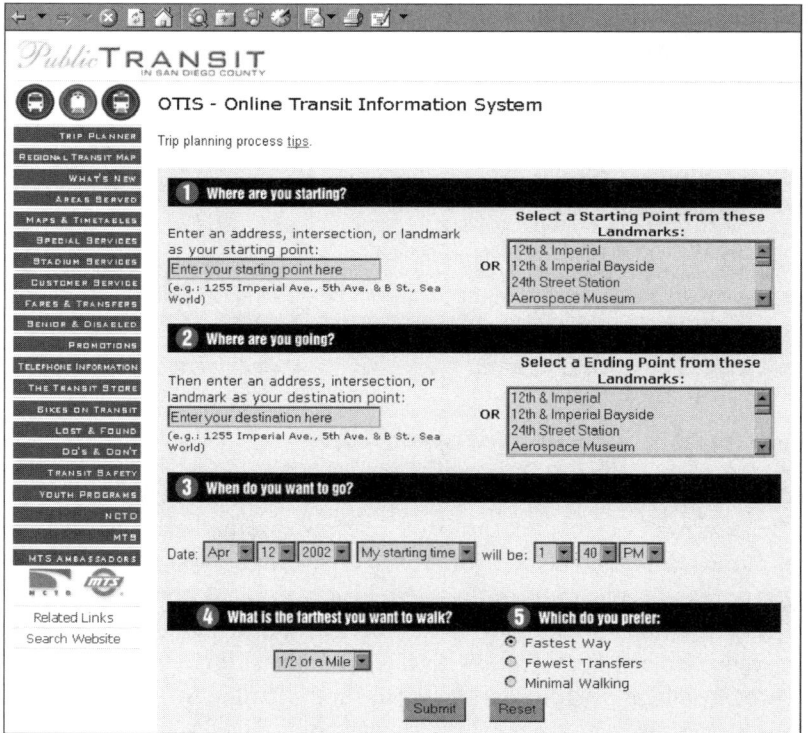

Exhibit 7-11. San Diego Transit's itinerary planning input page.

---

[5]Examples of screen reader software include such products as JAWS Screen Reader Software (Freedom Scientific), Window-Eyes (GW Micro) and Window Bridge (Syntha Voice).

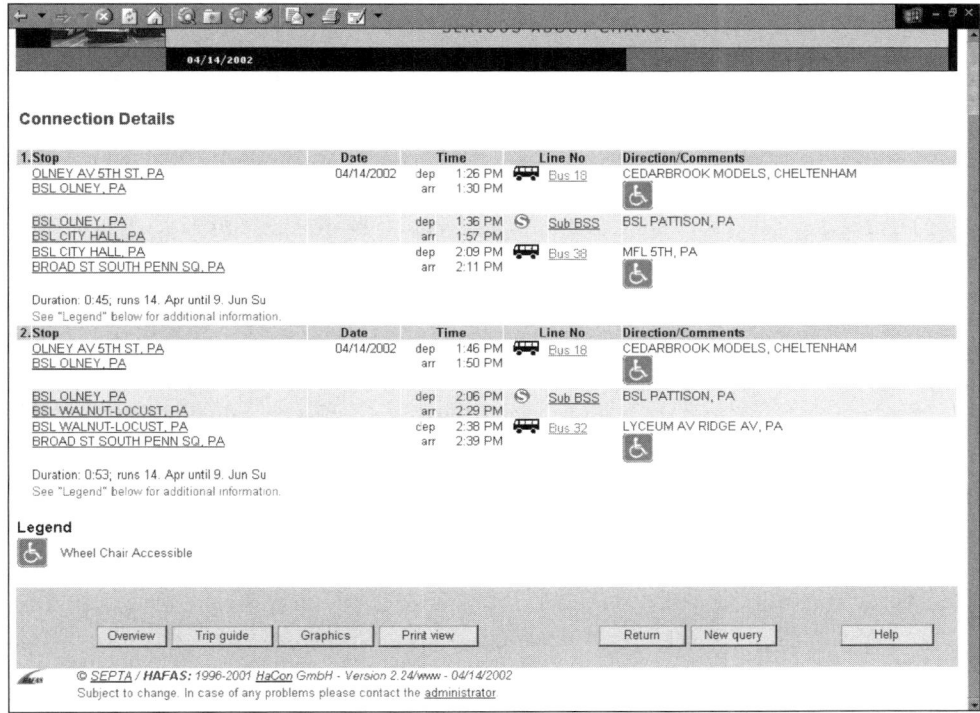

Exhibit 7-12. SEPTA TransitQuest itinerary details.

En-Route (and In-Terminal/Wayside) Transit Information

The importance of providing transit information does not stop once the traveler embarks on his/her trip. Quite often, and for various reasons, transit vehicles do not run according to the pre-trip information the traveler has received. En-route travelers may experience anxiety if their vehicles do not arrive on time according to the schedule, they are not sure where to go to catch their intended vehicle, or if they have missed the last vehicle (or do not know if they missed the last vehicle). Providing en-route transit information plays a significant role in keeping travelers informed about the status of their vehicle, reducing their anxiety, and directing them to the right stops, platforms, and bays.

Real-Time Information

Real-time or dynamic information informs riders of the current status of a particular route or line, including updates on service delays or diversions, as well as estimated vehicle arrival and departure times for stops along the routes. Obviously, such information must be updated frequently. At bus stops and in rail stations, real-time updates can be delivered to riders via DMSs, video monitors, and/or public address systems. However, updated vehicle arrival time and delay information can also be included on the agency's website or automated telephone answering system—or perhaps a local cable television channel. As these systems become increasingly interactive, an agency might consider disseminating updates or alerts to subscribing passengers via e-mail to personal computers or text messages to pagers, mobile phones, or PDAs.

The majority of real-time bus arrival information systems are based on the use of data from global positioning system (GPS) based AVL systems, although other types of AVL systems (e.g., signpost and transponder systems) are also being used in some real-time systems. The location data generated from an AVL system is used together with other information, such as current and historical traffic conditions, as well as real-time operations data from the last several buses that passed a particular stop, to predict the arrival time of the next bus at a particular stop.

In-vehicle Transit Information

In-vehicle transit information provides important information to travelers while they are on a bus or train. In-vehicle information provided by automated annunciator systems helps transit agencies comply with the Americans with Disabilities Act (ADA) by informing passengers of upcoming stations and major bus-stop locations in both text and audio formats. Furthermore, in-vehicle information reassures passengers that they have taken the right vehicle and route. On-board displays are also used for informing passengers about transfer points, service disruptions, or other events.

Most transit operators that are implementing these systems are supplying some combination of audible and visual information on next stop, major intersection, and transfer points to achieve both objectives. Two primary media are used: automated audible annunciators and in-vehicle displays. Both can communicate location-related information to customers based on location data from the AVL system, typically processed using an on-board microprocessor that is often used to support other on-board systems.

Another development is integrating bus destination signs with AVL systems to ensure that destination information display for waiting passengers is accurate. This is particularly important on multi-route corridors or multiple-branch routes. This integration takes the responsibility away from the vehicle operator by automating destination sign changes with the AVL/CAD system. Perhaps the most sophisticated examples of in-vehicle information involve transit agencies that are enhancing their fleet management systems so that passengers who are already on board can request and get confirmation on transfers to other transit services. This technology, called transfer connection protection (TCP) is being deployed in several agencies in the United States.

The technologies that can be used for accessing TTI can be categorized as follows:

- **Non-Interactive Displays**—These devices can be divided into DMSs at bus stops and train stations, DMSs on board vehicles (automated annunciation system signage), and video monitors. DMSs are more popular than video monitors as they come in a variety of shapes and sizes and are more versatile. Video monitors and wayside DMSs are mainly used to display arrival times, bay information, and service delays, while on-board DMSs are mainly utilized for announcing and displaying next-stop information. (An example of a DMS, from LACMTA, is shown in Exhibit 7-13)

Exhibit 7-13. LACMTA dynamic message sign.

- **Kiosks**—Kiosks are being deployed at major bus centers, train stations, and other public places such as hotels, airports, and commercial centers. The single most important advantage of kiosks is that they are interactive devices. This feature allows the users to access the information they need in a relatively short time. Moreover, kiosks can provide an infinite amount of information when they are connected to the Internet, by providing links to a host of sites like weather, traffic, and other local information sites. (An example of a kiosk, from Denver RTD, is shown in Exhibit 7-14.)

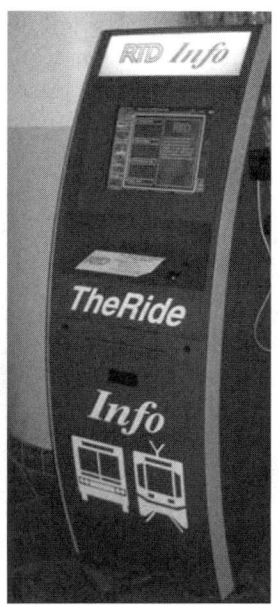

Exhibit 7-14. Denver RTD kiosk.

- **Personal Communications Devices**—This category includes traditional land-line phone and wireless devices such as cellular phones, pagers, and PDAs. Wireless devices are not limited to accessing real-time information but are also being used to provide static schedule information (e.g., providing transit schedules that can be downloaded to a subscriber's PDA, or enabling use of a cell phone to receive a trip itinerary).
- **Internet and E-mail Services**—Through the Internet, users can access a variety of TTI at any time to obtain schedules, real-time arrival information, itineraries, and other TTI. E-mail services, on the other hand, are usually limited to information on delays, incidents, emergencies, or real-time arrival information. Furthermore, unlike the Internet, e-mails are not interactive and are one-way messages. (An example of a page from Portland Tri-Met's Transit Tracker website, is shown in Exhibit 7-15.)

While many transit agencies lack the resources to consider implementing the more sophisticated information options, a growing number are automating at least the basic types of information on routes, schedules, and fares (e.g., through establishment of an

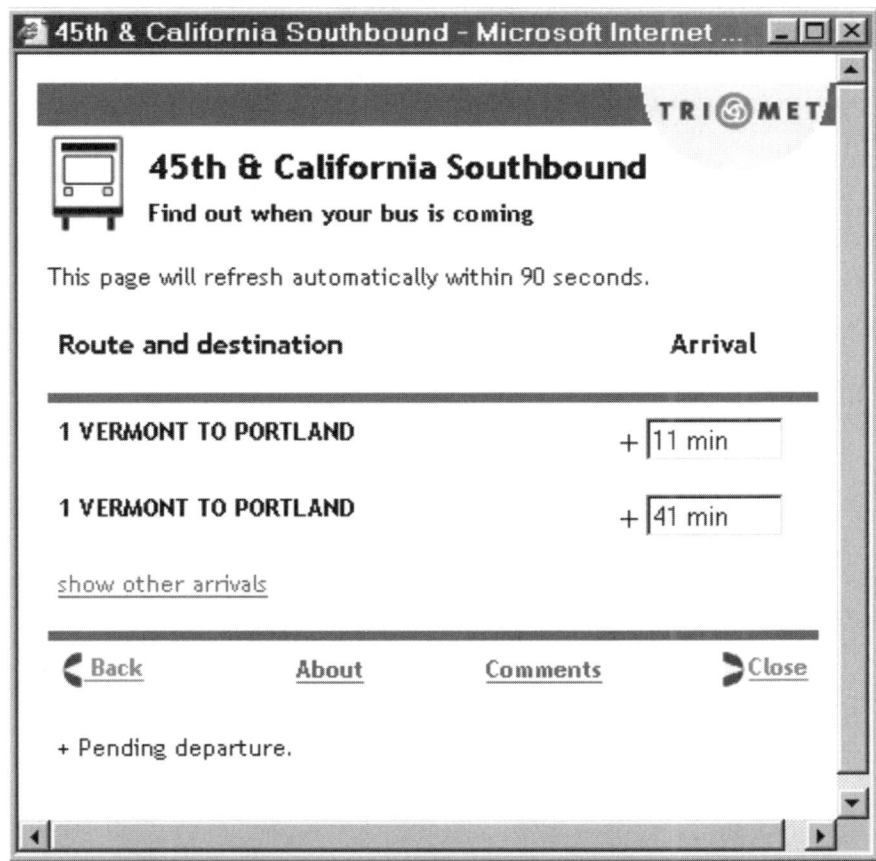

Exhibit 7-15. Tri-Met transit tracker website dynamic message sign.

agency website or perhaps including their information on a municipal or county website). As more and more agencies are able to take advantage of these emerging applications to disseminate up-to-date—and even real-time—information on the services they offer, they will clearly improve their ability to attract and retain riders.

VISTA
Implementation of a Countywide Bus Tracking and Arrival Prediction System
medium urbanized (200,000 - 1,000,000)

The Ventura Intercity Service Transit Authority recently implemented a countywide bus tracking and arrival prediction system. 100 buses were equipped with GPS tracking devices to monitor locations. Riders can check bus progress and estimated arrival times via the web. Riders waiting at transfer points throughout the county can see predicted arrival times on electronic signs. This service contributed to a 15% ridership increase in 2004.

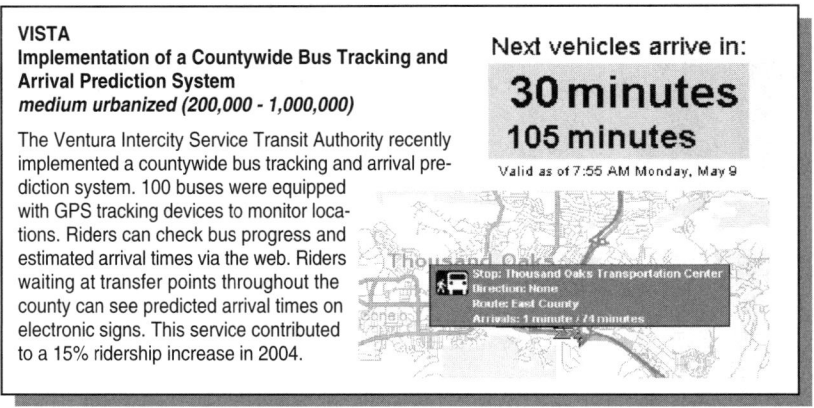

Tompkins Consolidated Area Transit
TCAT Trip Planning Interactive Website
rural area (Under 50,000)

In 2002, Tompkins Consolidated Area Transit of Ithaca, NY, added trip planning features to its website. Riders select their origin and destination, as well as date and time of travel. Riders can also choose from a number of preferences, including mode and accessibility. The system will display the best options available, which can be sorted by time, fare, and number of transfers. This project contributed to 3.8% increase in fixed route ridership between 2002 and 2003.

CHAPTER 8

Fare Collection/Structure Initiatives

Introduction

A widely used set of strategies, actions and initiatives that can contribute to efforts to increase ridership is fare collection/fare structure initiatives. The types of strategies—and specific actions/examples—included in this category are shown in Table 8-1. These types of strategies are generally intended to attract and retain riders by improving the quality of transit service or by making the price of transit use more competitive with the costs of using an automobile or other modes. Thus, each strategy should address one or more of the following mode choice factors:

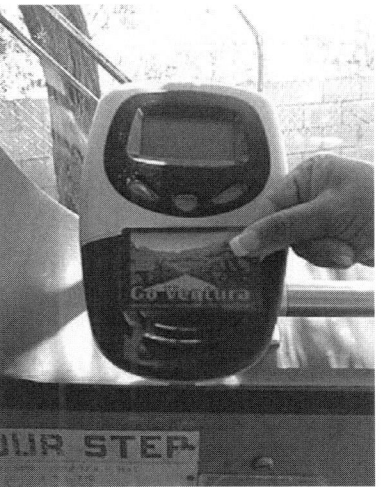

- Convenience,
- Cost of using transit, and
- Perceived "image" of the system.

Guidance on the development of appropriate fare-related strategies is provided below. This is followed by a section describing each type of strategy, including agency examples.

Design/Implementation Guidelines

The basic planning activities and types of considerations for fare-related initiatives are described below. Table 8-2 presents a checklist of the recommended steps an agency should consider in identifying and developing strategies within this category.

Applicable Settings

As indicated in Table 8-3, most fare collection/structure strategies are potentially applicable within any type of mode or service environment. One strategy, regional payment integration, will not be applicable in all locations (i.e., if the agency does not directly interface with any other agencies) and may not prove cost-effective in most rural areas. Moreover, smaller agencies may not find it cost-effective to provide expanded fare media distribution/reload options. As with other types of strategies, each specific action must be designed to reflect the agency's particular needs and constraints.

Table 8-1. Types of fare collection/fare structure initiatives.

Type of Strategy	Specific Actions/Examples
Fare collection improvements	
Improved payment convenience	Automated fare collection, new prepaid fare options, expanded fare media distribution/reload options
Regional payment integration	Regional smart card program
Fare structure changes	
Fare structure simplification	Elimination of fare zones; elimination of express or rail surcharge
Fare reduction	Deeply discounted options; reduced base fare; free transfers, free fare zone

Planning Activities

In identifying possible fare collection and fare structure changes, an agency must separately consider each of these areas (as indicated in Table 8-2), but it is also useful to consider the interrelationships between the two: the nature of the fare structure can affect decisions regarding a particular type of fare collection technology and, conversely, the selection of automated fare payment facilitates consideration of a range of new types of payment options. Ideally, policy goals and constraints should guide decisions in both areas, and planning for changes should be an iterative process.

Realistically, though, the most common approach is to make decisions on fare collection and fare structure independent of each other. Typically, an agency procures a new fare collection system and then reevaluates the fare structure and types of payment options offered. The key review/design processes an agency might follow in each area are summarized below.

Fare Collection System Design Process

The following process is often used by transit agencies in selecting a new fare collection technology and developing a conceptual design for a new/modified fare collection system. (This list represents an expansion of the fare collection aspects of the checklist shown in Table 8-2):

- **Identify agency goals, issues and constraints**—Gather input through review of any policy statements and working memoranda, as well as interviews with management/staff representing various agency functions (including administration, operations, finance, revenue management/accounting, planning, analysis, marketing/communications, customer service, and maintenance), and possibly with key Board members.
- **Conduct peer agency review**—Review experiences of selected other transit agencies that have previously implemented various technologies and methods that might be considered here.
- **Identify problem areas and opportunities for improvement**—Conduct an assessment of the current fare system and, based on the findings of the above tasks, identify potential areas of improvement.
- **Identify and evaluate payment/collection, technology, and equipment options (including fare media distribution/reload options)**—Develop screening criteria and conduct a review/ assessment of the alternative types of payment methods, technologies (e.g., paper media, magnetic farecards, and smartcards) and equipment (e.g., fareboxes, ticket vending machines, and faregates) the agency could consider.
- **Develop conceptual design**—Based on the above tasks, develop a conceptual design for a new system that addresses the agency's needs and goals. This should include a comparison of the benefits/costs of purchasing a totally new system versus upgrading the existing system

Table 8-2. Checklist—Developing and implementing fare-related initiatives.

Key Steps/Activities	
Fare Collection System Design Process	

Conduct needs assessment of fare collection system
    Identify goals, issues and constraints
    Conduct peer agency review
    Identify problem areas and opportunities for improvement	

Identify/evaluate fare collection options
    Identify payment/collection options (e.g., proof-of-payment, off-board payment)
    Identify technology options (e.g., magnetic farecard and smart card)
    Identify fare media distribution/reload options (e.g., autoload)
    Evaluate options	

Selection of strategy
    Develop conceptual design
    Identify costs of new/upgraded system
    Develop implementation plan	

Implement selected strategy
    Procure new equipment
    Hire additional personnel (if necessary) or train existing personnel
    Develop informational/marketing materials regarding strategy(ies)	

Fare Structure Development Process	

Evaluate current fare structure
    Identify goals, issues and constraints
    Identify ridership and revenue trends
    Conduct peer agency review
    Identify problem areas and opportunities for improvement	

Identify fare structure options
    Identify fare strategy options (e.g., elimination of zones or surcharges)
    Identify pricing options (e.g., reduction of base fare, free fare area, free transfers, discounts)	

Conduct market research/public outreach
    Conduct survey of current riders (e.g., on-board/in-station)
    Conduct survey of non-riders or infrequent riders (e.g., telephone)
    Conduct focus groups of riders and non-riders
    Meet with stakeholder groups (e.g., civic, government, business, institutional interest groups)
    Conduct public meetings or open house sessions	

Evaluate fare structure scenarios
    Develop fare ridership/revenue model
    Develop & evaluate alternative fare structure scenarios
    Select fare policy/structure modifications
    Develop implementation plan	

Implement selected strategy
    Procure new equipment or materials (if any)
    Hire additional personnel (if necessary) or train existing personnel
    Develop informational/marketing materials regarding strategy(ies)	

Monitor performance of strategy
    Identify actual ridership impact
    Make any necessary operational adjustments	

Table 8-3. Applicable modes/settings for types of fare collection/structure initiatives.

Type of Strategy	Mode		Service Environment					
	Bus	Rail	Large Urban	Medium Urban	Small Urban	Rural	Suburb	CBD
Improved payment convenience	+	+	+	+	+	O	+	+
Regional payment integration	+	+	+	+	+	O	+	+
Fare structure simplification	+	+	+	+	+	+	+	+
Fare reduction	+	+	+	+	+	+	+	+

Key: — = not applicable or inappropriate; O = applicable, but may not be cost-effective; + = applicable and appropriate

(e.g., replacing outmoded components and perhaps adding automated technology capabilities). The conceptual design should address such issues as data requirements, software/communications requirements, and labor/organizational implications of the new system.
- **Identify costs of new/upgraded system**—Develop detailed estimates of the operating and maintenance and capital costs of the new system; this should include annualized and lifecycle costs for both the upgrade and new purchase options.
- **Develop implementation plan**—Identify the steps needed for procurement and installation of the new/upgraded system, including final design, specifications, selection and award, installation, marketing, and training.

Once the agency has decided on a particular strategy, it can proceed with procurement and implementation.

Fare Structure Development Process

The following process is often used by transit agencies in developing fare policy/structure changes (This list represents an expansion of the fare structure aspects of the checklist shown in Table 8-2):

- **Identify agency goals, issues, and constraints**—Gather input through review of any policy statements and working memoranda, as well as interviews with management/staff representing various agency functions (including administration, operations, finance, revenue management/accounting, planning, analysis, marketing/communications, and customer service) and possibly with key Board members.
- **Identify ridership and revenue trends**—Review data and identify the agency's ridership and revenue trends over the past several years; also identify the impacts of past fare structure changes.
- **Conduct peer agency review**—Review fare structures of selected other transit agencies with similar operating characteristics.
- **Identify problem areas and opportunities for improvement**—Conduct an assessment of the current fare structure and, based on the findings of the above tasks, identify potential areas of improvement.
- **Identify fare strategy and pricing options**—Identify options for each fare structure element (e.g., base fare, transfers, pass types, multi-ride options, and reduced fare options) and the range of price levels that could be considered for each element.
- **Conduct market research/public outreach**—In order to identify potential reactions of riders (and possibly non-riders) to possible fare changes (e.g., to develop elasticity figures for inclusion in a fare model), it may be useful to conduct surveys. An alternative is to conduct focus groups and/or other types of public outreach (e.g., stakeholder meetings, public meetings, or open houses).
- **Develop fare ridership/revenue model**—In order to estimate the ridership and revenue impacts of alternative fare structure scenarios, develop an elasticity-based fare model (development of elasticity figures is discussed below, under **Expected Ridership Response**).
- **Develop and evaluate alternative fare structure scenarios**—Develop alternative fare structure scenarios (i.e., combinations of fare strategies, payment methods, and pricing levels for each fare structure element). Evaluate the scenarios based on ridership/revenue impacts (from the fare model) and qualitative criteria (based on fare policy goals).
- **Select fare policy/structure modifications**—Based on the above evaluation, select fare structure modifications that best address the agency's fare policy goals and needs.
- **Develop implementation plan**—Identify the steps needed for implementation of the recommended changes, including design/production of new payment options, marketing, and training.

Once the agency has decided on a particular strategy, it can proceed with implementation.

Cost/Revenue Considerations

Fare Collection Changes

Fare collection equipment is often a customized product, with many factors influencing cost. Much fare collection equipment is built in response to specific orders, partly because each agency's requirements impose somewhat different design constraints—even if major modules or subassemblies are the same among several orders. Final configurations of even very similar equipment for different agencies are rarely identical. The price for any type of equipment is therefore sensitive to such factors as

- The equipment specifications for the individual agency, including performance requirements and features; this affects the amount of customization required for a product, and this customization can represent a substantial portion of the overall price;
- The quantities of the particular equipment being ordered;
- The extent to which the new equipment will have to interface with other types of equipment (e.g., automated passenger counters or automated vehicle location systems);
- The nature of the vendor selection and negotiation process (e.g., type of contract: low-bid, two-step, or negotiated);
- The timing of the procurement (relative to the procurement of similar equipment by other agencies—and therefore the extent of refinement of the technology);
- Warranty terms: warranties are generally for 1 year, but this period can be extended based on other clauses associated with equipment performance;
- Documentation requirements (i.e., striking a balance between what is offered as manufacturer's "standard" and degree of customization for the agency);
- Software requirements: some software customization is expected, but requests for additional functions, features, and reports will be considered extra and will increase the cost;
- Vehicle/facility modifications: the cost of modifications to vehicles, bus garages, or other facilities also need to be considered; and
- Americans with Disabilities Act (ADA) requirements: fare collection equipment must address ADA requirements; these include provision of sufficient room on buses to pass the farebox in a wheelchair, compliance with height requirements for buttons on vending machines, and accommodation of needs of riders with visual impairments in purchasing and using fare media.

While farebox system costs tend to vary much less than systems involving extensive infrastructure modification (e.g., rail systems with faregates and large numbers of TVMs), the above factors can still result in a range of costs.

The ultimate cost of a fare collection system change to an agency will also be affected by such issues as the following:

- Will there be any additional labor costs associated with the change (e.g., additional maintenance, revenue accounting, or customer service personnel)?
- Will there be any cost savings associated with the change (e.g., lower overall maintenance costs due to replacement of outmoded equipment or lower fare media distribution costs)?
- Will there be additional revenue due to better revenue accounting and control of fare evasion?

Fare Structure Changes

While there may be some costs associated with fare structure changes (e.g., designing and printing new fare media), the principal financial impact any agency must be concerned with is the potential loss of revenue. Fare structure strategies designed to produce increased ridership typically result in reduced revenue. However, as explained below, under Fare Reduction, a carefully designed deep discounting strategy, if paired with a base fare increase, can result in increases in both ridership and revenue.

Expected Ridership Response

The most widely used indicator of the expected ridership response to a particular type of fare change is *elasticity*.[1] Chapter 12 (*Transit Pricing and Fares*) of *TCRP Report 95: Traveler Response to Transportation System Changes*) notes that "practically all the known observed values of fare elasticities fall in the range between 0 and −1.0, which, in economic terms, means rider response to fare changes is inelastic. Thus, if a transit system wants to increase total fare revenues, it should increase fare levels, but expect some ridership loss" (p. 12-7). In fact, while elasticities have been found to display considerable variation in different locations and for different market groups, general fare elasticity "exhibits relative consistency when expressed as averages. The effect of bus fare increases and decreases equates on average to an arc fare elasticity about −0.40. The effect of heavy rail transit fare changes is typically much less: short-run HRT fare elasticities average about −0.17 to −0.18, or about half the bus fare elasticities in the same cities" (p. 12-6).

While many agencies use systemwide elasticity figures, others use a different elasticity for each mode or even different figures for individual submarkets. Elasticities can be estimated from several sources and using different types of formulas. The key types of sources include

- Times series analysis of an agency's historical ridership data; this often includes a regression analysis to isolate the effects of fare changes from other factors such as service changes, employment levels, or fuel prices;
- Before-after ("shrinkage") analysis for a particular fare change;
- Use of a demand function often on the basis of the results of stated preference surveys; and
- Review of industry experience, particularly for agencies of similar size and with similar characteristics.

The most common types of elasticity formulas are those known as point elasticity, shrinkage ratio, midpoint arc elasticity, and constant arc elasticity. For small fare changes (i.e., less than 10%), each formula should produce roughly the same elasticity. However, where larger changes are involved—or where there may be a decrease in the fare level—the midpoint or constant arc elasticity formulas are generally preferable. As mentioned above, elasticity is a key element of a fare ridership/revenue model.

The different types of fare-related strategies, actions, and initiatives are described on the following pages.

Fare Collection Improvements

As transit agencies increasingly adopt automated fare payment technologies, they are recognizing the potential to attract—and retain—riders by improving fare payment convenience, offering a broader range of payment options, and facilitating seamless travel within the region; the major types of improvements that agencies have deployed are

- **Improved payment convenience** (e.g., automated fare collection, new/expanded prepaid fare options, and expanded fare media distribution/reload options); and
- **Regional payment integration** (e.g., regional smartcard program).

These types of actions and initiatives are described below, including agency examples of each.

Improved Payment Convenience

As the fare system is the means by which a rider gains access to any transit service, it is important to make fare payment as convenient as possible. There are several aspects to fare payment convenience, including the types of available payment options, the methods for purchasing and

---

[1] For instance, a fare elasticity of "−0.3" means that a 10% increase in fare would be expected to result in a 3% ridership loss.

reloading these payment options, and the ease of use of the fare collection system. This section discusses the types and capabilities of automated fare collection technologies (i.e., magnetic farecards and smartcards) and the various types of fare media distribution/reload options. (Exhibit 8-1 shows the Go Ventura smartcard from Ventura County, CA)

Automated Fare Collection

An increasing number of transit agencies are implementing automated fare collection (AFC) systems based on magnetic farecard and/or smartcard technologies. The technologies can be described as follows:

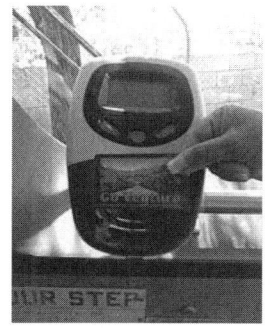

Exhibit 8-1. Go Ventura smartcard.

- A magnetic farecard carries a magnetic stripe, although there are two different types of magnetic media: read-only swipe cards and read-write stored-value cards. The read-only technology is similar to that used for credit or debit cards and allows the automatic determination of the validity of an unlimited-ride pass. In contrast, read-write technology, used with a ticket processing unit (TPU) or bus ticket validator (BTV), can accommodate stored-value and other automated payment options. A TPU can process an existing farecard, and some bus TPUs can be configured to issue some types of fare media (e.g., a transfer or a 1-day pass or even stored value). (The remainder of this discussion focuses on read-write technologies.)
- A smartcard carries a small computer chip and is thus capable of storing and processing a considerable amount of information. While there are two basic types of smartcards, contact and contactless, only the latter is considered appropriate for use in transit settings; contactless cards need not be inserted into a reader, but rather need only be held in close proximity—within an inch or so. Like the magnetic read-write technology, smartcards can accommodate stored-value and other automated payment options.

Both technologies can accommodate a wide range of payment options (discussed below). There are differences, however, in a number of parameters, including the cost of the cards themselves (magnetic media are much less expensive on a unit basis, although the cost of smartcards continues to drop), the cost of the card processing equipment (magnetic units tend to be more expensive to purchase and to maintain), data capacity and processing capability (considerably greater in the smartcard), ease of vending (magnetic media can be dispensed more readily, as discussed below), and ease of use (smartcards are particularly easy to use, especially for individuals with fine motor problems).

An agency considering implementing AFC should evaluate the relative advantages and disadvantages of the two technologies.[2] Most agencies opt for magnetics, although an increasing number of agencies are deciding to also include smartcard capabilities when they purchase new equipment. A few agencies have made the decision to forego magnetics when they implement new AFC systems. For instance, MARTA (Atlanta) is implementing an all-smartcard system; WMATA, which accepts both technologies on its rail system, has installed new fareboxes on its buses that read smartcards only; Exhibit 8-2 shows the WMATA SmarTrip card).

Exhibit 8-2. WMATA SmarTrip card.

New/Expanded Prepaid Fare Options

The use of AFC in general has influenced fare policy and has facilitated the introduction of a range of new payment options, as well as

---

[2]For additional discussion of the relative advantages and disadvantages of the technologies, as well as case studies of agencies that have adopted different types of systems, the reader is directed to TCRP Reports 32 and 94.

the opportunity for establishment of new types of fare media distribution methods; the latter are discussed below. Some agencies have used electronic media to essentially automate their existing options, while others have totally revamped their fare structures with the installation of electronic technology. The CTA, for example, took the former approach, replacing its discounted tokens with stored value (with a purchase bonus) and converting its passes from fixed calendar periods to a "rolling" (i.e., activate on first use) basis. The NYMTA represents the most graphic example of the latter approach, as it moved from the most basic fare structure in the industry—featuring no multi-ride discounts, prepaid passes, or discounted transfers—to an automated system (MetroCard; see Exhibit 8-3) that includes stored value (with a purchase bonus), several types of rolling passes, and free intermodal transfers; as discussed at the end of this chapter, these changes combined to result in a substantial ridership increase.

Exhibit 8-3. NYMTA MetroCard.

The basic payment options possible with electronic fare media and their purchase parameters can be summarized as follows:

- **Value-based or trip-based options**—These can be either *user-encoded* or *pre-encoded* (with a fixed amount). Agencies vary in their requirements for a minimum initial payment for user-encoded cards.
- **Time-based options**—These can either allow unlimited-rides (during the specified period) or be capped at a certain number of rides (during the specified period). The key pass development related to automated payment has been the conversion of fixed time period passes (e.g., "September" or "September 16–30") to rolling passes good for a specified number of days (e.g., "31 days" or "14 days"), or perhaps even a certain number of hours (e.g., "24 hours" or "4 hours"); an example of a rolling pass is shown in Exhibit 8-4. Such passes are activated the first time they are used. This increases the rider's flexibility considerably; for example, a rider can buy 4 weeks' worth of 7-day passes, rather than a single 30-day pass if he/she will be on vacation for a week during the month. The use of rolling passes can also reduce the administrative burden on the agency, since pass purchases no longer occur solely within a short time period (e.g., at the end of a month or during the first few days of the next month). Agencies are increasingly utilizing this approach as they introduce electronic payment.

Exhibit 8-4. Rolling Pass (CT Transit).

- **Combined value and time-based options**—Automated payment media are capable of carrying both stored-value and pass options. This may be in the form of stored value for use on one mode or operator's service, along with a time-based pass that can be used on another mode or service in the region. In an integrated regional payment system, a rider could have a farecard that has stored value for occasional use on all participating agencies' services, as well as a period pass specifically for the service he/she uses on a regular basis.
- An automated payment system can also automatically facilitate a *fare differential* (by time of day, mode or distance) or a *transfer discount* that would otherwise have to be handled using a separate paper transfer.

The other key parameter for farecards is the type and level of discount or bonus provided as an incentive to purchase and use the card (and to use transit in general). The basic types of discount/bonus options that might be considered are as follows:

- **Initial purchase bonus**—This is the most common form of stored-value bonus, as described above.
- **Frequency-based per-ride discount (above a threshold number)**—In this approach, a reduced fare is charged for each ride above a certain minimum number of rides taken with a particular farecard.

- **Farecard discount relative to use of cash**—A farecard can carry a lower per trip fare than if paying cash. For instance, the CTA recently (January 2006) changed its fares such that, on bus, riders pay a lower fare if they use either a smartcard or a magnetic farecard than if they pay with cash ($1.75 versus $2.00). On rail, the discount is available only with a smartcard; users of magnetic farecards must pay the full $2.00. In addition, riders receive reduced-price transfers (on bus and rail) only with a smartcard or magnetic farecard; a rider paying cash must pay a second full fare if transferring to another vehicle.

While the above strategies can be used with any type of electronic payment, the greater memory and processing capabilities of smartcards—coupled with the fact that they are intended to be used for a much longer period—make it possible to consider additional pricing innovations that would be infeasible with magnetic media; these include

- **Guaranteed last ride (or negative balance)**—In this option, a ride is guaranteed, regardless of the remaining value on the farecard. In other words, if a rider boards a bus or enters a faregate and the farecard is revealed to have insufficient value for that trip, a "negative balance" (up to the value of a single ride) is permitted. The next time the cardholder adds value to the card, the amount of that ride is deducted from the total value added. This strategy, being considered in a number of other programs, is attractive to riders in that it addresses concerns about running out of farecard value where it may be inconvenient to add value (i.e., on most bus routes).
- **Guaranteed lowest fare**—This option is a variation on the frequency-based per-ride discount mentioned above. It can take various forms, but the basic approach is to assure riders that they will automatically be charged the lowest fare for which they are eligible (i.e., based on their extent of usage of their farecards). A counter on the card would keep track of each card's use within a certain time period, and the fare system would be programmed so that the rider pays the lowest possible fare, based on his/her usage. For instance, once a cardholder has taken a certain minimum number of rides during a day, his/her card would automatically become treated like an unlimited-use day pass, and all subsequent rides that day would become free. Even at this point, however, rides would continue to be tracked; thus, if the cardholder used the card a sufficient number of times in a 7-day period, the card would become treated like a weekly pass (and subsequently a 2-week pass, and ultimately a monthly pass—assuming these are offered by the agency). Such an approach has yet to be tried in the United States; it is now being tested in London.
- A variation on this basic strategy is to use it in conjunction with post payment (i.e., in an account-based system; this is described below). Such an approach has not been tried in the United States; it is in place in Groningen, Netherlands, and is being tested in the Frankfurt region of Germany.

All of these strategies are intended to provide incentives to purchase and/or use a farecard—as opposed to paying with cash or using a token or paper ticket. With any of the strategies, the impacts on both revenue and ridership will ultimately depend on the exact nature of the bonus or discount relative to the full fare—and compared to the discount offered by other prepaid options (if any). A guaranteed lowest fare option in particular must be evaluated carefully, as it has the potential to result in some revenue loss: it converts rides that would otherwise have been paid for to free rides. An agency will thus have to balance the possible revenue loss against the likely gain in ridership—and general marketing benefit—associated with the strategy. A more straightforward frequency-based per-ride discount would presumably have a smaller revenue impact—since it charges for each ride—although it may not offer an agency quite as compelling a marketing angle.

Other types of prepaid fare media an agency might consider include short-term passes (i.e., good for 1 or more days, but less than a week) and multi-month or annual passes. The use of short-term passes, particularly day passes, is growing, and they are increasingly being targeted to both regular riders and tourists. Such passes have traditionally been provided primarily for out-of-town visitors, as many agencies have sold/distributed them only through hotels, convention centers, and other off-site locations. However, as discussed further under Fare Structure Changes, below, agencies are beginning to view day passes as alternatives to low-priced transfers, and several are now selling them on board buses and in rail stations. With the growth of electronic payment, we can expect to see an increase in the types of passes offered to riders.

Finally, multi-month or even annual passes are offered by a number of agencies, typically in conjunction with employers and universities. Such programs are discussed in Chapter 6, Partnerships/Coordination Initiatives.

Chicago Transit Authority (CTA)
Visitor Pass Program
large urbanized (over 1,000,000)

The Chicago Transit Authority started a Visitor Pass program in 1997. Prior to this time, visitors had to pay the full base fare for any ride on CTA. The new program allows visitors to buy unlimited ride passes, valid for 1, 2, 3, or 5 days. While overall system ridership has slightly declined, Visitor Pass usage has grown significantly since its inception.

Expanded Fare Media Distribution/Reload Options

A key to maximizing usage of prepaid fare media of any type—and thus maximizing their ridership potential—is to provide convenient card distribution and reload options. This is not a major issue for rail systems, as riders can conveniently obtain and reload farecards at ticket vending machines in stations. Other channels used by agencies for distribution of fixed value or pre-encoded fare media (e.g., monthly passes, packages of tokens, multi-ride ticket books, or pre-valued stored-value farecards) include the following:

- Purchasing at agency customer service centers or "ride stores";
- Purchasing at third-party sales outlets such as grocery stores;
- Ordering via mail or telephone;
- Ordering via the Internet (i.e., from the agency's website);
- Distribution by employers, educational institutions or social service agencies; and
- Purchasing on board buses.

Sale—and facilitating reloading—of automated payment media is more complicated than simply distributing fixed-value or pre-encoded payment options. Any third-party location would have to be equipped with a special card initialization and reloading device, and all employees who might have to operate the device would have to be trained. Many such outlets would likely resist adding another card-processing device on or near the counter, and training would be problematic, given the often high turnover rate at many retail outlets. Thus, this is not likely to be a viable option for most agencies. On-board dispensing (i.e., of magnetic stored-value farecards, day passes or transfers) and/or reloading requires that an agency's vehicles have the requisite processing capabilities (e.g., fareboxes equipped with some type of ticket processing unit).

Santa Clarita Transit (SCT)
Online Pass Sales
large urbanized (over 1,000,000)

Santa Clarita Transit, in the LA region, has an online pass purchasing program. Riders can create an online account, and use a credit card to purchase monthly passes. The passes are mailed to the purchaser at his or her home. Customers also have the option of receiving online notification (via e-mail) when it is time to purchase the next month's pass. The Frequent Rider program allows the customer to receive one monthly pass for free after purchasing eleven monthly passes online. Participation in the program has increased 37% over the last five years.

Employers, schools, and social service agencies, on the other hand, could be more willing to accommodate such functions. An employer, for instance, could directly issue a farecard to its employees who use transit. Alternatively, employees could be directed to obtain a farecard through another channel, and the employer would revalue its employees' cards; this would require the employer being equipped with a card sales/revaluing device.

Alternatively, an agency could establish an "autoload" program that facilitates automatic downloading of passes or value to a smartcard. In this approach, currently used by WMATA (Washington, DC) in its "SmartBenefits" program, the employer provides the agency with a list of employees to be provided passes. This list is downloaded into the fare collection system such that when the employee tags any smartcard reader (in a rail station or on a bus) with his/her smartcard near when the current pass is to expire, the next month's pass is automatically loaded onto the smartcard. At WMATA, the employee accounts are maintained via a special Internet site. Thus, the employer authorizes employee participation via the site; reauthorization can be required each month. Or, once an employee's information has been entered, the employer might only be required to enter any changes to an employee's account (e.g., to indicate that the employee is no longer employed or no longer eligible to receive a transit benefit.)

An alternative approach to offering prepaid passes to employees (or students) would be to implement a post-payment program whereby employers or schools would register employees for smartcards and be billed by the agency based on actual system usage. In other words, if an employee made only 10 commute trips in a month, the employer would pay only for those trips—rather than the cost of a full month's pass. A similar approach could be utilized for individuals (rather than employers/institutions) who establish a credit/debit card-based account with the agency. In an account-based system, a customer pre-authorizes the agency to initiate a credit or debit card transaction whenever the smartcard's stored value (or value in the active transit "account") falls below a designated threshold (e.g., $10 or $20). The value on the card or in the active account is then automatically replenished—or a specified period pass is activated—the next time the customer touches the smartcard to a smartcard reader (i.e., similar to many electronic toll payment systems).

The account-based/autoload approach represents increased convenience for customers (i.e., once they have established accounts and acquired the smartcards), since they subsequently do not have to worry about reloading their cards or obtaining new cards. Of course, this approach requires that an updated list of active card accounts be downloaded to every farebox on a daily basis. The CTA has instituted the first individual account-based transit payment system in the United States: the Chicago Card Plus program (See Exhibit 8-5).

Exhibit 8-5. Chicago Card Plus.

Finally, while transit AFC projects have thus far focused on internal (i.e., transit agency) issuance and acceptance of cards, the use of the type of contactless smartcard technology being adopted for transit has now spread beyond transit and thus introduces new opportunities for card issuance/acceptance partnerships in the coming years. In particular, a number of financial institutions (including MasterCard, Visa, American Express and banks such as Citigroup, Chase, KeyBank, HSBC, and MBNA) have begun to introduce contactless credit and debit cards (and smaller payment forms such as key fobs) targeted to use for quickly making small purchases. The emergence of bank-issued contactless cards creates the potential for transit agencies to equip their faregates and/or fareboxes (and possibly hand-held readers on commuter rail) to directly accept these cards for fare payment (i.e., not just for purchase of other fare media, as is currently the case). While this approach may not see widespread use on transit for at least several years, a trial of the concept was planned for New York City in mid-2006: the plan was for the NYMTA to accept contactless Citigroup MasterCards at faregates in select stations on one of its busiest subway lines. This type of arrangement is not likely to eliminate the need for transit agencies to issue their own farecards in the foreseeable future, but it would improve the convenience of fare payment—and thus using transit—as someone wishing to use transit would no longer be required to obtain a separate payment instrument. This could expand the potential transit market, particularly for occasional users.

Regional Payment Integration

With travel patterns increasingly requiring transferring between adjoining transit agencies' services, there has been a growing emphasis on the development of multi-agency agreements and integrated regional payment arrangements. As discussed in Chapter 6, agencies are increasingly moving from simple inter-agency transfer agreements to more comprehensive integrated regional payment systems. The emergence of electronic payment options, particularly smartcards, has facilitated the increasing focus on integrated multi-agency payment systems—i.e., introducing a regional farecard that is accepted at any participating agency.

The objective is to facilitate seamless travel within a region. True regional fare integration entails all agencies adopting a common fare policy, based on regional passes along with free or discounted inter-operator transfers. However, the use of electronic fare media effectively permits each agency to retain its own fare structure (i.e., passes, base fare levels, and discounts) while agreeing to accept a common fare medium. A rider can thus pay for rides on multiple systems with value from a common e-purse.

In a smartcard system, the rider typically would also have the option to load individual payment instruments (e.g., a pass) from one or more agencies onto the same card. Of course, a smartcard can readily support a regional pass as well; the card would track the use of the pass on the different services, permitting allocation of revenue from pass sales among the participating agencies. Finally, with regard to inter-operator transfers, a regional smartcard can facilitate linked-trip discounts for such transfers; the previous trip transaction record stored on a card would automatically indicate that the rider should receive this discount when he/she boards the second vehicle.

Of course, establishing a regional payment system is a complicated undertaking. As explained in the FTA's *National Guidelines and Technical Specifications for Electronic Payment Systems,* "Implementing a regional multiple agency payment system will require fundamental changes from the way each individual agency operates on its own. The integration of card/revenue management functions from several agencies can be challenging. Complex partnership agreements must be developed to address responsibilities, ownership, and allocation of costs and revenues. A clearinghouse or payment settlement process can be established to manage these processes, but all participating agencies must come to agreement on revenue management policies and procedures."[3] The types of issues/requirements that must be considered in developing a regional fare system generally fall under the following categories:[4]

- **Overall Policy and Business Rules**—includes establishing the business structure, including the financial and governance framework and system procurement strategy; addressing customer concerns; and setting fare policy for the region.
- **Technical Requirements**—includes developing system architecture and technology standards, and identifying effective implementation staging.
- **Administrative and Customer Support Functions**—includes establishing revenue settlement and data-sharing procedures, as well as customer service functions.

---

[3]USDOT/Volpe Center and Multisystems, Inc. *National Guidelines and Technical Specifications for Electronic Payment Systems—Regional Fare Integration Requirements (Summary)*, August 2000, p. 2.
[4]Ibid. (See this document for a description of these requirements. Regional fare system requirements are also discussed in *TCRP Report 32: Multipurpose Transit Payment Media*, 1998.)

Smartcard-based regional payment programs are currently being developed or implemented in several regions in the United States, including the San Francisco Bay Area, Washington-Baltimore area, and Central Puget Sound (Seattle) area, and Los Angeles, San Diego, and Atlanta. A regional system has been in place in Ventura County (CA) for several years (see text box). The potential scope of such programs is demonstrated by the plan to eventually expand the TransLink program in the San Francisco Bay Area to as many as 26 transit agencies in the region. A number of these programs are also pursuing smartcard-based partnerships with non-transit entities (e.g., parking authorities, toll operators, financial institutions, universities, employers, and social service agencies).[5]

Ventura Intercity Service Transit Authority (VISTA)
Go Ventura Regional Smart Card Program
medium urbanized (200,000 - 1,000,000)

In 2001, VISTA and five other municipal transit operators in Ventura County (CA) implemented a countywide smart card program that allows residents to travel easily on any of the systems. This follows completion of an earlier regional smart card demonstration, the Smart Passport project. Like the earlier Smart Passport system, the new system includes contactless cards. The cards are available for purchase and renewal at many sites throughout the county, as well as by mail. Riders can use the Go Ventura card as either a pre-purchased pass or an electronic purse (money added to the card is deducted each time the rider travels). With the e-purse option, a light will flash on the card reader when the amount remaining is below $5. Riders can easily add money to their e-purse smart cards on most buses. System ridership increased over 15% between 2003 and 2004.

Fare Structure Changes

Transit agencies sometimes use fare structure modifications to increase ridership; the types of changes that can be considered include the following:

- Fare structure simplification (e.g., elimination of fare zones, elimination of express or rail surcharge) and
- Fare reduction (e.g., introduction of deeply discounted options, reduced base fare, free transfers, or free fare zone/area).

These types of actions are described below, including agency examples of each.

Fare Structure Simplification

Basic fare strategies fall into two general categories: flat and differential. In a flat fare structure, riders are charged the same fare, regardless of the length of the trip, time of day, speed or quality of service. Alternatively, fares can be differentiated by one or more of those parameters, resulting in distance-based or zonal fares, time-based (e.g., peak/off-peak) differential, and/or service-based differential (e.g., express surcharge or bus-rail differential). Each of these approaches has certain advantages and disadvantages, mainly related to relative ease of use and administration versus ridership/revenue impacts; however, the principal arguments in favor of differentiation have focused on issues related to efficiency and equity. In particular, it has been argued that a higher fare should be charged to cover the higher operating costs associated with serving longer trips, operating peak-period service, and providing "premium" service such as express bus or rail; otherwise, the users of the higher cost services are effectively cross-subsidized by the users of

---

[5]For further discussion of such programs, including case studies of the SF, Washington, Ventura County systems, see *TCRP Report 94: Fare Policies, Structures and Technologies (Update)*, 2003.

shorter distance, off-peak, or local bus services. Differentiated fares are also seen as able to generate greater revenues than lower flat fares, since the users of the higher cost services (e.g., longer distance) have often been found to be less price-sensitive than those using the lower cost services.

The flip side of the argument in favor of differentiation is that a flat fare structure can produce somewhat higher ridership—depending on the relative price levels. In other words, simplifying the fare structure by removing a zonal (or peak or express) surcharge tends to boost ridership. The percentage of agencies using any of the basic types of differentiation is actually relatively low and has declined in the past decade.[6] Thus, despite arguments such as those cited above, most agencies have continued to display a preference for the simplicity of flat fares. In fact, several agencies have sought to simplify their fare structures in recent years typically by eliminating or reducing the number of zones (e.g., in Baltimore, MD; Norfolk, VA; Raleigh-Durham, NC; Albany, NY, Rochester, NY, several towns in Connecticut, and throughout Delaware, as well as on buses in Washington, DC). The Chicago Transit Authority is an example of an agency that has removed both a peak/off-peak differential (this existed on buses only) and an express bus surcharge in recent years.[7]

Another type of fare simplification involves transfers. Nearly 90% of U.S. transit agencies offer free or low-priced transfers. However, a number of agencies have in recent years eliminated such transfers (i.e., bus-bus), replacing them with 1-day passes sold on board buses. Agencies that have implemented this strategy include the Nashville MTA (see inset), Maryland MTA (Baltimore, MD), OCTA (Orange County, CA), DART (Dallas, TX), RGRTA (Rochester, NY), CDTA (Albany, NY), First State Transit (State of Delaware), and SCVTA (San Jose, CA). The day pass is typically priced so that a rider who must transfer pays roughly the equivalent of two to three linked trips per day. In other words, a transferring rider is not penalized with the elimination of transfers—as long as he/she makes a round trip. For riders who do not transfer, their fare payment is unchanged by the elimination of transfers. In Dallas, the full fare is $1 and the day pass $2, while Baltimore's full fare is $1.35 and the day pass $3—or the equivalent of 2.2 trips per day; OCTA's day pass of $2.50 represents 2.5 full fare ($1) trips.

A variation on the elimination of transfers can be seen at GBTA in Bridgeport, CT. In 2005, GBTA removed bus-bus transfers, but instituted both a day pass and a 90-minute "pass." In other words, rather than offering a free transfer with restrictions on use, the agency opted for a very short-term unlimited-ride pass, good for use on any routes and in either direction within the 90-minute window. The 90-minute "ziptrip" is priced at $1.50, i.e., the cost of a single ride. The day pass is $3. GBTA also introduced a 7-day and a 31-day pass at that time; the agency had previously offered no unlimited-ride passes.

Those agencies that have simplified their fare structures have generally increased ridership. Based on cases studies (covering elimination of zones and/or transfers at Baltimore MTA, CT TRANSIT, and OCTA) conducted as part of the TCRP study, *Fare Policies, Structures and Technologies (Update)*, the major impacts on and benefits to the agencies include the following:[8]

- The elimination of zone charges did not result in a significant loss of fare revenue, as might have been expected. In both Baltimore and Connecticut, the simplification of the fare structure, coupled with introduction of new fare options, attracted new riders and thus offset the loss of zonal surcharge revenue. Revenue in Baltimore actually rose following the fare restructuring and has continued to grow since that time.

---

[6]The exception to this trend is light rail systems, which show a slight increase in both zonal pricing and peak/off-peak differential. Moreover, most commuter rail systems continue to use zonal rather than flat fare structures—and this mode also has by far the highest incidence of time of day differentials.
[7]Of course, it should be noted that the CTA has recently introduced a rail/bus differential (using certain types of payment options), in response to a large budget deficit; this change is described on p. 8-12.
[8]TCRP Report 94, p. 19.

- The sale of day passes on board buses effectively offset the expected loss of ridership—as well as rider complaints—that might be expected with the elimination of free or low-priced transfers. Moreover, these initiatives resulted in significant revenue increases in both Baltimore and Orange County.
- These initiatives greatly reduced the extent of transfer abuse and the incidence of rider-operator arguments regarding the validity of transfers.

In short, all three of these agencies thought that they have benefited considerably from these fare strategy initiatives. However, it should be kept in mind that, while none of these strategies have any specific technology requirements, the on-board distribution of day passes requires some type of pass-issuing unit if the agency is to avoid having operators be responsible for manual distribution of the passes.

> **Metropolitan Transit Authority (MTA)**
> **Fare Restructuring**
> *medium urbanized area (200,000—1,000,000)*
>
> Following a comprehensive fare study, the Nashville (TN) MTA made several significant changes to its fare structure. Beginning in January 2005, the MTA reduced its base fare from $1.45 to $1.10, eliminated the $0.10 transfers and began to sell 1-day passes ($3.25) on board the buses. The agency had previously installed validating fareboxes capable of dispensing magnetic fare media, making the issuance of the 1-day pass feasible. As part of the fare change, paratransit fares were increased from $1.75 to $2.20 and the Downtown $0.25 Zone was eliminated. Pass and stored value farecard prices were also modified. The MTA had presented two alternative fare structures to the public, and this one was favored by nearly a 2-1 margin over a structure featuring an increase in the base fare to $1.60 (with retention of the $0.10 transfer, and no 1-day pass). The new structure has been readily accepted by MTA riders, and both ridership and revenue grew following the change. However, a larger than anticipated revenue shortfall later in the year forced MTA to raise fares: the cash fare was increased to $1.25 and the 1-day pass to $3.75.

Fare Reduction

As explained above, under Fare Structure Simplification, some agencies have effectively reduced fares by eliminating surcharges. However, another means of increasing ridership is to simply reduce the base fare or to offer some other form of fare reduction such as making transfers free, increasing the discount associated with prepaid options (i.e., passes and multi-ride options), or introducing a free (or reduced) fare zone or area. These types of strategies are discussed below.

Base Fare Reduction

Base fare reductions are relatively rare, given the general concern with maximizing revenue. Effective reductions have been widely introduced through prepaid discounts, but these typically accompany cash fare increases. However, several agencies have lowered the base fare in order to increase ridership. For example, Chapel Hill Transit eliminated its fare in 2002 (see inset); as explained in the inset, system ridership has grown considerably as a result, although operating and capital costs have increased as well as a result of the need to accommodate the additional riders. The other examples of base fare reduction within the past decade are also at relatively small agencies (e.g., in Ames, IA; Great Falls, MT; Savannah, GA; LaCrosse, WI; and Huntington, WVA). As explained above, Nashville MTA lowered its base fare late in 2005, but this was accompanied by the elimination of the reduced-price transfer. A few larger agencies earlier experimented with fare reductions, but the fares were subsequently restored to higher levels in these cases; examples include DART (Dallas), which lowered the cash fare from $0.70 to $0.50 in 1984 but subsequently reversed that change (due to excessive revenue loss), and SCRTD (the predecessor agency to LACMTA in Los Angeles), which lowered the cash fare from $0.85 to $0.50 in

1982, and then reversed the reduction in 1985.[9] Ridership impacts of these efforts are summarized below.

A second approach to reducing the base fare is to do so in conjunction with the elimination of low-price transfers. Rather than essentially replacing transfers with day passes (see Fare Structure Simplification, above), some agencies have considered the possibility of eliminating transfers in favor of a significantly lower full fare (e.g., reducing the fare from $1.25 to $0.75, but eliminating free transfers). While this will remove the administrative/operational issues with transfers, it can result in a substantial loss of either revenue or ridership (i.e., depending on the specific pricing and the extent of transferring). It can also result in major fare increases for those riders making more than one transfer on each journey. For these reasons, very few, if any, agencies have opted for such an approach to this point. As explained in the inset, Nashville MTA reduced its base fare in conjunction with the elimination of transfers, but also opted to introduce an on-board day pass.

Chapel Hill Transit (CHT)
Free Fares
medium urbanized (200,000 - 1,000,000)

Chapel Hill Transit (CHT) operates public transportation services within the towns of Chapel Hill and Carrboro, NC and on the campus of the University of North Carolina-Chapel Hill. The Town of Carrboro and the University of North Carolina are partners with the Town of Chapel Hill in the operation of the transit system. With the primary goal of addressing on-campus parking shortages, the University (and its students) pushed to create a free fare policy. Fares prior to the implementation of the free fare initiative were only $0.75, with various discounted fare mechanisms. However, the towns recognized that accessibility to free public transportation would permit easy access to jobs, educational and recreational ventures to students and the public alike. Thus, the three funding partners agreed to make all regular routes fare free as of January 2002. System ridership has increased considerably since the elimination of fares, monthly ridership in the initial year was as much as 50% higher than for the same month the previous year, reaching a high of roughly 400,000 rides in April 2002. However, service was also increased on some routes that were already at carrying capacity, and both capital and operating costs have increased due to the need for additional vehicles and drivers.

Transfer Price Reduction

Lowering the cost of transferring represents another type of fare reduction. As indicated above, most transit agencies already offer at least reduced-price transfers. However, a third of agencies do charge something for transfers to/from vehicles in the same system. A handful of agencies have implemented transfer reductions in recent years, although there has been a greater trend to move in the other direction—i.e., to charge the full fare (see Fare Structure Simplification). Examples of recent transfer reductions include the MBTA (Boston), which introduced free bus-bus transfers in 2000 in response to strong community opposition to a proposed fare increase, and the NYMTA, which introduced free bus-rail transfers in 1997 as part of the roll-out of its MetroCard automated fare system. An agency can thus consider lowering its transfer charge or making its transfers free if it currently charges something. However, as with any of these approaches, the resulting loss of revenue must be considered carefully.

Increased Discounting of Prepaid Options

The use of discounting, particularly "deep discounting" (i.e., offering discounts of 20% or more compared to the base fare) has been shown to increase ridership—or at least minimize the

---

[9]SCRTD was obligated to offer the $0.50 fare for a period of three years under the terms of the passage of a $0.05 transit sales tax initiative in 1980. Thus, once the three-year period was up, the agency reversed the fare change.

ridership loss that would ordinarily result from an accompanying increase in the base fare. The sale of discounted multi-ride options (e.g., 10-ride tickets or stored-value farecards) can also expand commitment to usage of transit by infrequent riders. When done in conjunction with increasing the base fare, raising the discount on multi-ride options or passes (i.e., keeping prepaid price levels the same when the base fare rises) has even been shown in some cases to increase both ridership and revenue.

CityBus of Greater Lafayette
Raising Fares and Increasing Ridership
small urbanized (50,000 - 200,000)

CityBus of Greater Lafayette has successfully used deep discounting in pass and multi-ride pricing to simultaneously increase ridership and revenue. CityBus offers a monthly pass discounted by 33% from the daily round trip fare for 21 days. CityBus also offers a 25% discount on tokens purchased in quantities of 10. This program resulted in significant ridership gains for CityBus; over a period of four years, ridership rose 117%.

With regard to the level of the discount offered, there is a fairly even distribution of agencies with discounts of less than 10%, 10–19%, and 20% or more. Approximately 33% of U.S. bus systems offer discounts of 10% or less, nearly 40% offer 10–19%, and just under 30% have discounts of 20% or higher. Among heavy rail agencies, the under 10% percentage is the same as for the bus agencies, but 50% have discounts of 20% or more. However, there has been a general shift over the past few years toward lower percentage discounts. While the incidence of discounts in the 10–19% range is virtually unchanged over the past decade, the percentage of agencies with discounts under 10% has nearly doubled—with the percentage above 20% declining accordingly. In some cases, this shift has occurred as agencies have moved from paper tickets or tokens to stored-value farecards—and now to smartcards at several agencies. In Chicago, for instance, the CTA offers a 10% discount (actually a purchase bonus: $11 value for $10) only with its stored-value smartcard (Chicago Card); the same bonus was formerly available with the magnetic farecard as well, but was discontinued in an effort to shift people to the smartcard. Prior to introducing electronic payment, the CTA had sold 10 tokens at a 17% discount; the discount had been as high as 28%, but had been reduced as part of subsequent fare changes. WMATA and NYMTA are other examples of agencies that offer a 10% purchase bonus with stored value, although like CTA, WMATA's bonus is available only with the SmarTrip smartcard.

Introduction of Free/Reduced Fare Zone or Area

Another strategy some agencies have utilized is introduction of free (or reduced) fare zones or areas. This is typically a specified downtown area in which all boardings are free (or at a fare considerably lower than the regular base fare). Some agencies have special routes or services serving the reduced fare area. For instance, MDTA (Miami) has eliminated the fare on its Metromover downtown people mover. GCRTA (Cleveland) operates two special low-fare Loop Routes in downtown Cleveland.

Such a strategy certainly generates additional ridership, especially if it is free; downtown workers or tourists who might otherwise walk to nearby locations will tend to use the transit system for shorter trips than they might if a full fare were charged. Approximately 60 U.S. transit agencies have reduced-fare downtown zones; about half of these are free, while the others typically charge on the order of $0.25 or $0.50.

There are a number of tradeoffs inherent in such a strategy, besides the lost revenue. In particular, unless there is a separate route/service, fare payment—and enforcement—for travel starting in the zone and ending in a full fare area tends to be an issue: riders boarding a vehicle within the reduced fare zone may not realize that they have to pay if they ride outside the zone, or they may purposely evade the fare in that way. Such concerns have led some agencies to eliminate their reduced fare zones; Nashville MTA, for instance, decided to end its Downtown $0.25 Zone as part of its recent fare restructuring, due to the combination of fare enforcement issues and the need for additional revenue.

Reducing fare levels through one of the above strategies clearly offers the potential to increase ridership. However, the magnitude of the ridership impacts obviously depend largely on the size and nature of the reduction; for instance, is the base fare itself being lowered or is the reduction only for multi-ride prepaid options? Impacts from several fare reduction efforts can be summarized as follows:

- In 1984, DART reduced its cash fare from $0.70 to $0.50 and the monthly pass price from $26 to $20, while removing the $0.10 transfer fee (in favor of free transfers). Ridership rose by 16% following this change, and by 1986, the combination of the fare change and a significant service expansion resulted in a ridership gain of nearly 50%. However, the fare reduction—as well as many of the service improvements—were subsequently reversed due to the resulting significant decline in the fare recovery ratio.
- In early 1990, the CTA introduced a new fare structure that featured an increase in the cash fare from $1 to $1.25, but a reduction in the unit price of ten tokens from $0.95 to $0.90. This created a multi-ride discount of 28%. By the end of the year revenue had grown (exceeding the target for the change) with no loss of ridership.
- As part of the introduction of MetroCard, NYMTA introduced free bus-rail transfers (only with use of the MetroCard) in 1997; previously, a second full fare was required to transfer. While the agency also subsequently introduced a stored value purchase bonus and unlimited-ride passes, the free transfer was considered to be a major contributor to a 15% ridership increase by 1998. This change was accompanied by a 4% revenue loss, as well as a significant increase in operating and capital costs—as the higher ridership required substantial expansion of the bus fleet.